AJ

The Life of Alfred Munnings

1878–1959

By the Same Author

Anything But Housework: Autobiography
Edward Seago: The Other Side of the Canvas
The Mond Legacy: A Family Saga
Royal Scotland (in collaboration with
Sir Iain Moncreiffe of that Ilk, Bart)
With Love from Bunty: A Biography
Debrett's books of the Engagement
and Marriage of the Duke and Duchess of York

AJ

The Life of
ALFRED MUNNINGS
1878–1959

ERSKINE PRESS
2000

First published as 'What A Go' The Life of Alfred Munnings
in 1988 by William Collins Sons & Co. Ltd

This enlarged edition published in 2000 by
The Erskine Press, The Old Bakery, Norwich, Norfolk NR16 2HW

ISBN 1 85297 061 8

Printed in England

In Memory of Lionel

The Finish
1952

CONTENTS

LIST OF ILLUSTRATIONS

Acknowledgements:
Colour Plates 1–7, 9–19 Copyright & Ownership The Sir Alfred Munnings Art Museum, Castle House, Dedham, Essex, 8 Private Collection

Black and White Plates and Drawings in the Text Copyright & Ownership The Sir Alfred Munnings Art Museum, Castle House, Dedham, Essex

SANDRINGHAM, NORFOLK

Every countryman recognises Alfred Munnings's deep affection for the countryside and for all the activities enjoyed by country people. Every artist recognises his quite exceptional talent as a painter. Everyone who knew him will remember him as a very special character. It is easy to see why the author decided that such a subject would provide a rewarding challenge. With new material available, she has now been able to widen the perspective of the first edition.

It is always intriguing to find out a bit more about the person behind the celebrity, but while it helps to understand an artist's motives and inspiration, it cannot explain the origins of natural talent and creativity. Anyone who knows East Anglia understands exactly why so many of our greatest landscape artists started their lives in this very special corner of England. The huge skies, the rolling landscape and, above all, the characteristic light, positively demand to be painted. For Munnings there were also the graceful lines of thoroughbred horses and the myriad bustle of fairs and race-courses. All this he managed to convey in his paintings with his own special exuberance.

The author has skilfully woven together Munnings's character, his work and his subject matter to give a rounded and fascinating portrait of an unusual man and a great artist.

Philip

ACKNOWLEDGEMENTS

To write about Alfred Munnings, the painter, is a joyous task. His pictures speak for themselves and tell, for all time, of a countryman's love for the land and for the horses and people who were as integral parts of it as the trees, the wide skies, the open landscapes and the slow-flowing rivers.

To write of Alfred Munnings, the man, who nearly forty years after his death generates strongly divergent feelings, is another story. Many older people refuse to talk, either from a strange sense of loyalty or because they feel some things are better left unsaid about a man described by the painter, Dame Laura Knight, as 'the stables, the artist, the poet, the very land itself!' 'What a go!' he would have said.

'The only genuine coward I have ever met,' wrote an acquaintance of the man who, time and again during World War I, displayed immense courage by painting for days on end within sight of the enemy.

I have, fortunately, had great help from very many people. Firstly from Mr Stanley Booth, Chairman of the Munnings Trust, who was an unfailing source of information about the painter. He gave me access to the wealth of material in the Trust's possession and I spent many hours working with him and his small team of helpers at their headquarters, Munnings's old home, Castle House, Dedham. It has been beautifully restored and, its walls crowded with many of Munnings's finest pictures, seems impregnated with the painter's personality.

I must also thank, in particular, Mr Reginald Pound, Munnings's first biographer, for his advice, permission to quote from his own works and from material which arrived after his biography was published.

Many others provided me with information and anecdotes. Among those who gave me a considerable amount of time and whom I should particularly like to thank – even if I could not always include their anecdotes – are Mrs Dudley Arnold, Mr Joseph Baillio, Mr William Bakewell, Mr Tim Barclay, Mrs Marjorie Bell, Mrs Tony Blackman, Dr John Bleby, Miss Muriel Boswell, Mr Humphrey Brooke, Dr Charles Bunting, Mr James Chamberlain, Miss Marjorie Coppin, Mr David Duff, Miss Janet Dunbar, Dr James Dyce, Mr Edward Ebden, Major and Mrs Timothy Ellis, Mr David Evans, Mr George Ewart Evans, Mr Francis Farmer, the Hon. Mrs Charles Fletcher, Miss Joan Forman, Mr George Fountain Page, Miss Caroline Fox, Mr Peter Garnier, Mr Leslie Gillett, Mr James Green, Mr and Mrs Roger Groom, Mr Michael Holroyd, Mr Sidney Hutchison, Mr Frank Jones, Miss R. E. Le Bas, Mr William Luscombe, Mrs F. Mackenzie, Mr Tom Mackley, Dr Hugh Maingay, Mr Edward Martin, Mr Richard Maxwell, Mr John Morant, Mr George Morris,

Mr Robert Moss, Lord Mottistone, Mr John Munnings, Mr W. Naunton, Mr Tony Nevill, Mr James Noble, Miss Jean Nurse, Mr Bob Osborne, Mr John Pank, Miss B. Parker, Mr Ralph Potter, Mr Robin Powell, Mr Charles V. Roberts, Mr Guy Schofield, Mrs Della Seward, Mr F. B. Singleton, Lt.-Col. George Springfield, Mr James Starling, Mr Bertie Stone, Mr Gerald Tealing, Mr R. J. Unstead, Mr Peter Upton, Mr M. Urwick Smith, Mr Stanley Wade, Mr Robert Walker, Mr Stephen Walker, Mrs M. Webster, Mrs Marion Wentworth Day.

I have also received help from the Royal Academy of Arts, the British Broadcasting Corporation, Eastern Counties Newspapers Ltd., Castle Museum Art Gallery, Norwich, Norwich Central Library, London Library, Royal Society of Medicine, Victoria and Albert Museum, Suffolk Records Office, the Jockey Club, Ascot Racecourse, National Racehorse Museum, Newmarket, *East Anglian Daily Times,* Page Bros. Printers, Norwich and Jarrolds, Printers, Norwich.

I should also like to thank the Society of Authors as the Literary Representative of the estate of John Masefield, for permission to quote letters from John Masefield, Michael Holroyd for permission to quote from *Augustus John,* Vol. II and Janet Dunbar for permission to quote from her biography of Laura Knight. I am also grateful to the Estate of Henry Williamson for permission to quote from his works. Also Eversley Belfield, Stanley Wade and Marjorie Coppin for letting me quote from their unpublished writings about Alfred Munnings.

I have also had valuable help with research from Mr Douglas Salmon, while Mr Correlli Barnett and Mr David Duff kindly read through certain chapters of the book.

'To be a great painter you mustn't be pious but rather a little wicked and entirely a man of the world.'

JOHN RUSKIN

CHAPTER I

A Background to Dreams

One mellow autumn afternoon, I stood in a clearing in a wood at Redgrave Fen, on the border of Norfolk and Suffolk. It was a timeless, secret sort of place. Sunlight filtered through gaps in the trees and glinted on two springs of water bubbling up through the damp earth, a few yards apart from each other, forming a pair of little trickling streams.

They were the sources of the Waveney and the Little Ouse, rivers that together form a natural boundary between Norfolk and Suffolk, the historical definition of East Anglia. It was the east-flowing Waveney that allowed Alfred James Munnings, or 'A.J.' as he was often called by his friends, to claim, from a geographical point of view at any rate, to be the most East Anglian of all the great East Anglian painters.

The river also cast a life-long spell over him. Sometimes, he was impelled to write about it, poetically and nostalgically, as well as paint it. 'I shall always long for the river,' he admitted, 'and the warblers' song going on and on, and now and then the wind through the willows turning the surface blue and purple .... And the wind comes in gusts, and the blown water is steely and puffed this way and that by unseen spirits.'

The source of anything so very much involved in a man's life was worth investigating.

So from Redgrave Fen, where the water first bubbled to the surface, I walked the narrow track beside the east-flowing stream. Gradually, it became a well-defined path, the trees grew sparse and the water splashed vigorously over stones, between clumps of overripe bulrushes.

Widening into a river, it meandered through the Norfolk towns of Diss and Scole, then into Suffolk at Hoxne where, legend has it, King Edmund was slaughtered by the Danes. Eight miles from its source it flowed more swiftly, through Syleham village where Henry II prepared for the siege of Bungay Castle, into Norfolk again, at Brockdish and the eighteenth-century town of Harleston and Mendham where it divided the village so that half lay in Norfolk and half in Suffolk.

There, by the bank of the river, Alfred James Munnings was born on 8 October 1878. He could, therefore, claim both counties of wide skies, wild unspoilt landscapes, fens and broads, forests and fine painting traditions, as his natural birthright. He was truly an East Anglian.

I stood on the single-span iron bridge over the river dividing Mendham village into two counties and saw the sturdy, red-brick Mill House, which was his birthplace. Adjoining it was the fifteenth-century white weather-boarded water mill owned by his father, John. It was surrounded by stables and stackyards, meadows and marsh-land, merging into miles of arable country where the mist drifted over in low-lying veils. Munnings's mill was the largest and finest of all the water mills in The Valley of Mills, as this rich lowland in the East Anglian countryside was called.

Endless stories and legends surround the towns and villages along the upper reaches of the Waveney. In childhood, Alfred and his three brothers never tired of hearing their mother relate them. Afterwards, when the boys lay in bed, the endless sound of the river under their windows might lull them to sleep or invade their dreams.

Emily Munnings was far more sensitive and romantic than her boisterous husband, who nevertheless, excelled at reading and often, on long winter evenings, they took turns at reading aloud from their favourite books, which included the works of Scott, Dickens and Thackeray, John Bunyan's *The Pilgrim's Progress* and Longfellow's *Hiawatha*. There was plenty of time for such homespun entertainment on winter evenings and on Sundays, in the days when family life was all important.

Then life in the little towns and huddled villages, surrounded by miles of open country, seemed a logical development of Chaucer's or Shakespeare's England and in those halcyon days of farming, before the advent of the tractor, was respected across the world. Horses were an integral part of the scene in the long hot summers in contrast to the cold winters, when the rivers froze and the untrammelled landscape sparkled with hoar-frost.

Alfred Munnings's generation was one of the last to enjoy a comparatively uncomplicated way of country living. It was governed largely by the changing seasons and by deep-rooted traditions and its well-defined standards offered a firm framework for adventure.

Alfred was the second of the four sons of John and Emily Munnings. When they were born nearly every riverside village in the Waveney Valley had its own water mill to grind grain from the surrounding farm lands and send down river to Lowestoft and out to sea to far away places like Hull and Newcastle.

At Mendham when there was a good harvest, waggon loads of grain would stand for hours waiting their turn to be unloaded at John Munnings's mill. Sometimes the queue stretched a quarter of a mile from the Suffolk mill, across the ugly little lattice-work iron bridge and down the main street to the red-brick school, which was in Norfolk. It was a grand sight; each waggon drawn by four great Suffolk Punches, their harnesses jingling with every move, their brasses shining in the sunlight, their manes and tails brightly plaited with the celebratory red, white and blue ribbons. Such splendid creatures made a life-long impression on a boy with an inherent sense of form and beauty.

As each waggon in turn drew up under the lukem – a platform of wooden planks suspended from the first floor over the doorway of the mill – the driver would hand a sample of corn or wheat to the miller. But as often as not the usually happy-go-lucky John Munnings would climb on the waggon and open up a sack or two to check the contents against the sample. It was not by chance that he was known as the best miller in all Suffolk.

Satisfied, he would signal for the sack to be chained and pulled up into the mill where the grain was ground by nine pairs of grooved millstones and then hauled up to the top storey for further processing. Sometimes the millstones rumbled on through day and night, except on Sundays, to clear the debts John Munnings had inadvertently acquired.

He was one of the youngest of ten children of a successful farmer, William Green Munnings, and his wife Susan Bugg and was born at Little Horksley Hall, an old farmhouse near Horksley

Church. Eventually, the family moved to Scotland Place Farm of about seven hundred acres at Stoke-by-Nayland in Suffolk. There William Green Munnings died at the age of forty-eight leaving his wife Susan to bring up their ten children and run the farm.

At fourteen John went to learn the miller's trade at Shonk's Mill at Ongar in Essex. After about a year he joined his cousin, Jeremiah Stannard, at his Nayland Mill and stayed for eighteen years. In his spare time he indulged in his fine sense of oratory and took part in the Penny Readings in the local hall, which took their name from the cost of admission. They were a popular entertainment in the country districts on winter evenings in the days when there was a scarcity of books and journals and many adults could neither read nor write. John Munnings's favourite dramatic renderings were from the essays of Charles Dickens who, some ten years earlier, had promoted many of his own writings in that way throughout England and America.

John Munnings was a diligent worker and by 1872 he had saved enough money to go into partnership with a corn merchant and miller, George Chase of Mendham, a businessman with well-spread financial interests including the building trade, retail shops and property. John Munnings's business association with him, however, only concerned Mendham Mill and its surrounding farm land.

He lived at the miller's house and, after three years, when he was thirty-six, married the twenty-five-year-old, dark, attractive Ellen Emily Ringer, one of nine children of William Ringer, a local farmer and agent for a nearby large estate. The Ringers were strongly opposed to the marriage so the determined Ellen went to Southsea and stayed with an aunt until her marriage to John could take place there at St Jude's Church.

A year later their first son, another William Green Munnings, was born followed at two-yearly intervals by Alfred James, Frederick William and Charles.

The four brothers whose parents each came from large families were never short of playmates. Their maternal grandfather William Ringer boasted he had sixty cousins, and many relations from both sides of the family lived close at hand while others were conveniently scattered throughout East Anglia.

William Ringer, however, also died comparatively young and

his widow Ellen, known to everyone as 'Grandma Ringer', continued to farm from Walsham Hall near Mendham. A tall lady, she dominated the whole family from her small Suffolk manor house whose size and status could be judged from the fact that in the thirteenth and fourteenth centuries its owners were expected to produce one knight whenever their overlord went to war.

In the 1880s to the young 'Alfy' as Alfred Munnings was called, Walsham Hall was a second home and much grander than the Mill House. Grandma Ringer had fourteen servants; the living-in ones slept in dormitories in the upper garret and there were cottages for most of the farmworkers. Servants were usually chosen at the annual hiring fairs at nearby Harleston where bargains were struck for board and lodgings and a sum of money at the end of the year with anything from a month's to a year's notice on either side.

Grandma Ringer and her kind prided themselves on running self-supporting households and every year, for six weeks, a travelling tailor stayed at Walsham Hall. His workbench was temporarily installed on a little landing half way up the beautiful carved oak staircase where he made clothes for the male workers and working suits for the men of the family.

Young Alfy loved to stay at Walsham Hall because, thanks to the three unmarried daughters who lived there, it was the centre of family fun and entertainment. His aunts were little more than girls and at every opportunity would organize singing round the piano and dancing and games in the low-ceilinged parlour. Boisterous games like 'Spin the Trencher' and 'Blind Man's Buff' were transferred to the large kitchen, hung with rows of home-cured bacon and smoked hams.

Beyond the kitchen was a bakehouse and a cold dairy where butter was churned and large round pans of milk, pots of cream and baskets of eggs stood. Then came the cheese room for cheese was a main item of the farmworkers' diet in the days when meat was very dear.

Homemade cream cheese was usually reserved for the family while for the farmworkers, Grandma Ringer used milk 'three times skimmed sky blue' to make great round cheeses the size of barrow wheels and a foot thick when dried. She made them each spring to use on cold winter mornings and they were so hard that the only way to eat them was to cut them in half horizontally, toast in a pan in front of the fire and scrape the hot cheese onto thick rounds of bread. 'Sandwiched with a slice of fat salt pork as red as a cherry between another slice of bread there could be no better food for farmworkers to start the day with,' Alfred's cousin William Munnings recalled, adding nostalgically, 'they would stick to your chest all morning.'

Beyond the cheese room there was a room where jams and cakes were stored and a brew house – essential in the days when the Three B's – bread, bacon and beer – were the staple items of the farmworkers' diet. At least twice a year Grandma Ringer supervised the delicate process of brewing – usually just before harvest time and before Christmas. For a day and a night, the task took precedence over all other household ones and the younger members of the family were often kept at home from school to help.

Home brewing was such an important tradition that schoolmasters accepted it as a legitimate excuse for absence. It demanded great care and vigilance from the moment, at Walsham Hall, when by tradition the head horseman supervised the cleaning out of the great fifty-gallon barrels, until hours later when Grandma Ringer saw the yeast start to work on the warm beer and pronounced with relief: 'the beer is on the smile'.

Attached to the brew house was a faggot and woodshed where the back-house boy chopped sticks, cleaned the knives and made candles by dipping wicks into boiling mutton fat.

Life at the Mill House was far more modest but, there too, bonds between employers and servants were strong and loyal, and Alfy Munnings grew up attaching no importance to class distinctions.

'They were marvellous times,' recalled Grace, the eighth and youngest child of John Munnings's horseman who lived in one of four workers' cottages and earned an average wage of eleven shillings a week:

> My eldest sister Rosie was the same age as Alfred and they used to play together. His mother loved to get us village children down there and give us lovely teas in the meadow. She talked so nicely to us about the flowers she liked and the river and horses. She'd wear a flowered hat and those old pattens on her feet and she carried a big wooden basket when she was out in the garden. She loved gardening.

> I remember the milk was carried from the farm to the house on a hoop with a pail hanging at each side. The wooden hoop kept the pails away from the legs.
>
> In the springtime we'd take the cows down to the marshes about eight o'clock and bring them home about four. It was nearly two miles to walk each time but we enjoyed it because we loved animals.
>
> Then I remember the gleaning; the men all in a row, each with a scythe, keeping time with each other. You'd hear the noise of the corn as they cut it; the swish of the mow. Then they would stop and all sharpen their scythes on the stone rubs they kept in their belts and start cutting again; swishing the corn with the scythes, the steel gleaming in the sun.
>
> On Saturdays my father always cleaned the horse brasses and blacked the little pony's feet – shined them up for the little gig. My mother and Rosie and I sometimes used to go for a ride in the little gig with Alfred and his three brothers. Some days we'd all go in the corn mill and watch the engine going round.
>
> When Rosie was eighteen she became a maid in the Mill House for a few shillings a month. Sometimes I went to tea and they'd say, 'Stay the night'. I loved that because I loved to go up the little winding stairs and on the way up look at all the little pictures Alfred had painted. Once he painted a picture of my brother fishing but he wouldn't let him have it because he liked it himself.

Bob Osborne's father also worked for John Munnings. Bob was one of eleven children and he acted as unofficial 'back-house boy' before he went off to school in the mornings and when he came home in the evenings. He cleaned the boots, carried bags of cinder dust up to the chickens and, as he grew older, was allowed to feed the pigs, look after the fowls and help to milk the cows. 'You got a shilling if you could get a froth on the pail when you milked,' he said. 'You used to have to rush down and show her the froth before it was off the milk.'

In the school holidays he often rode in the trap with Emily Ringer and held the pony while she went shopping. 'John Munnings was one of the best,' he said. 'She wasn't a bad old soul but she wanted a lot done.'

It was hardly surprising. At times, when money was short, Emily took paying guests, two or three at a time for a week or two's fishing or shooting. She charged £2 or £3 a week and once a party stayed for a month's duck shooting.

There was only one living-in servant at the Mill House and a woman who came to help with the washing. Emily did all her own baking. When Bob Osborne left school he was engaged to work full-time, from 7.30 a.m. when he made the fires to 4.00 p.m., for a wage of half-a-crown a week.

With so many farmworkers' children around, the lively Munnings boys were never short of playmates for their active imaginative games and the river near their front door provided an ever-changing playground. It was a perfect setting for endless adventures as pirates and Indians, ship-wrecked sailors or intrepid bush-rangers.

An old flat-bottomed boat, sharp at each end and rigged with an old sheet and a stolen clothes line, was a fine sailing ship and, in a March gale, with stones for ballast, could be made to shoot low through the water at great speed. Someone invariably fell overboard and ended the day with a sound thrashing on wet trousers. No-one was drowned for the children learned to swim almost as soon as they could walk by clinging to bundles of bulrushes in the shallow gravel-bottomed part of the river. Later they learned to dive in the deeper parts.

On lazy summer days they fished for perch, roach or dace or searched for moorhens' eggs or reed warblers' nests and, as the afternoons cooled, picnicked on the lawn with an assortment of aunts, cousins and friends. 'Moods for outdoor games and adventures came with the seasons,' Alfred Munnings recalled. 'Ice, snow and floods forgotten; Spring in the air; marsh dykes alive with spawning frogs; marsh marigolds along the river bank: pale, dead reeds bright in the sun – reeds for arrows! . . . The sound of the mill was the background to our dreams.' It was an idyllic secure background for a boy who was unworried by rats scurrying behind the walls of his home or realized that, through lack of money, many of the rooms were barely furnished.

What matter when, in turn, ice and snow brought skating and sledging at all hours of the day and often by moonlight and afterwards floods turned the surrounding marshland into an unfamiliar lake so that every day brought a new adventure? March was the month for making and flying kites and bowling hoops;

girls usually drove wooden hoops with a wooden stick, while the boys had iron ones forged by the village blacksmith and steered with an iron rod with a hook at the end.

As the days lengthened, it was time for hop-scotch and whipping tops on any flat surface on the village street. Marbles came later; the boys threw theirs ahead as they walked or hit them up against a wall and when they bounced back tried to span them with their fingers across to an opponent's ball. The girls bowled their marbles into a hole in the ground. Few sophisticated commercial toys could compete with the traditional homespun or simple games in the lives of children who lived so close to nature.

For Alfred, however, the most important toy in his life and one he would always remember was given to him by his father on his fourth birthday. It came at a time of insecurity in an otherwise happy childhood, when he and his elder brother had been sent to a dame's boarding school at Laxfield in Suffolk, kept by two sisters, Miss Alice and Miss Jane Read. The boys boarded there for a short time while their mother was ill – probably with one of her intermittent attacks of melancholia.

The birthday present was a dun-coloured wooden horse, whose head nodded up and down. It had a black mane and tail and Alfred called it Merrylegs after a picture of a horse drawn by Randolph Caldecott in the Christmas number of *The Graphic* taken by the Misses Read. Maybe Alfred, sent away from home at three-years-old, identified with the sentiments in Caldecott's picture of a young lady, about to be married, saying goodbye to her horse Merrylegs in the stables, just as he might have said goodbye to his father's horses. Missing his mother, he perhaps lavished his affection on a toy horse. Two years later it was still his favourite toy and he made a drawing of it for his mother. It was his first equestrian model; the forerunner of the many horses he would adore, draw, ride and often allow to become a part of his life itself.

At Laxfield he also rode his first dapple-grey, a steam horse on a roundabout at a country fair held in the wide village street. It was a magical moment he often dreamt about. He also remembered a dream-like quality about the piebald and skewbald ponies he saw later, through the strange mysterious light of a Big Top when a governess took him to the circus.

Horses, it seemed, were the focal points of many pictures in his mind's eye, almost from babyhood when he also learned the feel and scent and touch of them from being put up in front of an uncle or his father when they rode about the mill farm. Later he was often hoisted up on to the back of a great carthorse by one of the horsemen and, his legs too short to straddle its wide back, he relaxed, absorbing its every movement as if he were an extension of the horse itself. Driving with his father through the country lanes, it was the movements of the grey mare drawing their trap that held his attention rather than the passing scenery.

The appeal of horses was impregnated in him from childhood on two levels – the physical and the emotional. Every morning as he knelt at family prayers he fixed his eyes on an old oil painting labelled 'Grey Horse – Orinoco – the property of William Green Munnings of Stoke-by-Nayland. J. Hobart, Pinxt 1840' and speculated on the painter and his grandfather's attachment to the model. In later years he recognized the significance of horses in his life when he acknowledged 'They have been my supporters, friends – my destiny in fact.'

It was his father who first taught him to draw them. On winter Sunday afternoons, with the curtains closed on the family gathered in the parlour, John Munnings would split open a pile of used envelopes, flatten the paper and with commendable economy, draw horses on the clean insides. His sons did the same. This occupation, or browsing through the large family scrap album, were considered appropriate Sabbath pastimes by the religious-minded John Munnings who, every Sunday, read the lesson in Mendham Church with great gusto. He declaimed in such a theatrical way – an extension of his performances at the Penny Readings – that people walked miles from neighbouring parishes to hear him. Alfred could hardly have been unimpressed by his father's stentorian tones raised to the rafters of the little church. Years later, he frequently emulated them, but in very different settings on completely dissimilar subjects in a rumbustious way that belied his somewhat aesthetic appearance.

Ellen remained completely unimpressed by her husband's performances: 'The service was not, to my mind, refreshing or peaceful,' read an entry in her diary, which she wrote up only on Sundays. She was not nearly as religious as her husband, but she was an accomplished pianist and sometimes played the organ in church. Her diary entries also reflected her tendency to melancholia: 'I have been reading Longfellow's verses, *The Rainy Day* – it is typical of my feelings. At times the loneliness and the sense of loss overcomes me and I think "What use is Life?"' she wrote after she had visited the grave of the family dog, Joe, who had been killed by a butcher's cart.

Nevertheless, she ran a happy home and often played the piano and sang as well as joining her husband at reading aloud in the evenings. John Munnings's dramatic renderings to his family in the confines of the small lamp-lit parlour were even more enthralling to his diminutive audience than to the larger ones in the churches and village halls. 'What boys could ever be leading dull lives with a good story going on each night interwoven with their work and play?' Alfred recalled in a tribute to the happiest of childhoods, which gave him a life-long sense of security.

For the first seven years of his life, apart from the short period at the dame school, his education was entrusted to a series of governesses whose qualifications varied as the Munnings's family fortunes fluctuated. Some were well-educated spinsters who lived in the household; others were buxom village girls who made vain attempts to keep order in the nursery and took the boys out for country walks with Charlie, the youngest, riding in a little, four-wheeled cart pulled by a nanny-goat.

Alfred often rode the family's white pony, named Merrylegs after his favourite toy, but he was too small to mount her unaided. Some Sunday mornings he rode her the two-and-a-half miles to Harleston Post Office to collect the mail, for although there was a Sunday post, there were no Sunday deliveries. He would sit outside the Post Office on Merrylegs waiting for the postmaster or his wife to notice him through the window and bring the letters out to be stowed away in his stiff leather post bag. He enjoyed the ride on his own much more than he did the comparatively tame two-and-a-half mile Sunday afternoon ride to church with his brother mounted behind him and their father walking alongside.

John Munnings was a tireless worker and often drove his ponies to six markets a week, the furthest being Norwich, some twenty miles away. He sometimes arrived home rather the worse for prolonged stops at inns and public houses en route but this was accepted by the family as a matter of course. Drink merely induced a lively Rabelaisianism in him and it was hard to take offence.

He and Emily had been warmly welcomed when they had arrived in the parish, possibly out of respect for Emily's family at Walsham Hall. After two years, they joined four other founder members for the board of the new village school which opened the year their first son was born.

In turn all their sons went there to be taught with some hundred and twenty boys and girls between the ages of five and fourteen. Lessons were given in two classrooms by a 'headmaster and his wife or sister' as the advertisement for new teachers always read. Classes were co-educational but boys and girls were segregated at playtime by a wall down the middle of the concrete playground. Singing figured prominently in the syllabus, probably thanks to Emily Munnings who took her responsibility as a governor very seriously and frequently visited the school. She was an indomitable figure and, as the years passed, virtually ran Mendham village as she did her four high-spirited sons, particularly when her husband returned home later and later, delayed by ever-prolonged visits to the public houses.

William and Alfred Munnings were both pupils at the school on 23 April 1885 when the headmaster, William Garrett, declared a half-day holiday for the wedding of Miss Rosie Ringer, Emily's sister, and from eleven o'clock pupils were free to line the bridal route from the church to Walsham Hall.

Alfred's chief impression of his aunt's wedding day was of a pair of elegant dappled greys, sporting white rosettes above their silky silver manes. They had been borrowed from the Magpie Hotel at Harleston and trotted up to Walsham Hall drawing the carriage taking the newly-weds to their wedding breakfast, laid out on long tables on three sides of the low parlour.

Mingled with six-year-old Alfred's memory of the bedecked dapple greys with their arched necks was the sharp sweet taste of the syllabubs he ate hiding under the white tablecloth at the bride's feet. The rich creamy sweet, liberally laced with sherry, added to a day that delighted all his senses. Ever afterwards, grey horses remained his particular delight and stirred his imagination like no other horses.

He drew them all from memory and imagination; great Suffolk

Punches and gentle mares and foals, jousting scenes with knights on horseback inspired by *Ivanhoe* and mustangs carrying Indians into battle with cowboys, illustrating tales of the Wild West. Some spontaneous efforts were drawn on the white-washed walls of the garden house or privy, others on sheets of cartridge paper to be pasted up on the nursery walls. He was, he said, 'Drawing for no reason – in blissful ignorance – without intent or aim, and not a care in the world of dreams, excepting home lessons . . . .' But the artistic talent he displayed by the time he could read and write was clearly recognizable.

His first sale was a pencil drawing of a trace-horse that pulled the waggons of a wealthy farmer, Mr Sewell, who gave the young artist five shillings for it. His generosity may have encouraged Emily to send Alfred for twice-weekly drawing lessons to Miss Kate Brereton, the parson's daughter. It was the first step in acknowledging that drawing and painting might, perhaps, become more than part of a world of dreams in her good-looking son's life.

His talent was further encouraged when he, and in turn his brothers, went to Redenhall Commercial School, a small private establishment that aimed to train boys for commerce. It was a two-mile walk each way for the Munnings boys but it was worth it for the Headmaster, Christopher C. Hall, interpreted commercial training in the widest sense. The syllabus included history, French and other basic subjects but left plenty of time for physical activities such as football, cricket, drill and swimming in the school swimming baths. More important, the Head encouraged Alfred to draw. 'When you draw,' he told him, 'hold your pencil lightly – so lightly that if I flip it from your hand it will not mark the paper' and, suiting his words to action, he flipped Alfred's pencil away with his third finger and thumb at the first attempt.

Not that Alfred Munnings needed any encouragement to draw. A rag-and-bone man who pushed his two-wheel blue handcart round Harleston Market, left it outside the Magpie while he slaked his thirst and returned one day to see Alfred had found the blank surfaces of its sides irresistible and covered them with paintings of horses.

The uniform caps with R.C.S. embroidered on them, the canings and the Speech Days were good preparations for the large boarding school to which Alfred would go. Meanwhile, homework still left time for family reading round the fire on winter evenings and Alfred was happy at school for the last time. He had made three good friends: a form-mate, Philip Welham-Clarke, and his sisters, Mia and Lily, who were both fond of painting. Mia remained a painting companion for many years and a life-long friend.

Mendham Mill, in the interim, was beginning to pay its way. When Alfred was nine-years-old, however, the family fortunes suffered a severe set-back. It seemed that Munnings's partner, sixty-one-year-old George Chase, was well-cushioned against the agricultural slump by his diverse financial interests. But one winter's night, after celebrating too well at the Magpie in Harleston, he climbed into his pony and trap, whipped the pony up with a mighty flourish so that it jerked forward, the trap went up in the air, landed on a patch of ice and skidded over on its side. Chase was thrown out and broke his neck.

His sudden death came at a critical time in his financial affairs and it meant that John Munnings worked most of his life to clear Chase's debt involving Mendham Mill. Meanwhile, thanks to his wife's inheritance of a small farm at the top of Mill Lane, Mendham, family life gradually resumed normality – but too late for them to send their eldest son, William, to boarding school. Anyhow, he had already decided to be a farmer so it was felt he had received sufficient education and he left Redenhall Commercial School to help his mother build up a small stock farm, specializing in Red Polls, on land hired from her two unmarried sisters at Walsham Hall. Nevertheless, the fact that he was not as well-educated as his younger brothers gradually provoked a deep resentment – particularly between him and Alfred.

In the autumn of 1891, three weeks before Alfred's thirteenth birthday, there was enough money to send him to board at Framlingham College. Fees were £11 a term and a pound less for his younger brother who followed him there. They included, 'the Mending of Clothes and Boots, but not the soling and heeling of boots'.

The school had been founded sixteen years before Alfred's birth as Suffolk's memorial to Albert, the Prince Consort, whose bronze statue, eight feet high and mounted on a nine-foot granite pedestal, dominated the terrace in front of the main entrance. The fine,

T-shaped building, built to accommodate three hundred or so boys, stood in fifteen acres of grounds on a hill opposite the huge ruins of Framlingham Castle across the valley.

Alfred hated school. Separated once more from his family, he was one of four new boys in form Lower III, the next to the top form of the Junior School. The school's 221 boys slept about twenty to a dormitory, washed in cold water in the hundred handbasins in the corridors and ate together in the huge dining hall where projecting stones supported the roof girders. The stones were carried by carved angels holding painted shields emblazoned with the heraldic devices of the governors and patrons of the College. Alfred was not the slightest bit grateful to them. 'I was damned miserable there,' he complained.

School magazines of the time showed that he made no contribution to the social or sporting life of the school, despite the swimming prizes he had won at Redenhall. He hated Euclid, algebra and other compulsory subjects. Only history, taught by a kind and wise master, Mr C. O. Raven, held his attention when – shades of fireside evenings at the Mill House – he read aloud to his pupils from the stimulating works of the nineteenth-century historians, Thomas Macaulay and James Froude.

Discipline was strict and Alfred suffered plenty of canings including six of the best administered by Alfred Pretty, the under-Head, a former pupil at the school. He was the son of a country doctor and a strict Victorian disciplinarian who taught modern languages. He was also a keen athlete and heartily disapproved when he caught the non-athletic Alfred drawing during Prep.

Drawing and painting lessons, which mainly consisted of freehand drawing from copies, were given by Edward Walter Lynch, 'a peaceful, fat, curly-headed middle-aged bachelor' as Alfred described him. The description tied in more with Lynch's other role of Bathing Master which the boys were expected to subsidize from their pocket money along with a subscription to the Library Fund and games.

'Bug' Lynch not only supervised swimming in a large bathing pool near the College but, with other masters, took the boys for bathing excursions by train to Aldeburgh on summer afternoons. The cost was 7d, plus a little extra for incidental expenses such as boats to accompany the sea bathers. It allowed the boys, according to the School Prospectus, 'to have a dip in the Sea at less than ordinary risk, and five or six hours by the Seaside for about a Shilling'.

Alfred drew and painted in every spare moment. His letters home were usually embellished with lively drawings of knights in combat or illustrations of episodes from Wild West tales, always featuring horses. He and his great friend, Charles Hamilton Scott, eighteen months his senior, hit on the idea of painting in the Music Room before breakfast until they were met by Alfred's arch enemy, the zealous Mr Pretty. Their punishment was to get up at seven o'clock every morning, fill Mr Pretty's cold bath and parade up and down the school drive, from the statue of Prince Albert to the gates and back, before breakfast until further notice. 'We cursed that fool of a master,' Alfred said.

Ironically, Charles Hamilton Scott's name, not Alfred Munnings's, was recorded in the school records for winning a drawing prize. He was destined to become a stockbroker but drawing and painting remained his hobby, and in 1947 there was an exhibition of his Suffolk pictures at Framlingham. The next year he was also represented in the Royal Academy – not as an exhibitor but as a sitter in a portrait by Francis Hodge.

Alfred's impression of Framlingham College was made perfectly clear: in the 1940s the Headmaster, Mr R. W. Kirkman, invited him to present a painting to his old school and his reply was an emphatic 'No'.

After less than two years at a 'rotten place', as he described it, he left at fourteen-and-a-half, apparently fundamentally unaffected by his educational experience. He typified the roughly-spoken, bluff-mannered sons of the rustic bucolic farming fraternity who, with those of the local gentry and clergy and of Newmarket trainers and local tradesmen, made up the school community.

He ended his inauspicious career in the Lower IV but, unlike many of his form-mates, he had no intention of following in his father's footsteps. His future promised to be far more precarious. In the days when even great artists could barely scrape a living, his one determination was to draw and paint.

CHAPTER II

An Influential Trio

John and Emily Munnings were very concerned about how their sturdy fun-loving second son could be trained to earn a living. Eventually, John approached the well-established printers and publishers, Jarrolds of London Street, Norwich, the street where, more than a century before, the father of the Norwich School painter, John Sell Cotman, had run his silk mercer's business. Mr William Jarrold, the Chairman, was willing to take Alfred on as an apprentice.

Alfred was delighted. Norwich was the biggest place he knew. He had often gone there with his father to market or with his mother in the pony and trap on her excursions to find rare books – particularly first editions of Walter Scott's novels. His imagination was fired by the cobbled streets and gabled houses of the '... city of gardens, with its cathedral, its fifty churches, its river with wherries, boats and barges, quays and bridges ... towers on the ancient walls of the city, alley-ways [sic] leading to courtyards and back streets, with churches hidden away.... Such an unlimited wealth of motifs would tempt the dullest painter,' he wrote romantically.

Apart from school, his only other outings had been to Lowestoft on day trips with the family, where he had once spent a week on a steam yacht anchored by the quay. He had been a guest of one of the crew whose father worked at the mill.

The thought of living in Norwich thrilled him and he was about to sign his apprentice papers with Jarrolds when, quite by chance, a painting enthusiast visiting the mill was very impressed by a portfolio of his work. It included an illustrated moral tale of pigs told in seventeen pictures and fourteen verses, the first of which read:

Pigs were cheap and pig trade slow;
In a miller's stye was a fine old sow:
The time of year I don't know when;
But a pig would fetch as much as a hen.

The visitor was emphatic that such artistic if not literary talent might be lost in the world of publishing whereas in a firm of lithographers, he said, it would be developed and disciplined.

It was sound advice. The hundred-year-old lithographic method of producing prints from a drawing on porous stone had already been used effectively by the Spanish painter Goya and, in France, by the satirical cartoonist Honoré Daumier and later by Toulouse Lautrec. In Britain, however, it was not adopted by artists in colour to any extent until after 1900.

The head artist at Page Bros. & Co., the Directors and the Manager considered his pig story 'a masterpiece'. For a premium of £40, he was bound over for six years as an apprentice to the firm established since 1850 as letterpress printers, wholesale stationers, box makers and lithographers in a building off St Stephen's Street, near the heart of the city. For half-a-crown a week and two weeks' holiday a year, he would work from 9 a.m. to 7 p.m. with an hour for lunch and a half-day on Saturdays.

His mother paid for him to stay with her second sister, his Aunt Jane Read, who, after a farming venture of her husband's had failed, kept a small boarding house at Catton two miles west of the city. Alfred was happy there particularly because Aunt Jane, like many relations on both sides of his family, prided herself on being something of an amateur artist and took more than a polite interest in his work.

She was as dominating a personality as his mother. A silver chatelaine hung from her waist and among the paraphernalia dangling from it were a pair of tiny scissors, a button hook and a key to the caddy of best tea. When she entertained in the parlour, the caddy was brought in on a silver tray with the other tea things by the parlour maid and Aunt Jane ceremoniously unlocked it before her visitors. Another of her teapot rituals represented her personal addition to the thirty-nine Articles of religious belief. The fortieth Article, she decreed, should ensure that everyone would be physically cleaned out once a week. Therefore, on Friday evenings she served only senna tea.

Alfred cycled from her home to Page Bros. At first, he had the most menial task in the 'artists' room' where six besmocked lithographers sat on high stools and worked at their benches under tall north-facing windows. Frosted-glass partitions separated each man from his neighbour but, at times, particularly on dark winter evenings – the men used to sing in harmony in melancholy chorus.

The artists drew designs in reverse in greasy ink on highly polished limestone slabs about four inches thick. The ink was set and made waterproof with a solution of acid and gum arabic and the slab was then wiped over with a wet cloth. The greasy ink repelled the water while the unprotected area of the porous stone absorbed it. When printing ink was spread over the whole stone, it adhered only to the line drawing which could then be pressed off on to sheets of printing paper.

Colour printing was an exacting development. It involved using as many stones as there were colours. Each colour was painted on to a separate stone bearing copies of the master drawing and, in turn, each colour stone – sometimes as many as twelve – was pressed on to the final print. Needle-pierced register marks ensured the colours fitted exactly. Alfred Munnings's first job in this skilful process was to mix the saucers of special lithographic ink made from a composition of wax, lampblack, oil and soap, for his six companions.

He watched and learned and studiously mixed ink for many months and when, at last, he was allowed to try his hand and copy a fretwork design on to stone, he discovered it was not as easy as it appeared. He made a mistake in his free hand drawing and scraped it out without realizing that he was damaging the surface of the stone. In the press room his error was glaringly apparent as a bare white patch in the background. The stone had to be completely repolished and the design painted on to it all over again. Lithography was an art, Munnings learned, in which 'not a mistake could be made – even a finger touch on the stone would print'.

Over the next six years he created hundreds of clear-cut imaginative and arresting lithographic designs for posters and advertisements. In doing so he developed an assurance and an accuracy with his brush along with an ability to draw first and paint later, which were enviable assets for any painter. Perhaps, young as he was, he recognized the importance of this training for he never complained about the long disciplined hours nor found his work anything but 'thrilling' and 'engrossing'.

At seven o'clock after a nine-hour working day, bursting with enthusiasm, he tore off his artist's smock, jumped on his bicycle and pedalled down the narrow streets to the School of Art for two hours' instruction at a cost of sixpence a week.

The 'cabin'd, cribbed and confined' quarters of the Norwich School of Art, as the local newspaper described it, were conveniently situated above the Free Library so that Munnings could continue his love of reading started by his mother. He read avidly, from the works of Tennyson, Scott, Dumas, Thackeray and others and easily memorized long passages from poems and stories that took his fancy, so that he could quote them for the rest of his life.

Books were his passion while painting was his destiny. 'I could, if I had to, live without pictures, but without a book I might exist – but not live in the full sense of the word,' he once admitted. 'Without books I am lost.... Were I forced to make a choice between books and pictures in my home, without any hesitation I would say, "Give me the books".'

The cramped Art School was reached by a tortuous stone stairway, leading to rooms full of plaster casts, wooden stools, curtains and aspidistras. A cupboard housed a human skeleton which, when smallpox was about, was always decorated with a red arm-band.

Walter Scott, the School's seventh Headmaster, had managed to make some improvements to the appalling conditions he found when he arrived. He increased the ventilation so that students were no longer overcome by foul air seeping up from the Library's Reading Room, installed part electric lighting, a 'Tortoise' stove in the Antique Room and blinds under the skylights to exclude daylight and draughts.

Munnings seemed oblivious to any shortcomings in the School and saw only a pleasant studious atmosphere which filled him with a desire to study. Taught by Walter Scott and his four assistants, he worked his way through classrooms on either side of a long corridor. He always maintained that his artistic career really began at the end of the corridor in the Model Room, where new students laboriously shaded studies of white casts of cubes, cylinders, cases and triangles. 'There,' he wrote, 'my eyes were opened to all the never-ending wonders of perspective and light and shade.'

After a few weeks he moved to the Antique Room to copy an ornamental bas-relief, first in black and white and then in sepia. After copying a Trojan Scroll in sepia he progressed to anatomy starting with a study of Discobolos, the Greek discus thrower. However, he scarcely noticed the life-sized casts of mythological figures, including a replica of the famous marble statue, the Venus de Milo, surrounding him for his imagination was completely captured by the cast of a horse's head from one in the Parthenon. Would he always be more inspired by horses than by women? He was completely obsessed by it and wrote: 'All through the hours of work at lithography from nine till seven I lived only to go on with that splendid horse's head in sepia from seven to nine! The hours spent on it each evening slipped away too fast, but they were not wasted, for I learned all I know of a horse's head from that cast.'

The student of fifteen, who at six-years-old had used a toy horse as a model, still learned more by painting from a statue than from a living model. Steadily he grew more skilful and seemed to relish every opportunity to improve. In fact his acute awareness of the need for constant improvement was a driving force that never deserted him. He was never complacent and always, when confronted with a picture he admired, reacted in puzzled wonder with the searching rhetorical question: 'How did he do it?'

One of his teachers in watercolours was Miss Gertrude Offord, whose watercolours of flowers were exhibited in Paris, at the World Fair in Chicago and regularly at the Royal Academy. Her teaching was sound and, unlike many painters, he found watercolour an easier medium than oil. Moreover, from the beginning, he showed the true mark of the professional and was rarely satisfied with his work.

Eventually, he graduated from the Antique Room and the never-to-be-forgotten horse's head to the Painting Room to learn to work with oils, but it was many years before he was as happy with them as he was with watercolours. Finally he was allowed to work two evenings a week in the Life Room from live models. There, he proved the most consistent prizewinner.

During those formative years he had three significant, guiding mentors; three men for each of whom Munnings might have represented the son he never had. The first was Walter Scott, the

Art School's Headmaster, whom Munnings considered 'an honest soul if ever there was one'. Scott had, rather reluctantly, moved from Macclesfield School of Art to Norwich only on condition that the Committee offered him all the School's income from fees as well as the science grant from the local council, obtained by levying a penny rate to coordinate science and art teaching for the artisan.

Scott's marriage was happy but childless and when, four years after his Norwich appointment, he discovered a new student with a rare talent and a remarkable maturity in his work, it may well have helped to justify his decision to change jobs. Certainly he could rarely resist giving Munnings special attention, which the other students were quick to notice.

One day, Munnings and another boy were copying a cow from the same cast and Scott pointed out why Munnings's drawing was the better. The other boy exploded with rage and rushed from the room complaining bitterly about favouritism. Gradually, however, Munnings's extraordinary talent was accepted at the Art School as it was at Page Bros. and, because of his enthusiastic zest for life and his easy outgoing personality, he was never short of friends.

Walter Scott taught him the importance of sincerity in art – and made him aware of values, tones and shadow shapes. 'Munnings,' he used to say, 'whatever you do remember the tone.'

While Walter Scott was influencing Munnings in pure art his pupil's attitude to life and to commercial art was being developed and refined by 'the kindest, gayest, most happy and optimistic a friend a youth ever had,' as Munnings described his first patron. He was John Shaw Tomkins, managing director of A. J. Caley and Sons, one of Page Bros.' most important customers, whose chocolate and mineral-water factory was just next door. Munnings acknowledged that the tall fair curly-haired man with busy merry eyes, which took in everything that was happening, helped to direct the whole course of his life.

Shaw Tomkins was married with one daughter and lived in a fine house in Town Close Road, a mile from the city centre. He was bursting with energy, laughter and original ideas and, like many such men, indicated it by moving at about twice the normal pace as if to make time for everything he wanted to do. He was the complete opposite to the country boy from a prosaic slow-moving East Anglian background.

He introduced into the English confectionery trade milk chocolate blocks and bars, the first fancy chocolate boxes and chocolate-filled novelties, followed in 1899 by Christmas crackers. As Munnings's drawing and painting developed through his evening classes, he was invariably chosen to execute Shaw Tomkins's latest ideas and designs and, gradually, started introducing ideas of his own. At the same time he also designed posters and catalogues for other firms; from brewers to brushmakers, from political campaigners to poultry dealers and shoe manufacturers, but always Caley's ideas, as suggested or approved by Shaw Tomkins, took precedence.

Munnings found he could create eye-catching commercial designs with ease, purely from his imagination. He had no need to use models. Some of his posters became famous throughout the country, particularly the bright Christmassy ones for Caley's crackers.

At seventeen he won first prize of £3 in a competition for an advertisement for Waverley Cycles run by *The Cyclist* magazine. His entry showed a cheeky cyclist mocking an angry Satan sitting on a milestone and was captioned 'Satan's latest sorrow – those who ride Waverley defy pursuit.' By then his salary as a trainee had risen to £1.10s. a week.

He knew, however, that lithography, like his art classes, was merely a means to an end. He longed to be free to paint in watercolours out-of-doors, scenes of nature and horses and people reflecting the way of life he loved. He painted such pictures at weekends and during his fortnight's annual holiday when he went home to Mendham. Sometimes, his painting companion was Mia Welham-Clarke, his Redenhall school friend, whose untrained talent benefited from watching his technique. Often, Shaw Tomkins bought his better pictures for about five shillings each.

Meanwhile, his patron's infectious enthusiasm spurred the inherently lazy Suffolk boy to a prodigious commercial output that even surprised himself. Yet it seemed as if his commercial work added to rather than detracted from his progress in pure art which he described as 'strenuous'. This description reflected the effort he put into the three oils and eight drawings he produced during his six years of evenings at the Art School compared to the hundreds of designs he turned out, comparatively effortlessly, for Page Bros.

No commercial work, however, gave him as much satisfaction as the portrait of Shaw Tomkins's father which his patron commissioned. Munnings showed the benevolent old gentleman sitting in his garden against a background of hollyhocks and Canterbury bells, his faithful black collie at his side. It was a sympathetic and an immensely moving study of old age – a remarkable work to have been done by a rather raw youth.

He grew less raw thanks again to Shaw Tomkins. The enthusiastic businessman, whom Munnings described as 'the gayest teetotaller in the World', took the young painter on several Continental business trips on which he never tried to curb his protégé's love for strong lager. Their evenings were usually spent in good restaurants or local music halls. After a particularly alcoholic evening he watched indulgently when Munnings vainly tried to stand on his head to prove he was not the slightest bit intoxicated.

During the day, Munnings was introduced to other designers and exchanged ideas with them. Then Shaw Tomkins got down to business with buyers and suppliers and Munnings was free to visit the local art galleries. He was not expected to do any painting but spend his time absorbing the works of the great painters in France, Germany and Switzerland.

Leipzig Fair proved an exception. Before World War I the event was so popular that it was difficult to find reasonable accommodation near the town and often patron and protégé slept in a room with two or four others – or failed to sleep because of the loud snores of Caley's German agent.

At the 1897 Fair, Caley's had a particularly large and impressive stand. When it was erected Shaw Tomkins thought it could be improved by the addition of some extra posters. Caley's German agent took Munnings to buy huge rolls of calico-lined cartridge paper, paints and brushes with which he worked outside the stand, producing posters at an impressive rate while admiring crowds gathered to watch. It was one of Shaw Tomkins's best publicity stunts. Afterwards, Munnings painted a large impression of Caley's stand which the firm treasured.

'I can never pay sufficient homage to my old friend for those early travels,' acknowledged the boy whose boundaries, until then had been confined to East Anglia. The benefit to him was immeasurable. Often the direct influence of those travels could be traced in his work as in the oil painting that first brought him national recognition. It was undoubtedly inspired by a picture that had fascinated him in an Amsterdam gallery of a little girl wearing a bright overall of a particular shade of blue.

Until his travels with Shaw Tomkins his horizons had chiefly been set by artists of the Norwich School of Painters led by John Sell Cotman and John Crome, the weaver's son, who was so poor that sometimes he could not afford to buy brushes and had to paint with hairs taken from his cat's tail.

This only school of internationally famous painters in England had been started in 1803 as a literary debating society interested in artistic subjects. Two years later, in the year of the Battle of Trafalgar, it held its first painting exhibition. Its most vital phase ended about 1833, although the school continued until the 1880s.

In Munnings's student days only a modest collection of Norwich School paintings hung in the single little Art Gallery housed in part of the Museum in Norwich Castle, previously the County Gaol. The paintings were arranged two or three deep on chocolate-coloured paper behind a protective hand-rail.

Munnings studied those paintings by the hour, day after day. He longed to portray the beauty of nature all around him, as those financially struggling painters had done. There was John Crome's powerful scene on the River Wensum, filled with light and space; John Sell Cotman's quiet and tantalizingly unfinished view of his father's house in Thorpe, near Norwich; and Alfred Priest's strong study of a watermill that must surely have reminded Munnings of his own home.

Dominating them all in a riot of colour and pageantry, was Joseph Stannard's huge canvas of a Thorpe Water Frolic of 1824. The painting had been commissioned by John Harvey who organized the pageant when he returned from Venice to Norwich to live at Thorpe Hall. It was attended by twenty thousand people – two-fifths of the Norwich population.

The canvas was crowded with a rich impression of boats of all kinds and a mass of people. The patron could be identified standing on a huge gondola next to his own fine yacht, *The Sylph*, and the artist, also a keen boatman, had been unable to resist including himself, wearing a red coat, in the picture on the extreme right. The subject and its conception was in startling contrast to the calm landscapes of other Norwich School paintings surrounding it and the young lithographer would have been dazzled and captivated by the sense of pageantry.

It must have been agonizingly frustrating for an impatient boy, brimming with enthusiasm, to study and marvel at such works and dream of painting such pictures even while he recognized they were far beyond him. Confronted with translations of his own visions, he realized he needed expert help to sympathize with his longing and, at the same time, explain the significance of every line and nuance of the works he so admired.

Fate, in the short stiff personage of sixty-five-year-old James Reeve, was literally at his side. During his fifth year in Norwich, Alfred decided it was time to show more independence and leave his Aunt Jane's comfortable boarding house. He took lodgings on the other side of the city run by a rather formidable widow, Mrs Stubbs. He could not have made a more fortunate choice. By a sheer stroke of luck a few yards down the road was James Reeve's elegant detached residence. The Norwich-born curator of Norwich Castle Museum, during the last years of the Norwich School, was Alfred Munnings's third mentor.

He was a competent artist himself and when he joined the staff of the Norwich Museum in 1847, as Curator's Assistant with a wage of four shillings a week, he supplemented his earnings by giving private drawing lessons. By the turn of the century he was acknowledged as the greatest authority on the Norwich School and his bachelor home in the suburb of Thorpe was a treasure house of their drawings. He also helped Mr J. J. Colman, head of the Norwich mustard firm, to form a world-famous collection of their work. Most of his own collection was ultimately sold to the British Museum, because he perhaps hoped to consolidate national recognition for the Norwich School.

The Museum Curator knew Munnings from the student's frequent visits to the Art Gallery and also from the School of Art with which Reeve was closely connected. Before long the boy was a frequent visitor to Reeve's home where, after being initiated into the joys of cigar smoking, he was conducted from room to room, each crammed with Norwich School drawings, and lectured on the thoroughness of the work and on such finer points as Cotman's faithfulness to his motto 'Leave out but add nothing'.

Extravagance and insincerity infuriated Reeve and as a result of his detailed study of great artists he, as much as anyone, recognized the dangers of allowing an immensely talented and precocious painter to run before he could walk. Munnings, in return, acknowledged Reeve as the third of his guiding influences and he always kept the easel Reeve gave him, which had once belonged to a member of the Norwich School.

James Reeve's involvement in many civic artistic activities had resulted in the foundation in 1885 of the Norfolk and Norwich Art Circle with forty-six members. It aimed to bring together anyone interested in art, provide books and periodicals and stage exhibitions twice a year. Alfred Munnings considered the annual subscription of one guinea to be a good investment and became one of its youngest members.

In 1898 he sold fifteen pictures through the Art Circle, ranging in price from £2.10s. to £30. They included two studies of his friend 'Jumbo' Betts, a stone-polisher at Page Bros., which were his first attempts at out-of-doors figure painting. One showed Jumbo digging his allotment and was priced at seven guineas. In the smaller painting, priced at four guineas, he was pretending to fish in the river at Lakenham. Both were reminiscent of Millet's romantic pictures showing the characters and occupations of peasants which Munnings had admired on his visits to France with Shaw Tomkins.

The bi-annual exhibition of the Norwich Art Circle proved a lucrative and steady shop window. Through it, over the next ten years, Munnings sold more than a hundred and ten pictures ranging in price from single figures to £100 in 1904 for *In the Low Meadows*. Meanwhile, however, there would be other triumphs, disappointments and a tragic accident.

He was the Art School's most consistent prize-winner for life drawing and in his summer holiday, when he was seventeen, he embarked on his most ambitious effort which he was convinced would win the School's holiday competition. He was so certain that he persuaded his father to buy a fine grey mare for him to use as a model. Hour after hour she was held by a young horseman while he painted her and other horses against a background of the Suffolk marshes. Finally, for the sake of the composition, he introduced half a dark chestnut horse into the foreground.

It had been twelve long months since he had painted a horse out-of-doors and, after all he had learned, *Evening on the Suffolk Marshes*, as he called the large oil, would certainly be an immortal masterpiece. He was hurt and shocked when it won only the second prize because of the dark chestnut horse. According to Walter Scott, a painter could not cut a horse in half in the foreground and introduce it in profile into the picture unless it were in a crowded fair or a cavalry charge. The pupil, for all his admiration for the teacher, remained unconvinced.

He partially redeemed himself in his own eyes when he was nineteen and captured his impression of the Art School's Painting Room in a large oil on canvas measuring sixty-six by forty-six inches. He caught it all in paint, as vividly as in words, when he described how: 'Beautiful diffused top lighting by day and gaslight at night made work a joy. The faded grey colouring of the rooms was a perfect background to everything – students in blouses working at easels, large casts of Greek and Roman fragments with slight settlements on top surfaces, aged castor-oil plants in green tubs.'

The evocative study of five students engrossed in their work surrounded by detailed clutter was a study in subtlety of colour and skilful brushwork. It showed an amazing maturity and won a National Bronze Medal in 1898. When Scott's deputy, Percy Cooper, saw it with Munnings's other work in the School's Exhibition of 1899 he commented, 'That boy can become President of the Royal Academy if he likes'.

He could never have aspired so high. The failure of *Evening on the Suffolk Marshes* to win the Art School's holiday competition still rankled. He could not forget how he had revelled in every stroke as he modelled the shape of the quarters and caressed with his brush the painted head and neck of the beautiful mare: 'The white on the back and top of those quarters isn't white: the subtle grey tones are indescribable – what colour. Difficulties pile up, but I am undaunted,' he agonized and was unable to concede defeat. He also, perhaps subconsciously, needed proof that Scott's judgement was infallible. There was one way he could find out: he submitted the painting to the Royal Academy's Summer Exhibition of 1899.

With it he sent two smaller studies painted about the same time: *Pike Fishing in January 1898* was a large version of his original painting of Jumbo Betts in a black overcoat, gum boots and a cloth cap pretending to fish in Lakenham River. The wintry scene was in marked contrast to the second picture painted a few months earlier during Munnings's summer holiday at Mendham. It showed the direct influence of the picture of the little girl in a bright blue overall he had admired on his Amsterdam visit with Shaw Tomkins earlier that year.

During that summer holiday when he was eighteen, his cousin Nina had worn a dress of the identical blue. She was the twin daughter of his Aunt Rosie, the bride of the memorable wedding at Walsham Hall, with the syllabubs and grey horses. He persuaded fair-haired Nina in her blue dress to sit for him with her twin Cecil in the bows of a wide-bottomed rowing boat aground in a shallow part of the mill-stream between high green sedges. It was the spot where, as a child, he had learned to swim, grasping bundles of rushes. Once again, in that same place, he experienced the sheer happiness of achievement which continued for three sunlit mornings while he captured on canvas the intense concentration of country children on an idyllic summer's day. He called their moment of adventure *Stranded.*

Stranded and the wintry fishing scene were both accepted for the Royal Academy's Summer Exhibition of 1899. He received the official notification only four days before Varnishing Day. It was one of the greatest days of his life.

A country boy in a rough tweed suit, he made his first terrifying journey through London's traffic on top of a horse-drawn bus to Burlington House to find both pictures hung 'on the line' – at eye-level, the best position. He conceded that 'they looked quite well' among the other two thousand or so paintings. The fishing scene sold for the vast sum of ten guineas and eventually hung in Bristol Art Gallery.

Coincidentally, a letter telling him that another of his paintings, a small landscape called *Cloudy Weather*, had been accepted for exhibition by the Royal Institute of Painters in Water Colours arrived by the same post as the exciting acceptance letter from the

Academy. The thrill of having three pictures simultaneously on show in prestigious London exhibitions tempered his angry disbelief that the Academy, at the same time, had rejected 'the great masterpiece'.

The first rejection perhaps provoked a characteristic moment of humility by emphasizing that Walter Scott's judgment was right and that, as a pupil, he had much to learn. It also emphasized that, despite his natural talent, he should curb his impatience to paint ambitious scenes that were well beyond him and obey James Reeve's warning 'Don't run before you can walk.' With it all, however, his native stubbornness asserted itself; he was determined to prove himself right about his masterpiece and submit it to the Royal Academy yet again the following year.

Meanwhile the acceptance letters called for a day of celebration, suggested by a fellow lodger, Ralph Wernham, a Government Post Office Inspector. He was a scholarly sophisticated Cambridge graduate who, as well as furthering Munnings's interest in books and poetry, had already helped to justify the younger man's new-found independence by introducing him to the theatre and the best Norwich bars. He had already planned to spend the day at Bungay Races and insisted that Munnings should join him. So, drunk with success, the young horse-loving painter travelled first-class in the train to his first real race meeting.

It was a heady experience; a plunge into the most colourful phase of life at the very moment when he was dazed with the joy of knowing that, at last, he could truly describe himself as a painter. Norwich horse sales, local races and village fairs had done little to prepare him for a conglomeration of them all; ponies and picturesque gypsies, roundabouts, shooting galleries and swings, the blaze of colour of striped awnings, the confusion of sounds and, most exciting of all, the horses and riders.

'Such colour and action as I had never dreamt of,' he said and stood transfixed, burning with excitement, watching race after race. 'I saw the thoroughbred horses and jockeys in bright silk colours, going off down the Course. The peaceful School of Art, the smelly artists' room at Page Bros. faded away and I began to live,' he said. Fortunately he was near the end of his apprenticeship.

Wernham made £5 on the day's racing and celebrated by taking his young companion out to dinner. Alfred had been too engrossed in the thrill of the bright silks and the sound of horses' hoofs thundering down the turf or seeing men flying over great fences, to waste time betting – even if he had had the money. It was the start of a life-time's habit of going to race meetings but never bothering to place a bet.

The next day, lithographic responsibilities once more forgotten, they went to the races again. It had been no dream; horses and pageantry against a background of smooth green turf and wide skies, alive with drama just as he remembered it. He later preserved his impressions in a set of pastels.

The notice of his Academy debut in the *Eastern Daily Press* came as something of an anticlimax. 'Once again it is to be feared this year's Academy is somewhat characterless,' wrote their art critic adding, 'No young genius has sprung into prominence.' For a moment Munnings may have wondered if the writer had overlooked his contributions but he was denied even that consolation for the critic noticed 'his two small but interesting paintings, both well placed'. He added, 'There is truth of atmospheric effect and some humour of observation in the drawing of the fisher,' while of *Stranded* he pronounced that 'the artist would do well to avoid a tendency to paintiness'.

It made disappointing reading for a young man who, in local art circles, was acknowledged as quite a personality. The week after the Academy opened he had twelve pictures in the Norwich Art Circle's black-and-white Exhibition. They included the inevitable horses and a selection of highwaymen and other characters in period costumes inspired by stories of Dickens and Scott, all beautifully displayed in mounts cut, lined and made at Page Bros. works and in their time.

The Exhibition was enthusiastically written up in the local paper three days after the disappointing Academy review had appeared there. 'The chief attraction is the work of Mr A. J. Munnings whose rocket flight into the realm of local celebrity is just now an object of common discussion,' their critic acknowledged.

The 'rocket flight' had hardly begun but the signs were sufficient to tempt the brothers, Jim and Sam Boswell, whose shop in London Street sold fine antiques and paintings by the Norwich School, to become regular buyers of Munnings's pictures at very modest prices and to encourage him to produce others to replace them as quickly as possible. It was his first real attempt at painting purely for money.

He painted those pictures mostly at weekends when with a friend from the Art School, Savile Flint, he cycled round the countryside near Norwich and captured in oils or watercolours the endless variety of lovely scenes that caught his eye. He also painted corners of the city he loved; the Cathedral Close, inn yards, horse sales in the Cattle Market and the riverside at Thorpe Gardens in holiday mood with boats all along the river frontage, a faint echo perhaps of Stannard's water pageant.

Another of his painting companions was one of Page's lithographers, Phil Presents, whose enthusiasm, if not his talent, equalled Munnings's own. An Art School friend was Walter Starmer who had beaten Alfred and two hundred and fourteen other students to win a local scholarship of £20 a year for three years at the School. He was a student of stained glass and with him Munnings explored most of the churches south of Norwich.

If they found an empty unlocked church Munnings would try his hand at playing the organ with Starmer blowing. Then, ignoring his father's warning that he would never prosper if he worked on Sunday, he would set up his easel outside the church. At that stage, he had little alternative to painting on the sabbath if he were to record even a few of the scenes and the subjects he longed to paint.

At one village an elderly lady saw him painting in the churchyard and asked why he never joined in the church service. 'I'm sorry,' he replied politely, 'but I wouldn't know what to do with my hands.' His religious belief, carefully nurtured by his parents, had crystallized into a passionate longing to express his painter's visions. His consistent prayer, frequently murmured aloud in anguish, was 'Oh God, if only I could put down what I see.'

He worked hard and consistently although Norwich offered him many distractions. As well as his regular visits to the Library, there was the fine museum with its collection of rare birds and geological and archaeological specimens adjoining the Art Gallery. There was music and the theatre. He was absorbed by George du Maurier's play *Trilby*, with its story of Parisian painters in a world he promised himself he would one day see at first hand. He thrilled to performances of the familiar plays of Shakespeare he had read so often. With it all, his happiest evenings were spent with friends in the convivial atmosphere of the Norwich inns and public houses.

There he was usually the life and soul of the all male parties, for in conversation he had no inhibitions, particularly after a drink or two and, like his father, he was happiest holding the centre of the stage. Where girls were concerned he showed little interest apart from flirting in an open casual sort of way when he was with a group of boys. In fact, he was too shy to approach any of the pretty girls, who strolled invitingly in Chapelfield Gardens on summer evenings, while a band from a cavalry regiment played romantic waltzes or tunes from Gilbert and Sullivan. The gardens were hung with coloured lights and admission to the romantic setting was sixpence.

Towards the end of his apprenticeship he was often seen in Norwich with a beautiful auburn-haired model but, according to a mutual friend, their friendship finished when she shocked him by inviting him to her lodgings. Despite his good looks which must have made him a target for the opposite sex, it seemed that girls and women were subjects to be idealized in real life as in paint and his attitude to sex appeared most prudish except when transalated into the raucous ballads he wrote and declaimed to his friends.

As the beer flowed he sang verses of his own composition, long ballads or well-known songs for his companions to join in. If, at the end of the evening, he had insufficient money to pay his share of the bill, he would present the landlord with a drawing offered with such confidence that it was invariably accepted as good currency. At one inn, where no paper was handy to sketch on, he pulled down the white roller blinds in the bar parlour with a flourish and drew on them in crayon. This spontaneous gesture was so well-received that he mentally filed it away to repeat on future occasions.

'A glass of wine for a picture' was a bargain struck many times. Often his colleagues at Page Bros. lithographed one of his finer watercolours and friends and acquaintances at the Art School and in the Art Circle clamoured for copies.

One month after his debut at the Royal Academy his six years' apprenticeship with Page Bros. came to an end and he refused their generous offer to pay him £5 to stay on. His final gesture at the School of Art, where his studentship also ended, was to submit an entry for a competition run by the Poster Academy at the Crystal Palace.

He had no intention of severing his ties with Norwich but, for the time being, backed with a little financial capital from his sale of paintings and armed with a copy of Stubbs's *Anatomy of the Horse* as his bible, which he had bought second-hand for fifty shillings, confident but well aware that pride might come before a fall, he decided to try his hand as a freelance and returned to Mendham, his first painting ground.

CHAPTER III

Return to Mendham

The village of Mendham had scarcely changed during the six years Alfred Munnings had been away, apart from the absence of his life-long friend, Mr Fairhead, the carpenter. In Mr Fairhead's workshop all the Munnings boys had learned to use a hammer and chisel and Alfred had made several model boats. The carpenter and his men had always seemed to be part of life at the Mill, doing regular repairs or removing dead rats from under the floorboards of the Mill House when an unmistakeable smell indicated their presence.

The trained lithographer and painter found the village carpenter's shop and yard silent and deserted for its owner had sold the property to a neighbouring village carpenter, retired and gone away. Munnings saw the shop as an ideal studio.

He cycled over to meet the new owner who sold him the freehold of the whole place for £50. He then sweetened the deal by agreeing to cut a sky-light into the north side of the building and provide a tortoise stove with pipe and chimney at no extra cost. Alfred furnished it with a gate-legged table and a set of old elm chairs and installed his canvases, easels, portfolios, sketches, brushes and paints. The operation took most of his savings so, for the time being, he lived at home but revelled in owning his own studio at last.

He waited for the promised commercial commissions to materialize and meanwhile painted the country scenes all around him; farm sales, horses drawing the plough and countless studies of farm animals against the ever-changing background of his beloved river: 'A river does, without doubt make a place,' he reaffirmed. '... With a river you can paint.'

The farm horses could not be spared to model during working

hours but the family doctor, George Chandler, lent him his wife's fat pony for most of the summer. Alfred ecstatically painted him day in and day out. It was his first free summer since childhood and he basked in the new depths of beauty and tone he found everywhere, particularly in the horses and the pony. He wrote romantically of the pony, with almost a touch of sensuality: 'At last I was involved, entangled in the magic of his tones. I was coming to grips with a subject at last.... Only think of a white pony feeding two yards from the rush-grown pool by the flood-gates, the grey water showing under its belly, the young green osiers to the left ... the fall of the green weeping-ash bough trailing in the water.... His mane and tail were thick and like silk, and his head was beautiful.' Would any woman move him to express such admiration in either words or paint?

He had never before spent so much time on his own and working alone, day after day throughout that summer, even in his 'painter's paradise' he was aware of moments of loneliness, when he found it impossible to work. With the loneliness came introspection and, probably because of his maternal inheritance, periods of irrational depression, already familiar to the gregarious twenty-year-old: 'I admit I can't always understand why moods come,' he reflected. 'Why I want to work and why I don't; why I'm depressed and why I'm happy.' Eventually, when moods of introspection overcame him he left his studio and sailed the river for a few hours in the family's new boat. Usually, he returned to work with renewed vigour.

He had first been aware of moments of depression during anatomy classes at Norwich Art School when he made his first studies of skeletons. He found it a traumatic business until he was struck by the sheer beauty of the horse's head from the Parthenon. An early acquisition for his studio was the skull of a thoroughbred and he never ceased to marvel at its beauty. He allowed his imagination full play and wondered at the ghostliness about the dark, hollow eye sockets and the subtle modelling of the bridge of the nose. 'Where the velvety expanding surfaces above the nostrils used to quiver ... a lifeless object to examine, with a magic grain in the bone more delicate than the grain in precious wood. Ivory traceries and shapes. A miracle of creation – of God; a mere trifle in a world of mysteries, of millions upon millions of God's masterpieces.... The grain of the wood is God's design, the grain of the bone is God's design. I know less than nothing.' So, in characteristic humility, wrote the poet in the painter who accepted religion on his own terms.

He studied anatomy relentlessly, long after his Art School days. He knew that a detailed knowledge of the bones below the surface of the animals he wanted to paint was vital if he was to master their form and stance in every situation and portray their beauty and characters. He traced a similarity between equestrian and human anatomy. The horse's hocks, he said, were the man's ankles, each with six bones; its knees were the wrists; the horse walked on the equivalent of man's fingers and toes; the stifle joint was the human knee – and so on.

Stubbs's *Anatomy of the Horse*, with the author's own meticulous copper-plate engravings, was always near at hand along with other books on horse anatomy. Munnings also had access to a perfectly set-up skeleton of a man and a horse owned by a Norwich veterinary surgeon. The man was probably a murderer who had been hanged at Norwich Castle and the skeletons gave an eerie impression gleaming in the moonlight streaming in through the windows of the old stable loft. It started the painter wondering about life and death and the paranormal, but he found comfort in believing in some sort of continuation of life after death.

He went to Norwich to the veterinary surgeon's stables to study and sketch the horses there for shoeing, harness-measuring, treatment or for sale and frequented the yard at the railway station to sketch the patient cab horses waiting for customers.

He pursued his thirst for first-hand experience at the cavalry barracks, near the spot where John Crome had painted his immortal views of nineteenth-century Norwich. Doubtless, Munnings would have loved to emulate him but his purpose was more practical and he was sickened with horror at watching the skin stripped from a dead horse. At the knacker's yard he was almost overcome with revulsion at a similar sight.

It was a welcome respite when his twin cousins, Nina and Cecil, stayed at the Mill House again and Alfred painted them in the orchard with Cecil riding the white pony and two ponies in the background looking on. He was nearly defeated by the way the shadows of the trees patterned the grass in the sunshine – an effect of light for which the Art School had not prepared him. But he experimented with watercolours to capture the effect and practised until he was confident enough to transfer his technique into oil on canvas. The result, *An Old Favourite*, was another idyllic impression of country children on an English summer's day.

His loneliness was regularly alleviated by Shaw Tomkins's visits to his studio. Munnings would meet him at Harleston station with a pony and trap and drive him to the studio where they would haggle in fierce friendliness over the price of designs for tri-coloured chocolate and cracker box tops. Shaw Tomkins ordered them by the dozen and eventually agreed to pay the handsome sum of fifty shillings for each design. The astute businessman frequently concluded the negotiations by buying a sketch or two to take home.

Business over, patron and protégé would lunch at the local Magpie or the Swan Hotel at Harleston. Over glasses of vintage port they might plan their next Continental trip, for Shaw Tomkins continued to take Munnings abroad as his guest for many years and, to his eternal credit, the art-loving businessman broadened the horizons of the talented young countryman far beyond his native East Anglia. He also introduced him to local pleasures and, in that first summer of the painter's freedom, took him with a party of friends for a week's sailing in a wherry on the Norfolk Broads.

It was a scene he soon learned to love – both as a painter and as a participant in the exciting world of racing and an endless round of sailing regattas. Invariably, the sailing and the carefree social life surrounding it won and he participated.

He joined the Yare and Bure Sailing Club and crewed his friend, Herbert Mackley, at Beccles Regatta in his winning racing cruiser *Bonito*. Afterwards, they celebrated by painting the town red and finished up at the traditional fair at the quayside. There, full of beer and high spirits, they ran a coal cart into the river and, chased by the local policeman, ran off over the footbridge and along the river bank to *Bonito*, jumped into the river and held on to her bob stay, so their noses were just above the water. They ducked under when the policeman arrived so the skipper could truthfully say he had not seen any young bloods running along the river bank.

Such interludes provided essential respites for a gregarious and lonely young painter. A self portrait sketched in a friend's autograph album shows him sitting disconsolately in front of his easel. Captioning it is his own rhyme:

I feel very lazy and loose,
For pictures don't seem any use.
But days that are sunny
Are better than money.
So working may go to the deuce.

Work had practical advantages however. When Herbert Mackley became a dentist, Munnings always paid his dental fees in paintings. Mackley, at the time, was not very appreciative.

Munnings grew increasingly socially-minded and made several friends of his own age including the Read sisters, Chrissie and Ethel, daughters of the local squire who was a great hunting man, of Goswold Hall, Thrandeston. They spent much time brewing beer for parties where they played cards and made up parties to go to the Hunt and Army Balls at nearby Eye.

Munnings grew 'very keen' on Ethel, the younger sister, according to her son, Roger Groom of Diss. 'He chased after her quite a bit,' he said. 'But, according to my mother, he was spiteful and she didn't like him. He was an outspoken man and he didn't mind whose toes he trod on. He was hardly tactful. Most probably that was why my mother said he was spiteful. He was selfish. He was going to have what *he* wanted, and to hell with anyone else.'

Meanwhile, Munnings was always delighted to welcome friends to his studio. They included his Art School contemporary Savile Flint, Mr Bagge Scott, the President of the Norwich Art Circle who Munnings considered the best Norwich painter since Cotman and who remained equally impoverished, and the Boswell brothers, who invariably bought any picture within sight.

One day they noticed a painting of a beautiful girl in a striped gown and large hat on a panel of the canvas screen Munnings kept by the studio door to stop the draught. They persuaded him to let them cut out the panel and took it away, rolled up, to be framed. Thanks to their business acumen Munnings's depleted bank balance soon regained his self-imposed safety margin of £70.

Theirs was a happy, business relationship. Munnings made Boswells' elegant, double-fronted shop in London Street his Norwich headquarters and painted in a corner of the top room where an expert named Whiting restored old pictures. There he produced picture after picture from his imagination; illustrations of scenes and characters he had read or plays he had seen, which the Boswell brothers bought, before they were dry, for a few gold sovereigns.

He was also a modest customer, as well as a supplier, for each year he had his pictures for the Royal Academy framed there. Critical friends would gather round to praise or comment before the pictures were packed up and sent off, and wish him luck. Afterwards, the Boswell brothers usually took him to lunch at the City Club, just opposite their shop. The mildly exclusive establishment for the professional and more prosperous men of Norwich had been founded by twelve Victorian gentlemen who sought pleasant but non-political conversation. Each had a key to the place and could help himself to drinks and put the money in a box. In the evening Munnings and the Boswells might walk beside the river to Porritt's Fish Shop for an early supper with other friends, often followed by a game of cards in the back parlour.

Munnings's circle of acquaintances grew but there were no deep friendships. His Norwich trips were pleasant and financially profitable interludes in the quiet country life he preferred, beside the slow-flowing Waveney. His steadily increasing commercial work allowed him plenty of time to paint landscapes and scenes from his boyhood, viewed afresh with his trained painter's eye, in the place he considered the most paintable part of England. He promised himself that he would soon be free to paint only landscapes and scenes, his natural birthright. Meanwhile, he accepted a retaining fee from a London printing firm which, he felt, justified him joining London's Langham Sketch Club. He could congratulate himself that his first year as a freelance painter had not been wasted.

In the late summer he went to stay with Aunt Polly, the widow of his Uncle Arthur Ringer. After her husband's death she had married a wealthy bachelor farmer and lived at Lodge Farm, Mulbarton, eleven miles from Norwich. That visit completely changed Alfred Munnings's life.

One afternoon he and a farmer friend, George Gowing, were out on the farm with two dogs and a hound puppy when the dogs saw a hare and chased it through a thorn fence and across the fields. The puppy could not get through the fence so Munnings bent down and picked him up and dropped him over into the field. As he straightened up a thorny branch rebounded and struck his right eye. He felt a sharp pain and then saw only a grey fog.

The local doctor made light of the injury. He diagnosed a bruise and prescribed a lotion to foment it. That evening Munnings, wearing theatrical make-up, sang two songs at a charity concert in the village hall. His eye was very painful and he left the hall several times to bathe it. A few days later it was more painful and he was driven to Norwich to see an eye specialist, Dr Sidney Johnson Taylor.

Eyes were only one speciality of Dr Johnson Taylor. At his surgery at 41, Prince of Wales Road, he held a clinic every morning before nine o'clock where, for half-a-crown, the poor could have their adenoids or teeth removed without an anaesthetic. If the patient showed signs of desperate poverty the doctor might offer to toss him 'half-a-crown or nothing', a wager he could always be relied upon to lose.

He had no hospital appointment so operations were performed in his surgery. However, he also had London consulting rooms and was connected with Moorfields' Eye Hospital, where he sent Munnings for examination by the newly-developed x-ray. It showed a thorn had pierced the lens of his eye and a speck of foreign body still remained. Johnson Taylor operated but too late to save the sight of the right eye and the injury was already affecting the left. With both eyes bandaged Munnings was brought back to Norwich to a nursing home in a tall Georgian house in Surrey Street in the heart of the city.

For weeks he lay with his eyes bandaged and greeted his visitors with high bravado and spirited renderings of 'Sweet Rosie O'Grady' and 'The Blue Alsatian Mountains'. Beneath it all, however, he inevitably grew more depressed.

It was poor consolation to know that several great artists had suffered from imperfect sight: Sir Joshua Reynolds went blind in one eye; Degas grew so short-sighted that in later life he had to use photographs of his models; Monet and Turner developed cataracts; and Whistler and Constable were colour-blind.

Eventually, Munnings grew so depressed that his mother arranged for his cousin Ellen Ringer to stay at the nursing home and read to him whenever he wanted. She got through *The Decline and Fall of the Roman Empire* and several other books.

He relished the sound of words, either his own or voiced by others, but never more than when a nurse who, despite his shocking language, considered him her favourite patient, read an announcement to him from *The Morning Post*. It stated that he had won the Poster Academy's Gold Medal with his poster of a bewigged old gentleman peering mischievously over his glasses as he played the cello. It was one of three designs he had submitted before his accident and had forgotten about and he could hardly believe it had won first prize.

It had been chosen from two hundred and forty entries and the heavy gold medal arrived months after he had left the nursing home, when his savings were at their lowest for years. He sold it to Sam Boswell for six gold sovereigns and, in a characteristic fit of exuberance, spent the money the same night on a celebratory dinner. Later he regretted parting with his prize, particularly when he learned that the Boswells had sold it to one of his admirers, a Norwich builder, who resold it to them on hearing that Munnings wished he had kept it. But the winner never saw his medal again. Presumably, the Boswell brothers decided that, melted down, it was worth more than its selling price.

He had left the nursing home soon after Christmas and was advised to rest his good eye for at least six months. But invalidism was not for him and, instinctively anticipating more modern treatment, in half that time he was trying to paint again. For months, however, he found that he could not judge distance, and, time and again, he either missed the canvas completely with his brush and made fresh air strokes or hit it violently. Patiently he curbed his frustration and persisted until his brush could touch his painting surface at will. Because he was right-handed his right eye had probably been his master eye and it would have taken him much longer to adjust to the disability than had he lost the other eye.

The accident had not altered his appearance and new acquaintances rarely knew of his handicap. He hardly complained although his lack of binocular vision remained a life-long handicap. In a rare moment of self-pity he complained: 'It cramps my style – shortens my stride, so to speak. What wouldn't I give to see with two eyes again.'

He was a tenacious fighter, born to paint, and he never seemed to consider the loss of his eye might jeopardize, or even end, his vocation. His savings had gone in helping to pay for treatment at the nursing home and, as soon as he could control his brush, he concentrated on producing large easily-defined tri-coloured posters for Caley's which hardly taxed his eye. Moreover, he courageously determined to prove his confidence and assert his independence by leaving home.

He rented two unfurnished rooms in an old farmhouse opposite his studio for £10 a year from a farmer, Alfred Wharton. The rest of the house was occupied by the farmer's horseman, Jonah Corbyn, whose wife agreed to look after Munnings and feed him for fifteen shillings a week. He sensed another occupant of the house, the ghost of Damaris Shearing, the wife of a former owner, but this did not worry him. In fact he rather enjoyed the thought of the dead keeping in touch with the living – providing his dog, Friday, was close at hand.

One of his rooms was the low-ceiling parlour which, over the next six years, he gradually furnished with interesting antiques. He acquired rugs and carpets from the Boswells in exchange for pictures and was delighted if he could find a bargain, restore and sometimes exchange it for a better one. When he bought a new treasure, he would spend hours rearranging his room to show it off to its best advantage. An original touch was a collection of different-shaped palettes displayed on one wall.

He was extremely house-proud and took particular delight in an old walnut-veneered bureau, a tall ormolu grandfather clock, its door emblazoned with a gold cockerel, and a pair of Sheffield-plated candelabra he could ill afford but which he thought added tone to the place. He had bought them from Ted Ellis, a dealer's buyer in Norwich, who attended auction sales to buy for other dealers, including the Boswells, and also to bid for fine wines and pictures for several county families.

Munnings often joined the crowd of regulars who met in the evenings in Ellis's back parlour behind the shop to sample his new acquisitions of port or wine and listen to tales of his sale-room exploits or stories of his youthful adventures when he had looked after the elephants in a travelling circus. The young painter did a wickedly clever charcoal drawing of the roguish bespectacled dealer sitting among the clutter of his curiosity shop. It was a brilliant likeness but Munnings's talent was scarcely recognized in those days, beyond his immediate contacts in the art world, and Ellis apparently never thought of asking for the sketch or even offering to buy it. He next saw it hanging in an important exhibition, but Munnings always refused to part with it to Ellis or to members of his family, probably because it recalled to him one of the happiest and most carefree stages of his life. It suggested that he could well have concentrated on portrait painting had it not been for his love of the outdoors.

At Mendham, Munnings was perfectly content to spend evenings at home among his treasures and read the works of Thackeray or Surtees. He could quote whole chapters of the latter for the rest of his life. Occasionally, he gave parties when he mixed a steaming punch made from an eighteenth-century recipe acquired from the landlord of the Swan Hotel at Harleston.

As the days lengthened he was back at his easel out-of-doors, trying to paint the familiar scenes and characters. The locals passed by with a friendly nod, accepting him as one of their own, and never stopped to look at his work. It was just as well because, for a long time, he found it difficult to avoid a flat look in his pictures and convey depth to them, features which, because of his lack of binocular vision, he could only imagine.

He fought such battles privately and when a waggon load of sightseers stopped to watch him painting he lost his temper and hurled the canvas into the river. Another day, a cousin saw him painting down in the marshes. Evidently the work was not going well because eventually he swore loudly and daubed it all over with brushfuls of red paint.

His frustrations were endless and extended to the Royal Academy's Summer Exhibition of 1900, when two of his four submissions were rejected. They had been painted before his accident. The acceptances were *An Old Favourite*, the picture of his twin cousins in the orchard, and a landscape, *In the Suffolk Marshes*. Not surprisingly, 'the masterpiece', defiantly submitted for the second time, was one of the rejects.

He always dreaded rejection but in the summer of 1900, as he learned to paint again, he found it almost intolerable to have his days coloured by 'the discordance, the jolt, the shock, the pause in life,' as he described the feeling of knowing, after weeks of suspense, that his work was not good enough.

Only his old terrier, Friday, witnessed the hurt and misery as his master agonized over the wasted effort incurred after the high hopes with which he had embarked on his subject and the blissful hours and days spent translating his vision into paint. All was rendered meaningless and his unvoiced query must have been when, if ever, would he be able to paint well again?

An effect of his accident, which probably resulted from his imagination, was that, after months of darkness, he was more aware of colour than ever before. Nevertheless, a new brilliance was certainly apparent in *Feeding the Chickens*, a small canvas alive with a sunburst of multi-coloured fowls clustered round an old countryman. It hung, with two of his other paintings, in the 1901 Royal Academy's Summer Exhibition – proof, at long last, that the accident had not ruined his career. On the contrary, *Woodcutting in October* hung on the line. It showed a countryman in an old smock and soft felt hat trimming long boughs stripped from the willows beside a bend in the river. The third picture, *A Suffolk Horse Fair*, was the most ambitious subject he had ever tackled.

He had used his first big canvas, measuring fifty by eighty inches, to show the tented fairground at Lavenham Horse Fair with heavy draught horses and farmers crowding the fields, which stretched back to a distant view of houses clustered round Lavenham Church.

It had been produced by the same technique he had used to capture the elusive shadows on the grass in *An Old Favourite*, but he had gone to the length of first painting the whole scene in watercolours on the spot and afterwards translating it into oils in his studio. 'Fools rush in where angels fear to tread,' he admitted. 'Painting so large a picture from a watercolour version was asking for trouble. I worked away at it all through the winter. The tone of the grass gave me the same trouble as it does today.... I was wretched.... That ambitious effort should have taught me my limitations.'

Having won the battle for his eyesight, he could afford to belittle and criticize his work again. Nevertheless, the preliminary watercolour version of the large picture was accepted for the Annual Exhibition of the Royal Institute of Painters in Water

Colours and sold for £25. The oil painting sold at the Academy for a few pounds more. It was a forerunner of a series of action-packed country scenes involving country folk and their horses in typical English settings, destined to be rated among his best work. At the time, however, his overwhelming feeling was that he had much to learn.

The credit for introducing Munnings to Lavenham Horse Fair goes to a character in the picture, one of his favourite models, a Suffolk showman, old Nobby Gray. 'A natty, wise-looking old bird,' as Munnings described him, who was bald and clean shaven and wore a pair of horn-rimmed spectacles when he read the newspaper or mended umbrellas, which made him look like a crafty old lawyer.

He lived with his gypsy wife, Charlotte, and their son, Fred, in a gaily-painted gypsy waggon, parked in winter in the meadow behind the Red Lion, Mendham and in summer round the Suffolk fairgrounds. All the family were happy to pose for their painter friend, even without the incentive of a pint or two of ale or the gold sovereign with which he invariably rewarded them.

The friendship was strengthened when the Grays organized Saturday sausage suppers in Munnings's studio. They would arrive with a basket of fine sausages made from a pig killed at the Red Lion every Friday and fry them with chips on the tortoise stove. As the sausages sizzled, pints of ale were served to whet the appetites of the company.

After the meal Munnings brewed up a special punch while the others smoked and talked. When it was served he was ready to strum on the amber-coloured Broadwood grand piano he had bought from a Norwich dealer. He vamped an accompaniment to ballads, some of his own composition. One extolled the virtues of punch, in his seven-verse ballad which started:

Oh punch, it is good!
It is brimming with joys,
If you only lose count of your glasses;
And the fellows who say,
'No, thank you, my boys!'
Are nought but despicable asses.

But as the level of drink in the punch bowl sank, the bawdiness of the songs and stories rose and the women drifted away to their homes, leaving the men to continue their riotous revels until the small hours. After everyone had gone home Munnings often had a final nightcap from the dregs of punch left in the glasses.

On a more sober occasion, the Grays persuaded Munnings that he must see Lavenham Horse Fair. Nobby and his son offered to take him, although it meant leaving their pitches at Walsham-le-Willows Fair where Nobby was looking after the swing boats, Charlotte the shooting gallery and Fred the coconut shies.

They met Munnings at the Swan Hotel, Lavenham, where he had spent the night. After breakfast they showed him round the inn yards, the narrow streets and the little greens where horsemen were grooming their huge animals, plaiting their tails and manes with the traditional red, yellow and blue ribbons and trotting them up and down. Munnings, full of a fine breakfast of Suffolk-cured bacon and the busy exciting atmosphere, could not wait to get started. He set up his easel at the edge of the showground and, thanks to the perceptive travelling showman, Nobby, began the first of a series of pictures that marked the start of his lucrative career in pure art. His commercial bread and butter designs would soon be things of the past.

The next year the three Grays could be seen in the Academy's 1902 Summer Exhibition in a picture called *The Gossips*, which sold on the Private View Day. Dwarfing, but not outshining, it was an ambitious canvas, eighty inches by fifty, called *The Vagabonds*, showing a straggling group of horses and gypsies in a long narrow lane. It might have been Munnings's attempt to outdo Lucy Kemp Welch's *Colt-hunting in the New Forest*, which had been the talk of the Academy's previous Summer Exhibition, but he had to admit it was a comparative failure. It toured several other Art Galleries before it was sold for £30.

By then the 1903 Academy had provided him with his record of five acceptances, four on the theme of country fairs. The smallest, *A Gala Day*, portraying half-a-dozen countrymen at a fair, hung on the line. Munnings was persuaded to sell it for less than half what he intended to an astute Preston Alderman, who had quite a collection of his pictures and consistently entertained him and wined him too well. Munnings was always prepared to repay such hospitality in kind and was impulsively generous when the irresistible combination of wine and good company heightened his sense of well-being.

He had apparently inherited his father's tendency to drink too much, which he made an ineffectual attempt to justify: 'Working against the climate through the seasons wears an artist out,' he wrote. 'That is why artists should be forgiven for all the exaggerated stories told of them. No indulgence in pleasures of all kinds can be too well-deserved a reward, or can recoup the wearied soul of the painter, whether he loses or wins the struggle. He deserves a jolly dinner if he wins and needs a jollier if he loses.'

There was a happy sequel to the sale of *A Gala Day*. The hospitable Alderman bequeathed it in his will to Preston Art Gallery where it hung beside the *The Last of the Fair*, Munnings's study of an exhausted boy asleep between the shafts of a cart surrounded by three horses and a donkey. It had been one of his five paintings in the 1903 Academy where Preston Corporation had bought it for £150.

Another of Munnings's favourite models was Old Norman, well into his eighties, who the painter described as his 'staunchest friend'. He lived in the poorest house on the village street near the entrance to Shearing's Farm and he could neither read nor write. He had always been hard up and in 1851, desperate for a job, had walked a hundred miles to London with a workgang to get taken on at the Great Exhibition in the Crystal Palace.

As Munnings's odd job man, for eighteen shillings a week, he made the fires and gardened, held the horses for the artist to paint, cleared up the studio after a party and sometimes acted as a model. His wage was twice as much as he had earned in the forties when he left home at four o'clock in the morning and walked five miles to work as a trench digger on the marshes, often going without breakfast to leave more food for his children.

In the 1904 Academy he could be recognized in Munnings's only exhibit; a sun-filled painting called *Whitsuntide*, showing Old Norman standing in a field of buttercups with a mare and foal and some of his grandchildren. It was the only time Munnings was represented by a solitary picture but *Whitsuntide* saved his lifetime's unbroken record of annual acceptances, interrupted only by one year in World War II.

Munnings always proved a good friend to someone he liked. When Old Norman was taken ill, the painter climbed the rickety stairs to his bedside night after night to read aloud to him – usually passages from the Bible which the old man loved, just as much as Munnings loved a captive audience.

About that time he finally disposed of his 'masterpiece', *In the Suffolk Marshes*, when he exchanged it with the landlord of the Trowel and Hammer public house in Norwich for a bay mare. She was his first hunter and had proved too hot for the landlord to handle. Munnings, who felt he had been born in the saddle, called her Music and found her an exciting challenge. She shied at every bird in sight and one night, when he was riding home from the Swan at Harleston, she shied at the reflection of the moon in a puddle, caught him unawares, shot him off and left him to walk the two miles home where they were reunited.

He bore her no malice and constructed a loose box for her in an open shed at the end of his studio where, over the half-door, she could watch him at work. She was the first hunter Munnings had been able to use as a model and she was groomed meticulously, by Old Norman in summer and Fred Gray in winter. He painted her many times ridden by Fred Gray, wearing a hunting pink coat or other riding clothes bought from a Norwich second-hand dealer. He learned a great deal, about both riding and painting from Music, but as far as painting was concerned, he was never satisfied and always felt he had more to learn.

He was encouraged in this belief by a sixty-year-old bachelor artist, Edward Elliot, who with Sam and Jim Boswell and their friends could usually be found in the bar of the Castle Hotel, Norwich on Saturday mornings. One Saturday, Elliot held forth so glowingly about his student days at L'Atelier Julian in Paris that, there and then, the whole group decided to go.

Eventually everyone except Munnings backed out and he found himself sharing a large bedroom in the Hôtel Jacob, near Julian's Atelier in the rue du Dragon, with a lazy and sociable acquaintance, who was soon discouraged by bedbugs and shortage of funds and returned to England. But Munnings stayed, secure in the knowledge that there was more than £70 in his Harleston bank account.

He then shared his room with a young Irishman and spent the days jockeying for position to paint a nude model in Julian's huge over-crowded ground-floor studio. His fellow students, mainly English or Americans, of all ages drew lots for places to stand their easels. Those lucky enough to get in the front row were so tightly crammed in that they could hardly lift an arm or keep their balance as the crowd behind milled about trying to catch an occasional hazy glimpse of the model through clouds of dense cigarette or pipe smoke mingled with a strong smell of human bodies and the reek of oil from an ancient stove. Munnings felt completely at ease.

At last he was in the world he had seen portrayed in *Trilby*, working alongside superior painters as well as his peers, where everyone seemed prepared to be his friend. This mitigated the shortcomings in tuition given by three visiting professors, the chief of whom confined his comments to 'Pas mal' or 'Continuez toujours'.

The models changed every fortnight, which Munnings found was plenty of time to do them justice. He had considerably speeded up his work and produced a fine sensitive study of a female nude. The picture conveyed something of the studio atmosphere apparent in his prize-winning impression of the Paint Room of Norwich School of Art which had taken more than a year to produce.

Every second Monday he was reminded of Norwich Cattle Market. An assortment of would-be models of all colours and races arrived and paraded in turn on the dais, accompanied by cries of approval or disapproval by the students until the right number had been chosen. He felt sorry for the rejected ones.

The token tuition he received at Julian's was compensated for by the glorious sculpture he saw in the gardens and squares of Paris, where he and his friends studied and sketched and held endless conferences at the base of one lovely nude statue after another.

On fine weekdays they often went to Versailles by train or boat. There, Munnings was unceasingly drawn to the gallery of huge battle canvases and stood fascinated before Morot's *Charge of the Cuirassiers*, thirty feet long and with a life-size wounded grey horse in the foreground. 'I was spellbound at every visit,' he recalled, 'though others were never impressed. Thus do we differ in our outlook.... Such an effort requires a lifetime's study and knowledge.... Only an artist born of a military nation could conceive the tragic moment – the mad rush, the fury, the fright, all shown on this wide canvas. I wondered where all Morot's first drawings and designs would be? How large were they? How did he paint the studies for the wounded horse?'

Once again a grey horse had dominated his experience and it was as if, standing before that painting, he pledged himself to a lifetime's study to that end. The answers to his questions about it seemed more important than any concerning the nude drawings he made at Julian's, his dream-like sketches of the statues in the Luxembourg Gardens or the beautiful landscapes which, to his eternal regret, he only had time to represent by sketches of whispering poplars growing beside lazy rivers.

In Paris, however, he also discovered the work of Théodore Géricault, perhaps the Michelangelo of the nation who, in a sense, had devoted his short existence to the horse. He also found the answer to perhaps the most important question of all, 'What are pictures for?' In the art galleries, he knew a feeling of admiration – amounting almost to reverence – when he studied the works of Degas, Fantin Latour, Tissot, Bastien Lepage and others. Such painters, he felt, aimed 'to fill a man's soul with admiration and sheer joy, not to bewilder him and daze him'. It was an extension of the appreciation he had known for the Norwich School of Painters and it stayed with him for ever.

His social life kept pace with his studies: he ate cheaply at small dinner parties in little restaurants where, in halting school-boy French, he managed to dominate the conversation. He went to drinks parties in wine shops and artists' studios and at the Bal Bullier watched bearded Frenchmen twirl girls in tight-waisted, long-skirted frocks round the dance floor at great speed. He had learned to waltz at dancing classes in Norwich but, in Paris, he apparently preferred to remain a spectator. He was not shy but he seemed uninterested in forming even a casual relationship with a girl. 'Such days were too perfect to be true,' he wrote. 'No income tax; no letters....' Nor, it seemed, were there any romantic interludes for a handsome twenty-four-year-old on his first stay in Paris.

That first visit to Julian's lasted for just a few weeks but it was the forerunner, over the years, of other short visits from which he invariably returned stimulated by 'blissful experiences'.

HOTEL RITZ
ADRESSE TÉLÉGRAPHIQUE
RITZOTEL-PARIS-81
Hotel Ritz
Place Vendôme
Paris

CHAPTER IV

Marking Time

He returned from his first period at Julian's with a new confidence in his work which entitled him, he felt, to ask £300 for a painting measuring thirty inches by fifty, which he had not submitted to the Academy. *The Horse Fair* centred around a white-suited figure, recognizable as Herbert Blackmore, one of the most knowledgeable judges of horse flesh in East Anglia, showing off a chestnut shire to five countrymen against a background of tents and horses.

When Munnings came to sell the painting, however, it was the old story. The would-be purchaser gave him a lavish dinner and countered his asking price with an offer of £150 in cash. 'The dinner, the champagne, the rustling of the notes were too much,' Munnings confessed, and he took the cash. Eventually, the picture received wider acknowledgement when its owner donated it to Norwich Art Gallery where it held pride of place.

Another result of his Parisian trip was a large canvas called *Leaving the Fair*, probably influenced by Lucien Simon's *La Procession* in the Luxembourg Museum. But, as in the case of Munnings's attempt to out-paint Lucy Kemp Welch, he was rarely successful when he deliberately allowed himself to be influenced by other painters and his picture was rejected by the Academy.

The essence of his work was distilled from his own rugged independent East Anglian character in which a sturdy bluffness was mixed with a romantic lyricism. The results, at their best, were his personal celebrations of English idylls, and there was a magic joy about his country scenes with unselfconscious villagers and horses in their natural settings. He was no businessman and discerning buyers eagerly acquired his paintings at bargain prices, and, at the same time, many were delighted to make a friend of the young artist who was becoming known as 'a bit of a character'.

One of them, Edward Adcock, a Norwich market gardener introduced to him by the Boswells, specialized in growing asparagus and, like the Alderman from Preston, drove a hard bargain. But, if the Boswells were not around, Munnings was comparatively unconcerned as long as his bank balance stood above the magical £70. He willingly sold Adcock six small pictures for £90. At this stage he just took life as it came.

He was genuinely modest although increasingly confident about his work and, providing he earned a living, he found his true reward in the intense excitement of capturing his impressions of the scenes and landscapes he loved; scudding clouds under great skies, the dazzle of light on water, the texture of a leaf, the toss of a foal's head, the stance of a pretty girl, the sheen of a horse's coat. 'Who knows?' he wrote of the bargains acquired by Adcock. 'They may have been dear, even at a low figure. But they were at least sincere efforts.'

Moreover, Adcock and his wife offered him an introduction to a more sophisticated life-style. He often stayed in their well-run home in the best residential part of Norwich, 'where,' he said, 'they indulged in a good, full way of living'. He joined them at bowls on the manicured lawn and at pianola parties when the guests sang and danced to music pumped through perforated paper rolls, which revolved in an upright piano when 'the pianist' pedalled vigorously.

Munnings recognized the jovial Adcock was 'part of the core of provincial England' and he delighted to welcome him to Mendham. His patron would arrive at the studio in his splendid Silent Night Minerva, unload a great basket of food and champagne, buy some pictures and then drive Munnings about the countryside searching for antiques, looking at churches and stopping at inns. Often, Munnings drove back with him to Norwich.

Another of the Boswells' introductions was to Prince Frederick Duleep Singh, who lived at Old Buckenham some thirty miles from Norwich. Munnings spent a week with the Indian potentate in his magnificent treasure-house of a home where, every evening after dinner, his sad-eyed host played and sang to him in a fine baritone voice. That first intimate glimpse into the world of royalty was exciting for a twenty-four-year-old who was barely accepted by the East Anglian county set. It was a memorable reward for fulfilling a commission to paint a twenty-five-inch picture of the Prince's bull and cows, the last of an ancient breed of Suffolk Dunn Poll cattle, a picture for which he received £10 from the Boswell brothers.

A few weeks later the Prince paid an informal call at Munnings's Mendham studio. He was on his way home from inspecting a squadron of Suffolk Hussars at nearby Harleston and Munnings took him to see his rooms at Shearing's Farm. The Prince made a point of asking how much the Boswells had paid him for the picture of the bull and cows and a few days later sent a charming letter enclosing £5 because he felt Munnings had been inadequately rewarded.

Munnings was widening his conception of life and, accordingly, soon after his return from Paris he lengthened his studio to forty-five feet. It certainly impressed his friends from Julian's who came, one or two at a time, to board with him at Shearing's Farm for fifteen shillings a week or, when they were more than two, to stay in rooms in the village.

At first the locals were amazed by the sight of the strangely dressed young gentlemen, some wearing painters' symbolic wide black hats, but they were soon placated by their readiness to stand them pints of beer. They were completely mystified, however, by the long involved art discussions the painters conducted in the local inns – just as they had in the Luxembourg Gardens and the Paris studio.

During the day the visitors tended to paint in a group in the quiet Suffolk valley that had never been so immortalized by as many artists at the same time. Munnings recalled the scene: 'A sedge-grown bank of a river; the poplar's sound; willows whitening in the breeze rippling the river where swallows skim the surface. Along the bank, not far off, sits one figure with his Paris easel; yet further on, another, and just over a bridge, where cattle are standing, two more blithe spirits sing and paint away.'

One of them, a Captain Warden from a well-to-do family, had taken up art after fighting in the Boer War. He returned Munnings's hospitality by inviting him to join him in late summer at a school of animal painting run by a specialist in it and in other outdoor subjects. He was Frank Calderon, a remarkable teacher, and his school was held at the village of Finchingfield in Essex.

It was a show-place of a village where the main street curved up from a little river bridge on the green and wound its way between an intriguing variety of fairy-tale houses. The street led Munnings to an Arcadian scene, strangely reminiscent of the Fragonard paintings he had seen in the Louvre.

Elegant maidens in flowing painting clothes and wide-brimmed picture hats worked in a field at their easels, painting two tethered cows, placidly chewing clover. Munnings soon realized that many of the ladies were members of the County set and, for the first time in his life, he was conscious of his own coarse country clothes and social inferiority. One student arrived at the school from her nearby ancestral home driving a four-in-hand drawn by fast-trotting donkeys.

Students who had enrolled for the summer term were of all ages and included one or two men. Some students were from London or further afield. Munnings, no doubt bolstered up by his unbroken record of paintings in the Royal Academy and his exhibits with the Royal Society of Painters in Water-Colours, soon made friends. As usual he was eventually moved to record his impressions in verse as well as in paint and composed a ten-stanza poem ending:

> Our painting embraces a score
> Of most interesting diversions;
> A party of four – two less or two more –
> Can go off on sketching excursions
>
> And gaze at a church or a tree,
> When our talk gets fearfully clever;
> And we all then agree such parties should be
> Continued for ever and ever.
>
> We're sure to have brilliant careers!!
> Nobody will ever forget us!!
> And people for years will remember with tears
> The very last day that they met us!!

The parties did continue. Munnings's friendships made at the School of Animal Painting resulted in visits to London where he was introduced to well-known painters and furthered their acquaintance at the Langham Sketch Club during Friday night suppers. Before the meal, he and other members sketched a nude model and to his delight, many fellow members identified him with his Academy paintings.

Arthur Gough, the famous boxer and swimmer, who drew for the *Illustrated London News*, sometimes invited him to spend the night at his home in West End Lane. He went to the London Sketch Club with Dudley Hart, designer of the Gaiety Girl poster which could be seen all over London, and with Phil May the cartoonist and John Hassall. He drank with his new friends at the journalists' famous Cheshire Cheese in Fleet Street, sometimes went on to the theatre or music hall where Dan Leno and Marie Lloyd might head the bill and, driving home in a hansom cab after a late supper, led his companions in rousing choruses from the hits of the day.

'What nights they were! And what girls we met at the old Empire! What figures! What dresses!' he exclaimed. But, it seemed, as far as girls were concerned, there was no semblance of a personal relationship in his full life. Days were spent visiting the Academy, the New Gallery and the National Gallery and nights enjoying the company of fellow artists. There were few quiet moments to reflect on the spectre of his bank account plunging towards £70.

He found London more expensive than Paris but more exciting because, in his own words, he was 'climbing into higher circles'. He needed new clothes for city life and for when, 'satiated at last with the sights', he returned to Mendham.

Back in Mendham the loneliness returned because he felt that both socially and professionally he had outgrown the place. So much of his life centred round Norwich that he decided, as a temporary measure, to make it his working headquarters. He rented furnished rooms there above the offices of a lawyer friend, Nick Everitt, in Prince of Wales Road, which led down to the river flowing through the heart of the city. From his office windows he had a fine view of the tall spire of Norwich Cathedral. He accepted all the work that came his way, including commissions for horse pictures at £10 each.

Such commissions took him to many East Anglian villages where he put up at local inns for 14s 6d a week for bed and board. The Norwich rooms served as his office, not his studio and anyhow, wherever possible, he chose to paint out-of-doors.

On his travels he could rarely resist buying attractive antiques because his feeling for old furniture was growing and he loved to surround himself with it even if it meant that he sometimes ran out of money. He was always confident that wherever he stayed, his landlords would let him settle his bills with a sketch or two.

There was no shortage of work. A London literary journal, *The Athenaeum*, described him as 'perhaps the most vigorous of the younger nature painters', and commented that his pictures indicated considerable natural talent although they showed no refinement of colour. The critic could not have known that at about that time he was probably starting on the colour experiments whose results would ultimately prove a trademark of his work.

Colours in his pictures were no longer absolute. He saw their relationship and reaction to the other colours he used. The blues and violets in his shadows imprisoned the sunlight rather than quenched it. He was the first to realize that the coat of a living horse was coloured by the reflection of blue and grey from the sky.

At Easter he spent a month in the Black Forest. He stayed at the Hotel Poste in Hornburg, walked through valleys and pine forests and painted goats by streams surrounded by trees heavy with blossom. He travelled alone and in the evenings shared a bottle of fine hock with his landlady's son.

He made another European trip with Shaw Tomkins. In Dresden he stood in front of large paintings that literally took his breath away and in Munich he was so impressed by pictures of peasant life, painted out-of-doors, looking as if they had been completed in one session and on one spot, that he admitted he 'gave up all hopes of ever being anyone at all'.

> 'I stood gaping,' he wrote, 'in front of a huge canvas of a girl walking towards me through luminous greenery . . . . Another was of some Baltic fishermen in the late evening light – the men coming ashore in their boat on the crest of a wave, all life-size. The wave in the near corner must have been painted with a brush six inches wide.'

He bought a small colour reproduction of the painting, framed it and kept it by his bedside all his life.

He returned home through Paris where he again studied at Julian's for a few weeks and delighted in the companionship of his fellow painters and student friends. He gave them gifts of bottles of wine and drank and sang in their studios, just as in the old days. He went to the art galleries and again stood before the works of the great masters he had admired and confirmed his initial reactions. Time and again, he found himself lost 'in profound contentment and admiration'.

In 1905 he was commissioned to paint his first oil portrait of a horse and rider. It was presented by the Dunston Harriers to their Master, Thomas Springfield, showing him on his favourite hunter, Mangreen, and the painter was paid the princely sum of £75 for it.

The sittings took place at the Mulbarton farm of Munnings's Aunt Polly where, seven years previously, Munnings had lost his eye. He painted Springfield astride a wooden saddle horse and later introduced the fine hunter, Mangreen, into the picture. While he painted, he remembered that Aunt Polly's first husband had owned a partly-occupied farm at Swainsthorpe, which now belonged to his aunt. One day it might make him an ideal home.

Meanwhile, the portrait of Mangreen and his rider was so successful that Springfield invited him to do a watercolour of his favourite horse, Beacon, and took him down to the stables to see it. Munnings, probably flushed with self-importance after that first commission, took one look at it, dismissed it as 'the most dreadful animal I've ever seen in my life,' and refused to paint it.

According to Springfield's grandson, Lt.-Colonel George Springfield, his grandfather did not say a word and the two men walked off. Then, as George Springfield narrates: 'Grandfather slipped back and said to the groom, "Now when we get to the top of the path just lead out Beacon from the stable and let's see what happens." He then rejoined Munnings and they walked to the top of the path where Munnings looked down and saw the animal being led along. The sun was out and the chestnut looked absolutely glorious.

'"Tom you old fool, *that's* the horse I want to paint, not that dreadful old thing in the stable," he said.' At twenty-seven he could still be outwitted by a fellow East Anglian.

Meanwhile, he bought other horses and ponies and took them to Mendham. His best bargain was a little skewbald acquired for £10 together with an antique bureau after a long drinking session with the dealer. Munnings painted that pony many times and in the 1906 Academy it could be recognized in *Ponies at the Fair* standing at the end of a row beside a fence. The fence was a boundary of the Red Lion's meadow where Munnings repeatedly practised his belief that 'draughts of shandy gaff were the true painter's potion'.

He painted a sturdy little shaggy chestnut pony, led beside a well-clipped hedge by a very sturdy Charlotte Gray wearing a white apron over her blue blouse and a full black skirt. Her sleek black hair and dangling silver earrings glinted in the sunlight. Over the hedge was a glimpse of Mendham, a farewell glimpse, for *Charlotte's Pony* was one of his last Mendham pictures to hang in the Academy. He had made up his mind to move to Norwich.

Just before he left the village he stood near the church portraying the village thatcher at work. He was using a swift technique – one used by Fragonard – applying his paint in sure thick strokes as if there was not a moment to spare. He was so engrossed that he hardly noticed when Farmer Wharton, the landlord of Shearing's Farm, paused to watch him. Suddenly, his gruff voice penetrated Munnings's concentration: 'Don't leave this part of the country,' he advised. 'It's brought you luck.'

The advice came too late. Not until some fifty years later did the determined, self-opinionated painter, who would always remain a bluff East Anglian countryman, acknowledge: 'Were I then as I am now, older, experienced and loving the soil more and more, wild horses would not have drawn me from that studio and those sausage nights.'

Charlotte's Pony was one of Munnings's three pictures in the 1907 Royal Academy Summer Exhibition, which was one of the brightest for many years. The interest caused by his three paintings, among its two thousand or so exhibits, entitled him to return to Norwich in good spirits.

'The paintings of the horses are superb,' wrote the art critic of the *Eastern Daily Press* describing *Going to the Meet* which hung on the line with *Charlotte's Pony*. The third painting, *Into the Spinney*, he noted was 'a very spirited hunting picture'.

Munnings read the report at his new home, Church Farm, Swainsthorpe. It was a pleasant house set well back from the road in a village five miles from Norwich. His Aunt Polly had let him half of it, consisting of two rooms up and two rooms down, for £10 a year. The rest was occupied by an elderly couple, Mr and Mrs Lodes. Mr Lodes was the farm's yardman and his wife ran the dairy. She agreed to provide all Munnings's meals, clean his rooms and do his washing for fifteen shillings a week.

'The rocket flight' prophesied by an art critic eight years ago seemed underway and the painter decided to raise his life-style accordingly. He engaged a groom-cum-model, George Curzon, to do the work of Old Norman and the Grays and his first job was to organize a harness room. Horses dominated the painter's life and on days when he was not riding to hounds – often with Lord Stradbroke's Harriers – he planned to paint in the mornings and in the afternoons ride the six-year-old mare he had bought for thirty-five guineas from a Norwich friend, Richard Bullard. She served as hack, hunter and model and with her he planned to explore the tracks and bridle paths that passed just outside his front door.

He bought a custom-built wooden sectional studio designed by a friend, with the roof pitched at the correct angle to allow a northern light to be inserted. It arrived in two parts and he was very proud when it was assembled in the meadow behind the house. At first, however, he found it strange to work there without the companionable scufflings of a mare surveying him over the stable door as at Mendham.

He felt nostalgic and lonely when he thought of Mendham, but consoled himself that Swainsthorpe certainly provided a more sophisticated atmosphere. Its open railway platform raised high above the level of the fields, was the first railway station on the line from Norwich to London and instead of riding or walking into Norwich, he often made the quarter-of-an-hour train journey there.

A countryman born and bred, he was completely at home in Norwich probably because, as his writer friend James Wentworth Day said, it was 'a city of the land' which had scarcely altered from the Norwich immortalized three-quarters of a century before by the poet George Borrow. Droves of bullocks, strings of horses and waggon loads of squealing pigs still blocked the narrow winding streets. 'The country is never far away,' Wentworth Day wrote of the Norwich he and Munnings loved. 'You smell it on the winds of spring and the sweet gales of autumn and, at night under the stars, when the market stalls are shuttered and the bullock pens are empty, the factories are still and the lights are out, you may hear the wild geese chanting overhead, the wings of wild duck sibilant under the moon. . . .'

When Munnings rode into Norwich he left his horse in the livery stables at the home of the veterinary surgeon, Fred Lowe. On Saturday market days some of the hunting and farming set would meet in the parlour for afternoon tea, after they had whiled away an hour or two in one of the city's many inns when the market closed.

There was an inn for every day of the year and at least six sported signs painted by Old Crome, the father of the Norwich School of Painters. One, a sign for the 'Labour in Vain', showed two women ineffectively trying to scrub a negro white. In that sphere, Munnings outshone Crome in quantity if not in wit, for every Bullard's public house in and around the city displayed, as their logo, Munnings's picture of a jovial landlord holding a mug frothing over with beer.

Munnings had earned £10 when he designed it for Bullard's calendar. He received no more when they later adopted it as their logo. It pleased his ego but did nothing to ease the financial strain caused by his improved life-style, his love of antiques, his new clothes and the cost of keeping up with his growing circle of acquaintances.

The farmers and huntsmen accepted him as a fine horseman and a good companion, in spite of his blunt earthiness and his readiness to speak his mind regardless of the effect on anyone's feelings – particularly after a drink or two. They regarded him as one of the crowd who happened to be struggling to earn a living as a painter, and few were aware of the genuine talent he nurtured and cherished above everything else in life.

He enjoyed the lively Saturday tea parties at Fred Lowe's, which he found far more stimulating, if less riotous, than the sausage suppers at Mendham. They usually centred round the great Jack Cooke, the best horseman in Norfolk and the legendary master of the Norwich Staghounds of which Munnings became an enthusiastic, if rather controversial, member. He thrilled to the excitement of the chase but hated the kill and never concealed his dislike and disgust at such cruelty.

At first, he turned up dressed like an amateur in a grey whipcord suit, bowler hat and leggings, probably because he was short of money and anyhow he liked an excuse not to conform. There were objections, but Cooke was his champion: 'Munnings is the artist to the hunt,' he declared. 'We'll allow him to wear boots and cap like a farmer.'

Such tolerance and understanding from a man who ruled his field and spoke his mind was a boon to Munnings, because hunting had become an essential part of his life. 'I saw many things on those days,' he recalled. 'Bright winter sunlight on clipped horses and scarlet coats; on bare trees; stacks; on farmhouse gables; the riding home with a frost beginning and a young moon in the sky; puddles already crisping over as I said goodnight to friends. Such were needed to freshen my mind and vision.' They were also needed to alleviate his moments of depression.

He often visited Jack Cooke at his home, Brooke Lodge, a handsome red-brick Elizabethan-style house six miles from Norwich. Cooke lent him horses to ride or hunt and he painted them in the sweet, warm atmosphere of the stables where Cooke sometimes watched him at work and offered booming homilies such as 'Good hay's a luxury. You can always buy good oats; but a piece of hay is what a horse likes and he'll eat it all night.'

Munnings delighted in the country talk of his boyhood and the colourful East Anglian characters he met in Norfolk, often through riding. They included the Revd Humphrey Barclay of Kings Lynn, later Domestic Chaplain to King George VI, who was such a keen horseman that sometimes his marriage sermons sounded like hunting adventures. His son, Timothy Barclay, a farmer and Huntsman and Master of the West Norfolk Foxhounds, said:

> Munnings and my father were great friends. A lot of my family were eccentrics, like Evelyn Barclay and his family who lived at Colney Hall, near Norwich and used to keep lions in the back garden. The youngest son was mauled by a lion and subsequently died.
>
> There's no doubt Munnings was an eccentric. He was a great character, humorous and great company and somewhat out of the ordinary. I think we could do with one or two more like that today, although to be an eccentric these days is much too expensive.
>
> Munnings was very keen on an aunt of mine, Margaret Bond Cabbell of Cromer Hall. They met through riding and, the story goes, he chased her round the orchard and she went

> up an apple tree and he got sick of it and that was the end of the romance.

More serious distractions were visits to the Theatre Royal in Norwich to see performances by Frank Benson's Shakespearian Players or Ouida's *Under Two Flags* and to the Hippodrome for Boswell's Circus, or Variety perhaps, featuring the King's mistress, Lillie Langtry. He went to concerts in the intimate thatched Assembly House and for twopence admission, watched Henry Wood conduct in the spacious St Andrew's Hall, once a Dominican Friary.

His happiest evenings, however, were spent with friends in inns, or small bars where drink took the edge off any feeling of loneliness or depression and allowed him to give full vent to his lack of inhibition before an indulgent audience. His favourite haunt was the little Dickensian panelled bar at the Maid's Head, the oldest inn in Norwich, whose bow window looked out on to the coaching yard.

He and others, with no particular reason to go home, usually found their way there after Fred Lowe's Saturday teas to dine round the large polished, mahogany table. They talked and drank and sang, until Munnings forced himself to collect his restless horse and ride off to Swainsthorpe. He preferred the five-mile ride home, however late, to spending the night in his Norwich rooms.

He joined the City Club where the Boswell brothers had often taken him to lunch and, very soon, he made his mark there. One night in 1907 he had a violent argument with another member who, awed by the mystique he supposed surrounded art, insisted a painter needed the correct equipment for his work and the 'right atmosphere' of a studio.

A reverent attitude to painting unfailingly annoyed Munnings and he tended to ridicule an intellectual approach to it. Primed with drink, he declared that the member's belief was pure nonsense and to prove it he tore down one of the four-foot-square, blue spring window blinds, seized a piece of billiard chalk and drew a splendid sketch of a steeplechaser taking a fence. Playing to his admiring audience, he ripped down the other blind and covered it with a sketch of a clown talking to a saucy Pierrette. Across the tops he wrote with a flourish, 'A.J.M. 2 a.m. Nov 29th 1907'. The next year the club moved to new premises and the blinds were framed and hung and insured for £500 each. The third time the Club moved they were rolled up and left in a drawer.*

Far from needing 'the right atmosphere of a studio' Munnings preferred painting out-of-doors, even on the coldest days when he had to drag out large canvas screens to protect his easel from the wind. Painting in the open air was, to him, 'the easier, slacker way'. He recorded his first impression on the spot, and later saw it in a new context and more objectively when he worked on it in his studio. There, he sometimes turned a painting to the wall for a week or two in disgust and then looked at it again, coldly and critically, before tackling it once more.

He liked to paint the same subject in oils simultaneously on two canvases; the smaller carried his impression of mood and atmosphere in case the weather changed and on the larger he added the details. He worked on the pictures alternately, which allowed the paint to harden off at each stage in both and also, he explained, let him 'gain a stride now in this one, now in that'. Eventually, he modified the practice so that before he started work on a large canvas he tried the subject out on a small one, measuring about twenty-five by thirty inches.

Sometimes, he was so carried away by a new subject that, in the thrill and excitement, he swept his oils too lavishly on to the canvas in an initial orgy. Then he had to abandon the painting until he could look at it calmly and correct the results of his over-exuberance.

He was always on the look-out for new challenges and inspirations and, as long as he painted purely to please himself, he found them everywhere. One came from a friend who lent him a handsome chestnut for a season while he was abroad. The animal's clipped coat, contrasted with its flowing mane, fired Munnings's emotions in the way that the sheen on a woman's hair might have affected another man. 'I have had painting thrills in life, but never such a one as when I began the horse on a sunny November morning,' he said, recalling how that clipped coat had provided 'a new inspiration – an entirely new exercise in paint'.

The sheen on the coat, its texture and the pale, subtle beauty of

*In the 1970s they were sold at Christie's for £1,600 and eventually went to America.

the first clipped horse he had ever painted, offered him a colour challenge he needed. His mastery of form was already something he could take for granted so that he could focus on how muscle action and structure were revealed by lighting and colour. He experimented with colour reactions and the texture of paint; the way a touch of purple placed close to a splash of green reflected in the horse's coat could light up the brown hide. Hunting and riding were forgotten as, day after day, in a sheltered corner of the meadow, he painted George Curzon wearing a scarlet jacket posed on the clipped chestnut in the sharp winter sunlight.

More ambitious subjects took him further afield to country fairs at Peterborough, Stourbridge, Tavistock and Nottingham. But with complete freedom to go and paint wherever he wished, he had time for misgivings which were confirmed when a Norwich builder wrote to suggest he was capable of handling more important subjects.

> I know it well enough, Munnings replied. But to conceive a great work and carry it out is not as easy as one thinks.
>
> I myself know just what I ought to do and no one better but it is the *Idea* I want. It's no use painting just anything.... I am at present in a state of unhappiness and unsettlement. Simply because I cannot hit upon *just* the *good* thing.

His mother was quick to recognize any signs of depression. An entry in her Sunday diary read: 'Alfred has been over. He seems to be happy, at least as happy as it is possible for him to be – he really very seldom seems quite satisfied or happy.'

Loneliness might have contributed to his unhappiness. He had no close friend to feed him back the regular criticism or praise he needed at the end of a day's work; no yardstick apart from his acceptances by the Royal Academy and other galleries, and the rising prices fetched by his pictures. But money brought him little lasting satisfaction because he regarded it primarily as a means of maintaining a comfortable standard of living rather than as a measure of success.

He valued criticism and it sometimes came from unexpected places. In Norwich, he occasionally painted in the stable loft attached to the surgery of Dr James Bremner in St Giles' Street. He was working there one day painting, from memory, a sepia and colour picture of Augereau tied to a caravan. Watching him

1. Daniel Tomkins & his Dog, 1898, 22″ x 26″

Daniel Tomkins was the father of Munnings's earliest patron, John Shaw Tomkins, a director of A.J. Caley and Son of Norwich, for whom Munnings designed posters.

2. A Suffolk Horse Fair, 1901, 50″ x 80″

Lavenham Horse Fair where Munnings saw the scenes which started him off on this subject.

3. The Path to the Orchard, 1908, 29½″ x 42″

Munnings purchased this white pony, Augereau, from a horse dealer in Norwich.

4. Nude, 1902, 32″ x 26″

This subject was one of a number of nudes that Munnings painted in the over-crowded ground floor studio at L'Atelier Julian in Paris.

5. Portrait of Nelly Gray, 1907, 29″ x 37″

Munnings came across Nelly Gray at the Bungay races – his first real meeting. She was a strikingly handsome tall Gypsy who was once model to Frederick Sandys, and was acquainted with Rossetti and Millais.

6. The Timber-gill, 1902, 55½″ x 43½″

Jim Boswell, the antiques and paintings dealer, once asked Munnings why he did not paint horses pulling a great tree-trunk. This picture was the result.

7. Augereau (The Old Gravel Pit), 1911, 50″ x 80″

The pony in a sand-pit in Norfolk originally was the sole subject of this painting; the boy was added in 1956.

8. Florence Munnings on Horseback, c. 1913

Munnings's first wife was the subject of many paintings, of which this oil sketch is an excellent example.

9. The Ford, 1910, 54″ x 64″

)ne of three large versions, one of which was exhibited at the Royal Academy in 1911, which
Munnings considered a failure.

10. White Canoe on the Stour at Flatford, c. 1922, 20″ x 23¾″

The subject of the white canoe on the river at Dedham had a great fascination for Munnings, and he painted many versions, the first in 1922 and the last in 1956.

paint were Dr Bremner's niece, twelve-year-old Freda Fortune, and her friend, inexplicably nick-named Rabbit Pie. Suddenly, Freda proclaimed in a piping voice: 'I don't like that. I don't like that at all.' Munnings said nothing, but afterwards he presented her with the finished sketch in a gilt frame. 'Here you are,' he said. 'This is for your damn cheek.' On the back he had written: 'To my friend Freda Fortune from her friend A.J. Munnings. – When "Pie" was there.' He was nearly thirty and badly needed a friend.

CHAPTER V

A Boy Called Shrimp

Alfred Munnings could never have considered finding a friend through James Drake, a Norwich horse dealer, who was always at the Saturday markets. The Romany had green fish-like eyes and a dark face, carried a long brass-bound whip and had a lurcher at his heels.

To Drake's delight, Munnings changed his equestrian models every two or three months. The painter not only wanted the stimulation of having a new horse to paint, but also the challenge provided by riding the more temperamental ones through the quiet local parishes at a brisk canter. Although his life-style was geared completely to art, few painters could have derived more joy from its appurtenances.

To Drake went the credit for supplying Munnings with his two most famous models. The first was a beautiful unbroken white pony. He had never been driven or ridden but Munnings found his arrogant wild looks irresistible. Curzon secretly trained him to draw an old gig and the moment Munnings found out he insisted on celebrating by harnessing him up and driving to Norwich to see *A Royal Divorce* at the Theatre Royal. The painter watched the play from the circle, his groom from a seat in the pit.

His imagination was fired by a sentence repeatedly exclaimed by one of the characters in the play, Marshall Augereau; 'I swear it on the word of an Augereau.' Driving home the phrase echoed in his mind and, whenever the pony flagged, he tried the name out with a variety of inflections to spur him on. He responded willingly so that Augereau became his name, well-suited to one of his innate dignity.

The pony made his double debut at the 1908 Royal Academy. In *On the Road* his ability was commemorated in a picture of him pulling a yellow-wheeled gig, driven by a nonchalant George Curzon, wearing a wide sun-hat and reading a newspaper, while other ponies trotted freely ahead or trailed behind on halters fastened to the gig rail.

He could be seen again in a sun-filled study of *The Old Gravel Pit* which hung on the line. It measured fifty inches by thirty and showed Augereau, the white of his coat echoed in a single cloud in the blue sky, standing in masses of white marguerites and scarlet poppies blooming in the red-gold gravel. On Varnishing Day, Munnings was congratulated by many painters and at the Private View the picture sold for £150. Munnings painted several versions and in 1984 a small study in water and body colour, measuring just fourteen-and-a-half inches by ten, went for £14,000 at auction.

There was a wild untamed quality too about the second model Munnings found through Drake. He was a scruffy young brigand who looked after Drake's horses and slept under a caravan with the dogs. He rode bareback and handled horses so well that other dealers often borrowed him to run their horses up and down before a potential buyer and gave him a shilling 'luck money' if they made a sale.

He was stockily built and just over five feet tall, which accounted for his name, Shrimp, and during his early transactions with Drake, it was doubtful if Munnings even noticed him. But George Fountain Page, to give Shrimp his full name, had certainly noticed Munnings and, years later, his elder son, also named George Fountain Page, revealed his father had laid a plan. He explained that Shrimp liked the look of 'the toff', who Drake regularly succeeded in 'stitching up' when he came to buy horses. 'Shrimp was cunning and, like a fox, made his moves well in advance,' his son remembered admiringly.

Shrimp could neither read nor write, he explained, had no family ties and a father represented only in his misspelt, second name. His mother had been a maid at Narford Hall, near Swaffham, the home of the old-established Fountain(e) family, a current member of which, it was alleged, had got her in the family way.

Her small son had apparently inherited a touch of aristocratic independence and was so ashamed of his illegitimacy that he hated living in the village and repeatedly ran away from school. Twice he was caught and sent to the Workhouse, but each time he escaped as soon as it got dark. After a third and final escape, he made a living buying and selling or working with horses and slept rough.

'Pa was tough,' Shrimp's son said. 'He was a survivor. After they made him they threw the mould away.' Eventually, Shrimp teamed up with Drake who, although he too was illiterate, was a sharp dealer but a good provider and made sure Shrimp always had money in his pocket, which was not usually the case for boys in that position.

Money and possessions, however, meant little to the young vagrant and Shrimp's son firmly believed his father worked for Drake simply because he saw it as a way of getting to know Munnings, the handsome flamboyant 'gent', who was around at most Saturday markets. Shrimp watched him from a distance and gradually developed an irrepressible urge to team up with the painter who, like him, seemed something of a loner.

All his life Shrimp had lived by his wits and he formulated the idea that if he could somehow attach himself to the painter he was on to a winner. It would never have occurred to him that, for the first time in his life, his motivation might be to find a surrogate father to replace the aristocratic one he had never known.

Standing, arms akimbo, he shrugged his shoulders disdainfully as he watched Drake sell Munnings another supposed horse bargain. Cunningly, his son said, he worked on Drake. As a result, one Saturday morning in 1908, Munnings was taken aback when Drake invited him to spend a week with him and his family. They lived in a gypsy waggon on the green of a little hamlet near Aylsham and Drake hurriedly suggested that Munnings should put up at the nearby Horseshoes public house.

Munnings hesitated, but Drake persisted and talked persuasively of the geese, ducks, cows and ponies that roamed the common and of many other paintable subjects to be found near the Horseshoes. Munnings, still seeking a new 'idea', accepted Drake's invitation and, two days later, he arrived at Aylsham railway station with his painting things, his dog Joe and the horse blanket he had been advised to bring. He was met by Drake with a horse and cart and driven through some of the most beautiful country he had seen for a long time. The first person he met at the Horseshoes was Shrimp who, according to Shrimp's son, had masterminded the whole idea.

For a week they worked together. The 'undersized, tough, artful, young brigand,' as Munnings described Shrimp, rode or held Drake's ponies in a country lane for Munnings to paint. Every evening Mrs Drake provided satisfying meals from the succulent hares or pheasants caught by the lurchers, and afterwards Munnings and Drake strolled over to the Horseshoes for country talk over pints of ale.

A week later they all returned to Norwich. Drake and his family slept in their waggon, Shrimp slept with the horses, and Munnings, wrapped in the horse blanket, slept under a hedge with his dog. Thanks probably to Shrimp, he had tasted the freedom of the road and, more important, he had forgotten his loneliness and recovered his zest for living.

It had been an exhilarating experience, but by the spring it seemed like a dream. He decided to test its validity and, after he had sent his pictures off to the Royal Academy, he saddled his mare and rode off with Joe to meet Drake and Shrimp again at his early painting grounds near Norwich. He put up for a week for seventeen and sixpence at the Falcon Inn at Costessey, where he and Savile Flint as students had stopped for high teas after their painting expeditions on bicycles. In that week he proved to himself that, in the right company, the landscapes around Taverham and Costessey, where the golden gorse blazed against the blue woods, could never be beaten as settings for the right models.

Drake supplied the models. His waggon was parked near the infamous Bush Inn at Costessey, frequented by prostitutes and patronized by some of the local trotting fraternity. Munnings painted Shrimp with Drake's horses in the inn yard and out in the surrounding heathland and found in Shrimp a model with whom he felt a complete affinity.

The boy needed little food, but insisted on having half a pint of ale to get in tune with Munnings's mood. He would then, almost instinctively, group the horses and ponies just as Munnings wanted, or ride at the head of a string or encourage the animals to graze in contrived disorder against Munnings's chosen background, just as if he had read the painter's mind.

Mounted at the head of a static procession of animals, he could hold a horse firm with his knees and sit for hours with his arm outstretched, his thumb pointing stiffly upwards, to give the one-eyed painter one of the three points needed to judge distance to compensate for his lack of binocular vision.

'Sit there, Shrimp. Stay still!' Munnings would shout. He swore abominably if the boy, aching with holding the same position, showed by his restlessness that it was time to dismount and have another pint.

Suddenly, Munnings realized that the stocky boy, with his straight nose and close-set eyes, was indispensable to him. 'The best model I ever had,' he vowed. That spring, according to Shrimp's son, 'money changed hands one night between Drake and Munnings'. The vagrant's scheme had come to fruition. He had a new master; a hard taskmaster he knew, but one he worshipped.

Their main common interest was their understanding of horses as personalities. Both preferred them to people. Munnings still bought his horses from Drake but, while bargaining, kept his eye on Shrimp standing in the background to indicate by a toss of his head when the price was a fair one. Guided by his young adviser, he bought a beautiful old Welsh mare for £20, a fat little five-year-old Dartmoor pony for £5, a bay yearling colt, a small, dun-coloured horse, another pony and a patient donkey.

Shrimp found a blue, horse-drawn, gypsy waggon in Norwich and a baker's old, open cart complete with horse harness for fifty shillings. The waggon was for shelter during the day and for Shrimp to sleep in; the cart was to carry a tent, painting gear, cooking pots and Munnings's pictures.

Shrimp's proudest moment was when 'A.J.', as he called the painter, sent him to a Norwich tailor to be fitted with a model's outfit. It consisted of a pair of tight-fitting, cord, 'dealer' trousers with pockets slanted well to the front; a Georgian-style, pearl-buttoned, black-fronted, sleeved waistcoat with grey cloth back and sleeves; a cloth cap; a bright neckerchief and a pair of Luton boots. In those clothes, the boy was immortalized in some of Munnings's finest paintings and for the rest of his life he never varied from that style of dress.

So began one of the most propitious and happy periods of Munnings's life. Riding his brown mare he led his strange procession to painting grounds around the Ringland Hills. He was followed by the blue waggon drawn by the Welsh mare with Shrimp in charge, Augereau on a whipple at the mare's side and two ponies tied to the van. Then came Bob, a dour handyman and a replacement for Munnings's groom, George Curzon, who had left to better himself.

He and the terrier, Joe, brought up the rear of the procession in the long cart pulled by another pony, behind the mare, the colt and the donkey. The name, chalked on the sides of the caravan and cart, as required by law, was 'Jasper Petulengro, Swainsthorpe, Norfolk'. By adopting that *nom de plume* Munnings proclaimed his intention to follow the life-style of a famous Norfolk gypsy.

He admitted to feeling 'a thrill of adventure about the whole thing,' when they set off on the fifteen-mile journey to two meadows he had rented at Ringland. Bob and Shrimp camped there with the animals while Munnings stayed at the Falcon Inn and rode to the meadows every day.

He experienced a renewed joy in living which resulted in a wealth of fine pictures, painted in the haze or sunlight of the next two English summers. With an abundance of personal equestrian models he took great pleasure in a peace and companionship such as he had never imagined. Those two summers proved to him that work done spontaneously and on the spot was, for him, the truest in terms of colour, harmony and the relationship of his subjects to nature.

Having his own models gave him endless themes: 'The mere sight of the ponies, coming or going, or different placing of groups gave me fresh pictures,' he wrote. 'Like a game of chess there was no end to it.'

He painted feverishly and canvases of all sizes were piled up in the long cart together with an assortment of unfinished pictures, temporarily abandoned because of changes in the weather.

At the heart of it all, stage-managing from the wings, was Shrimp. Despite his illiteracy he was intelligent and he had realized, probably even before Munnings, that by that time he had succeeded in making himself indispensable to the painter.

It was confirmed on a day when he was posing on the white mare in a quiet stackyard and the peace was shattered by the arrival of a Police Inspector and the Village Constable with a summons for his immediate arrest. He was accused of a breach of the peace and assault at Bungay Fair months before, but the summons had taken a long time to catch up with him.

Munnings, not Shrimp, was more shocked by the intrusion. The situation, for him, had the quality of a nightmare. 'No model! No Shrimp! All would be finished! There was only Shrimp, and I must keep him or shut up shop .... There sat the figure on whom my hopes were centred,' he revealed, hysterically and unashamedly.

Shrimp's crafty roguish expression remained unchanged. Without bothering to dismount he admitted the offence and from his lofty seat watched impassively as Munnings paid the alternative fifty-shilling fine, gratefully and with an unfamiliar humility, in order not to have to part with his prized model. Probably, Shrimp never bothered to thank Munnings or explain that the assault had been caused when he had seen a woman whipping a horse at Bungay Fair and had jumped on her waggon to stop her forcibly.

'Pa told us that never a week went by but there was a blow-up between them,' Shrimp's son said. 'They were two of a kind. Each saw in the other something of himself. Each was needed for the job Munnings was doing. They were both short-tempered and outspoken and Pa gave as good as he got.' They had other things in common; neither valued money for its own sake, both often needed a drink to face life, had iron wills, strong constitutions and tremendous courage.

One day Shrimp had drunk too much and, while sitting for Munnings, just could not keep his horse still. Munnings, in a fit of temper, hurled his palette at him. Shrimp solemnly dismounted, let the horse go and walked off down the lane. Before he had gone far he was overtaken by Munnings riding the mare, intent on stopping him, 'If you ever do that again I'll knock your other fucking eye out,' the servant told the master. He meant it, too, because he loved a fight. Probably because he was small, but very strong, it was his way of proving he was as good as the next man and, after a drink or two, he was prepared to take on anyone in the pub.

His verbal threat to Munnings, however, had hit harder than any physical blow. 'Don't ever talk to me about my eye again,' Munnings warned him bitterly. It was the unmentionable handicap for a painter, which he forced himself to try and ignore. Shrimp told his son that, from the moment he heard the mare's footsteps following him down the lane, 'I knew I had A.J. over a barrel.'

There were other violent incidents. Shrimp, unlike Munnings, was fond of the girls and could never resist a roll in a hayloft with a young maidservant. He ignored A.J.'s warning that there was no time for that sort of thing and it would only cause trouble. If he was caught with a girl her master's fury was usually vented on Munnings, who might be renting a meadow from him for his horses. When any trouble started Shrimp always managed to be well out of sight.

Shrimp's drinking bouts increased. Sometimes Munnings found him flat out by the side of the waggon sleeping it off and the painter often vented his fury by taking a running kick at the boy's behind. Several times, he threatened he might end up by killing him. Time and again, after regular bitter arguments, Shrimp threatened to run away. He was bluffing but, if he disappeared for a night in Norwich and failed to return by morning, Munnings could rarely resist going the rounds of likely Norwich pubs to find him. 'Had he known his value to me, Shrimp might have struck again and again for anything. This never entered his head,' the painter conceded.

It was an unlikely friendship with a strange inevitability about it. The painter who prided himself on his independence found the cheeky young vagrant not only the key to his new-found life-style but also, in some strange way, his inspiration and, for the first time in his life, he realized his dependence on another person. 'Without Shrimp all was ended – finished,' was his constant cry after their rows when the boy landed them in some new trouble such as the day when he allowed the horses to stray on to a farmer's crops.

Moreover, Shrimp certainly had an eye for a picture: 'A.J., you've got that tail all wrong,' he would say, or 'the bridle's not hanging right.' Munnings inevitably accepted his criticism.

Shrimp's prophecy of a change in the weather one day resulted in one of the most outstanding paintings of their travels. There had been weeks of unbroken sunshine and the heat was oppressive as Munnings worked on a landscape in the Ringland Hills. It was a favourite scene he had painted many times and he chose to ignore Shrimp's warning about the thunder clouds gathering on the horizon. Suddenly, the light changed dramatically, the canvas was laid in the cart and replaced on the easel by an unfinished impression of the same scene painted on a dull day.

The partly finished canvas became the background for a swift impression of Shrimp riding the white mare and leading Augereau to shelter, caught in the spotlight of the last ray of sunlight piercing the ominous sky. Light shone from them. The effect was spectacular.

Munnings must have sensed the picture's potential for, when the storm broke and the canvas was stowed away and men and horses disappeared, he stripped off his clothes and in an ecstatic moment danced and sang stark naked like a young dervish in the pelting rain, watched only by his dog, Joe. Afterwards, he dried himself on his old flannel trousers and made for the Falcon.

Later he worked the picture up on a canvas measuring about fifty-nine inches by seventy-two, and heightened its dramatic effect by painting a huddle of fairground tents in the background and adding a string of dark horses following Shrimp and the white mare and pony. The additions, like supporting characters in a play, heightened the impact of a boy and two white horses riding before a storm. Here and there a flash of light illuminated a horse's dark coat and in the far distance, like a hieroglyphic, Bob could be seen riding another white horse.

The Coming Storm, as it was called, was exhibited in the Royal Academy and afterwards was bought by the National Gallery of New South Wales for £850. When the Duke of Gloucester went to Australia as Governor General it was one of the paintings he chose to hang in his official residence. 'What a go!' Munnings commented in a letter to a friend when he heard the news.

Australia also acquired *Shade*, a study of Shrimp under the trees with Augereau and other ponies. It hung on the line in the Academy and was bought by Sydney Art Gallery. A version of Augereau in a sandpit, painted at the same time and called *The Old Sandpit*, was not shown in the Academy until thirteen years later.

Another series of grey day studies involving Shrimp resulted in three large versions of *The Ford*, showing the boy at the head of a string of fifteen horses and two men crossing a ford in the River Waveney. He was riding the brown mare, with Augereau on a short leading rein. The position of his outstretched right arm, with his hand grasping the rein, indicated that originally he might have posed with his thumb pointing upwards to give Munnings an eye-line.

To introduce a feeling of movement into the picture Munnings had repeatedly shouted instructions to Shrimp to 'Wake that dun horse up! Shove his head up!' and had employed a boy with a long pole to stir up the water, for he preferred to paint exactly what he saw rather than rely on his imagination. He had stationed himself on rising ground so that he looked down at the leading ponies coming out of the grey water with its multi-coloured reflections. He made several five-foot studies of the scene. 'What a subject!' he exclaimed in joyous satisfaction, time and again.

Often he was short of ready cash on their travels. Then, he would go into the local pub to sell a painting closely followed by Shrimp. 'What yer trying ter do? Buy the place?' Shrimp would comment with amazement, when he heard the asking price for a picture. 'Shut up, Shrimp. Go away!' Munnings would bellow, but the landlord and his customers appreciated the repartee and Munnings always got a fair price.

Gradually, the heated rows between Shrimp and the painter lessened as their nomadic life settled into an easy routine. When Munnings was intent on a day's painting Shrimp agreed not to go into a pub until the evening and survived on a bottle of beer supplied by Bob, while Munnings lunched on a cold chop with half a loaf of bread.

In return, Munnings stifled his misgivings when Shrimp decided gleefully to 'puve the gruy' which, in his language, meant fielding the horses for free for the night. He chose a field lush with grass and clover, checked for gaps in the hedge, put the horses in after dark and let them out before daylight.

Sometimes for the sake of a scene Munnings wanted to paint, they trespassed with the horses. If an irate farmer turned up and could not be appeased, the painter and model would hurl such a stream of joint abuse at him that the startled man would stagger away in a daze, grateful to escape out of earshot. Munnings could be foul-mouthed, but Shrimp could outshriek him and swore like a maniac.

When the November rains came they made their way back to Swainsthorpe where Shrimp kept an eye on the horses, apart from his occasional trips to Norwich for a little wheeling and dealing. He bought and sold for the excitement of the contest, not for the sake of money or possessions. Otherwise he smoked and hibernated.

Munnings also went into Norwich. When he travelled there by train, he often went on to his destination in one of the hansom cabs that plied for hire in the station yard. George Morris, a cab proprietor, frequently drove him, despite the painter's tendency not only to have no money to pay the fare at the end of the journey but often to borrow five shillings from the driver with the promise to 'pay you the lot later'. 'You'd give him half-a-crown to get rid of him,' Morris recalled. 'And yet when he was in the money he was one of the best spenders around. He'd want a cab here, a cab there – go and drive there and drink there . . . .'

One year he attended the cabmen's annual dinner at the Criterion Café in Norwich and during the meal, did several sketches which he handed around, charging half-a-crown for each. 'They were all tearing them up,' George Morris told his son, who added: 'Well, what would they do with them? He was not a known man. He was doing it to earn a few shillings. My dad kept one, a sketch of a fellow called Spinks, eating his meal using the top of the cab as a table.'

During the winter, while Shrimp hibernated, Munnings returned to Swainsthorpe as something of a celebrity and children from the village school were sometimes allowed to go to his studio and watch him paint.

> 'He was a real gentleman and very kind to us,' eighty-seven-year-old Jimmy Chamberlain recalled. 'But if we made a noise we'd be outside in no time at all . . . . He had a dog, an Irish terrier, that used to wander down into the village. If we spotted it we'd grab it and put it on a leash and take it home for the day. Then, in the evening we'd take that up to Mr. Munnings's house and knock on the door and say, "Please sir, we found that wandering." And Mr. Munnings would kick it up the behind and give us a penny.'

The painter also hunted enthusiastically and felt he looked 'A hell of a fellow' in his black velvet cap, dark grey melton coat, white cord breeches and dark brown-topped boots, the uniform of the farmer members of the Norwich Staghounds. He bought another thoroughbred, Rebecca, to join his brown mare, for forty guineas at a Norwich sale and sometimes rode her as far as fifty miles a day.

He was a fine rider, but not foolhardy and had a great respect for his horses. Friends often lent him their best horses to ride, and at one hunt he was entrusted with a fine powerful hunter called Duhallow. Jack Cooke warned him he would probably be thrown and, after he had collected the horse from Attleborough station and ridden to the site of the meet, astride the animal's great wide saddle, he thought it quite possible.

The meet was at a hotel in the town and, before joining his friends there, he nipped into a chemist's shop, bought some powdered resin and rubbed it into the leathers of his breeches and down the insides of his boots. Stuck to the great horse he had the ride of his life as it soared over jumps and kept at the front with the Whip, the Master and one of Cooke's young horses. Afterwards Cooke congratulated him on his fine performance. 'He carried me and I just sat there,' said Munnings, modestly, but truthfully.

Such first-hand experience of his subjects was partly responsible for his success as an equestrian painter. He described his method of painting in an article in *Country Life* analysing how his idol, Stubbs, worked. Describing how Stubbs painted a particular equestrian portrait* Munnings might have been writing of himself:

> Picture to yourself Stubbs being shown the horses he was going to paint [he wrote]. Surely the grey veteran filled his eye – I would bet all I am worth that Stubbs had a thrill when he saw him led out. Then he sees the other horse, or horses, and does not miss the little stable lad meanwhile, nor the curious pinnacled structure outside the riding school, of which he makes a memory note....
>
> His picture would grow in his mind. He would make drawings and finally place it on canvas ... the outline of the white horse shows distinctly enough where he has painted that dark transparent shadow up to and around it. He decided to place the pinnacled structure within an ace of the centre of the picture, and the duke on his white horse under it, also in the centre; and what consummate art it is! For there, with all his surroundings – the trees, the buildings, the other figures and appurtenances – the duke is the picture; ... in looking at that painting of that head alone, I am certain that it was painted on to canvas from life, as were the horses and other figures. The painting of that figure and of the others is great portraiture. The claret-coloured coat, the breeches and boots are well

* Portrait of William Bentinck, Duke of Portland.

> worth studying; and the same with the green-coated huntsman which is, if anything, even greater as a portrait than that of the duke. See his attitude and his expression of trusty devotion. The understanding is there between the servant and master .... Look at the little stable boy in his long waistcoat – the painting of his waistcoat is delicious.

The same could often be said of his own paintings of Shrimp's much-prized, pearl-buttoned waistcoat.

In mid-July he always moved on from Ringland, and travelled with his little procession through the drowsy South Norfolk villages to Suffolk, near Hoxne, for a change of scene for both himself and the ponies. Often artist friends from Paris joined him there and Gerald Stones never failed to turn up for a week or two's painting.

One summer, before they set off on their travels, Shaw Tomkins took Munnings to Munich again where he saw an exhibition of paintings by German artists that staggered him with its virility. He studied large open-air pictures of horses, sheep and cattle that were more full of life than any paintings he had ever seen. All that summer he visualized Zugel's vigorous manipulative brushwork in his brilliant painting of a peasant washing his yoked black and white cows in a shallow stream. The broad strong handling of paint to emphasize texture was a feature of his own technique but, looking at Zugel's masterly brush strokes, he must have felt he had a long way to go.

That summer he also discovered that Shrimp, for all his tough manner, was capable of genuine grief. The old white mare broke a fetlock and had to be destroyed and Shrimp cried like a baby. The boy remembered the mare every time he picked her white hairs from the seat of his cord trousers and he could not forget the long days he had sat on her broad back while Munnings painted.

Perhaps her passing brought home to Shrimp that his only experience of companionship and a secure if irregular life-style, was also transitory. This was emphasized when Gerald Stones joined them, as usual, for a week or two, because his presence seemed to dilute Munnings's strange dependency on Shrimp. One cold October day when Munnings saw Stones off from the southern corner of Norfolk where they had been painting, he had a sudden urge to return to Mendham. The Shrimp episode was over as far as he was concerned.

Shrimp received the verdict impassively. Munnings sent him and Bob in the waggon to take the paintings and horses to Swainsthorpe and when he returned he gave him the money he had saved up for him over the years, for it would have been fatal to have paid him each week. He also gave him the dun horse and the blue waggon with the name 'Jasper Petulengro' deleted and that of 'Fountain Page' painted in its place.

Shrimp had never before owned anything in his life, apart from the clothes he stood up in, and he could not have dreamt of having such possessions. Speechless, he drove away leaving Munnings to ride the mare and Augereau to Mendham.

Early the next morning a horse-dealer from the next village arrived at the farm where he was staying and asked if the painter wanted his dun horse back. It seemed that Shrimp had stopped at his village and, after a few drinks at the local public house, had traded him the waggon and horse for a pony and cart and a little money and had driven off to Norwich.

For a moment Munnings thought of buying back the dun horse, but suppressed the idea. That period of his life was over and he must go to Mendham and work out his next move. At the back of his mind, however, there remained a nagging doubt as to whether he had done as much as he might have done for the boy who had helped him to create some of his finest paintings. Time would show, however, that in fact the strange friendship had benefited the boy a great deal more than the man realized.

CHAPTER VI

Life in Cornwall

Munnings went back to his parents' home, the Mill House at Mendham and, on grey days, worked up a large canvas from the small studies he had made of Shrimp driving his horses across the ford. He still needed to copy the subject from life and he used his father's ponies as models, with Fred Gray driving them through a shallow part of the River Waveney. The skies were dull enough but the picture just would not go right. Gray stood in the water in gum boots and held the ponies. Augereau was there, but there was no Shrimp to keep the animals alert or give Munnings an eye-line.

At the end of every afternoon, miserable with frustration, he carried his canvas back to the kitchen and stood its face to the wall. His only satisfaction came from knowing that his visit was giving his mother pleasure. Later, she wrote in her Sunday diary, 'Alfred has been with us part of the winter, and in spite of his erratic ways and hasty temper it has been a better one than the last. I have had no time to be dull or lonely.'

For her sake, as much as his own, he invited a young sculptor friend, Whitney-Smith, to stay who did a bust of John Munnings and two small statuettes of Nobby and Charlotte Gray. Whitney-Smith also encouraged Munnings to try his hand at modelling. The result was a small statuette of Augereau who was prepared to pose for hours as long as he could eat hay where he stood.

On bright days, Munnings painted Fred and Nobby Gray dressed as huntsmen in scarlet coats. The watercolour of Fred riding through the trees was called *The Gap*. It was exhibited at the Royal Institute of Painters in Water Colours the following spring and was eventually reproduced as a popular colour print. Nobby sat for hours on a wooden saddle horse and blew a hunting horn but the painting of him was never finished.

Whitney-Smith left, and to complete Munnings's misery, his dog, Joe, was run over by a butcher's cart. His master was 'utterly heartbroken'. He was also experiencing lack of confidence in the value of his work, which could be deduced when one of his contemporaries, Michael Warren of Swardeston, got married. He sent him one of his paintings as a wedding present, a small oil of sheep among the trees, and accompanying it were instructions to 'hang it so that the light catches it from the side – that is on a side wall to a window, not opposite'. Munnings explained, rather apologetically, that it was an old favourite of his, 'a decorative style of thing for a living room'. Then, still doubtful if it was a good enough wedding present, he sent a pair of Sheffield-plated candlesticks as well.

There was no shortage of grey days in late November and he struggled on with his picture of *The Ford* while, in his mind's eye, were probably images of Zugel's river scene of a peasant and his cattle, and his bedside print of the Baltic fishermen bringing their boat ashore.

A group of English artists, who painted such scenes of everyday village life out-of-doors and on the spot wherever possible, lived around Newlyn. He remembered them from several short holidays he had spent in Cornwall. He had been fascinated by the difference in scenery between East Anglia and that strange, comparatively treeless county with its narrow fast-running streams and granite cliffs towering like giant sculptures above the pounding surf. It was great riding country too, he remembered. He decided to go there for an indefinite period in the spring.

Before he went, he sent off six pictures to the Royal Institute of Painters in Water Colours' Exhibition and three, including one version of *The Ford*, to the Royal Academy. He was still dissatisfied when he saw it hung there and some years later he cut off the top part, which was mainly sky, and allowed the horses on the bank at the far side of the water, to form the background. He preferred the result and one version was bought by the Wolverhampton Art Gallery.

Before he went to Cornwall he had to make arrangements for his horses: he gave Augereau to his mother to pull her gig and one thoroughbred mare to a farmer to be mated. The brown mare and his new dog, Taffy, a large Welsh terrier, were to follow him to Cornwall by train. Then he set off to find the Newlyn Painters, who lived in the small fishing villages on the slope of a hill above the western shores of Mount's Bay, near Penzance.

A painting colony had been formed in Newlyn in 1880 by artists who were influenced by the work of the French realist painter, Millet, and by Bastien Lepage whose work Munnings had admired on his Paris visits. Lepage painted in muted colours and subtle tones absolutely true to nature.

The Newlyn colony originally spent their summers in Brittany, but eventually gravitated to south Cornwall because of its similar scenery, mild climate and good light. Their realistic earthy pictures of Cornish fishermen made a striking impact in the Royal Academy against the fashionable Victorian paintings of staid maidens, fluffy kittens and stiff portraits of high society.

By 1890, however, many of the original group had left Newlyn to go their own ways, but Stanhope Forbes, 'the grand old man of Cornish painting' as he became known, and his Canadian wife, Elizabeth, stayed to found a school in three huts in the green wilderness of an old orchard called The Meadow. In the smallest hut, beginners drew from plaster casts; in the largest, they painted and drew from live models – mostly local people including elderly fishermen and young girls, glad of the chance to earn a little extra money. The third hut was the life room where professional nude models from London posed, to the grave suspicion of the locals.

Stanhope Forbes, as well as running his school, was the centre of the little painting community and held it together. It contained a few of the original group including Walter Langley, the first figure painter to depict incidents in the lives of the fisherfolk, Thomas Cooper Gotch with his 'imaginative symbolism' and the impressionist, Norman Garstin. They were joined by the landscape painter, Samuel John (Lamorna) Birch, who settled a few miles away from Newlyn at Lamorna, where a stream flows through a wooded valley into the sea at Lamorna Cove. Birch took the name Lamorna to distinguish himself from another Newlyn painter, Lionel Birch, and as a tribute to the beautiful valley, with its trout streams surrounded by quarries and cliffs, which was his life-long inspiration.

A second generation of Newlyn painters moved in including Ernest Procter, the best student of his time at Forbes's school, who married a gifted fellow student, Dod Shaw, and stayed in Newlyn. He painted very successfully in many styles and he and his wife were commissioned to decorate the Kokine Palace in Rangoon helped by a team of Burmese, Indian and Chinese plasterers, carvers and gilders.

Geoffrey Garnier, a specialist in etching and engraving, also met his wife, Jill, at the school. His studio, above Newlyn at Trewarveneth, was sometimes visited by Orpen. Another occasional visitor to Newlyn was the sculptor, Frank Owen Dobson. While there, he produced potboilers by the half-dozen – vivid watercolours of moorland scenes. He sold them through a Penzance dealer to subsidize his chalk drawings and sculpture, the true vehicles of his genius.

The Newlyn artists worked quite separately from each other, although a few tended to continue the tradition of their forerunners and paint with uncompromising realism, directly from life and, whenever possible, in the open air. They also introduced brilliant colours and intimate studies of home life.

The permanent community of painters was supplemented by students at Stanhope Forbes's Art School. Many lodged in the sturdy, little terrace houses above the harbour with fine views over the slate or thatched roofs of the lower terraces, across the bay to the gentle outline of Tregonning Hill. They paid thirty shillings a week for full board.

Some of the male students stayed in buildings surrounding Trewarveneth Farm and groups of girls also boarded at Myrtle Cottage and other large houses. Married couples could often be persuaded to act as chaperones for, in spite of the high spirits and hectic social life, the hard-working professional painters were determined their colony should preserve its moral reputation. At the worst the students were regarded by the locals as 'a godless though profitable nuisance', according to one student, C. E. Vulliamy, who eventually became a writer. 'They brought a lot of money into the place but also brought frivolity and rebellion,' he wrote in his autobiography. He described Sundays when the locals pelted with stones any students painting out of doors, and threw their pictures and easels into the harbour.

Every Saturday morning Stanhope Forbes criticized his students' work. It was shown anonymously and occasionally 'The Professor', as Forbes was known, could be quite merciless; justifiably so because his school, in its idyllic setting, attracted not only serious students but also girls who studied art as a pleasant pastime. They could be identified by their picturesque tussore silk dresses. Their male counterparts could be recognized by their bow ties. When these young romantics were not playing at painting, they wrote poetry, dabbled in writing, read and discussed daring books and revelled in a brave new feeling of complete emancipation.

At the end of 1907 Laura Knight and her husband, Harold, arrived. They took rooms in a large house in the centre of Newlyn belonging to Mrs Beer, who let rooms to several other artists. The Knights also rented two lofts with skylights for their studios. From 'Beer House' as their lodging was called, they could see the whole stretch of the surf-fringed bay with a line of hills beyond. At night the sweep of the Lizard arm was pinpointed by the winking lighthouse.

The Knights were both just over thirty and reaching the peak of their careers. They intended to paint, not take lessons in the school, but Stanhope Forbes invited them to visit his studio whenever they liked. They soon made friends with the students and painters in the colony and participated in its non-stop social life. Laura joined in the local activities enthusiastically; Harold with more reluctance.

They found the life stimulating: eminent painters arrived for short visits and stayed at Trewarveneth or at the Cliff House Temperance Hotel, Lamorna, run by Jessie Jory, wife of the stout complacent landlord of a rival establishment, the Lamorna Inn down at the cove. The two were not on speaking terms. His Inn was the centre of village life and was known as 'The Wink', a name usually associated with a beerhouse without a spirit licence. In Mr Jory's case it most likely implied a place where the landlord tipped the wink to local smugglers when customs' men were around.

Musical evenings took place in the studio of Stanhope Forbes's pleasant house at High Faugan. The host loved to play the cello and everyone who could play a musical instrument performed. There was also a Beethoven Society and formal concerts took place in local halls. Summer dances were held in private gardens illuminated by Chinese lanterns, and picnics were held at Lamorna Cove or Land's End.

Laura Knight thrived on a sense of youthful fun and freedom she had never known. Her new exuberance was reflected in her paintings. She might be 'the wildest of the wild' at a party, according to a fellow guest, but would be out very early the next morning painting huge sun-filled canvases all day.

Her picture called *The Beach*, showing seven almost life-sized children playing by the sea in brilliant sunshine, was a big success in the 1909 Royal Academy. Alfred Munnings was represented there by *The Edge of the Wood* and, more spectacularly, by a study of Augereau called *The Path to the Orchard*. It was a colour-filled picture of the white pony, his coat iridescent in the summer sunlight, being led along a path beside the river by a blue-frocked girl whose white cap and apron were pale echoes of the golden white of the pony. White flashed again in the foreground where clumps of fragile phlox mingled with crimson ones.

The Path to the Orchard, however, did not attract as much interest as Laura Knight's beach scene which Munnings greatly admired. Perhaps it reminded him of his own visits to Cornwall. He remembered what bliss it had been on an August or September day 'to lie on the sweet-smelling turf, watching sea-pinks trembling in light winds, and listening to the unceasing sound of the surf and cry of gulls.... Nothing [he wrote] quite like this coast exists anywhere, gives peace and rest to body and soul. There were spots where I could laze and be idle and drowsy enough in Norfolk, but of all places, on the right day, I find myself more often longing to be back on those Cornish cliffs, lying in the sun, listening to the incessant sound of the surf.'

When the day came for him to return to Cornwall for an indefinite period, his mother wrote mournfully in her Sunday diary, 'Now I feel I have lost Alfred.'

He arrived at Newlyn in flamboyant style, accompanied by a group of girl models. When he was not painting them they went with him for long walks. He lodged at Chywoone Farm in Trewarveneth opposite Gotch's studio, and Laura Knight saw him for the first time chatting to his girls in the street. Her first impression, recorded in her autobiography, was of a fine figure of a young man with a pale face and light brown hair combed forward, who might have sat for a portrait of Robbie Burns. He wore a shepherd's plaid suit with close-fitting trousers belling out at the foot. Her artist's eye recorded every detail. He made an arresting sight, 'standing straddled there; strong, upright, small head, wide shoulders, narrow hips....'

She heard that he had invited a group of male students to a dinner party where he served a punch based on his formidable recipe from the landlord of the Swan at Harleston. It required a pint of rum, a pint of brandy, a pint of sherry, sugar, lemon rind and cloves simmered with boiling water. Four guests had got hopelessly drunk and had been laid out on the veranda. Such a scandal had never before sullied the Newlyn colony's reputation for, although the artists were unconventional, they stopped short of anything more than colourful clothes, mild flirtations and noisy parties. In that remote corner of England, in their free time they tended to behave like overgrown children let out of school.

Laura met 'A.J.', as she soon called him, a few evenings later at a musical party in Gotch's studio. There the newcomer took complete control of the entertainment and sang choruses of hunting songs with great gusto and rhythm so that the whole company soon joined in. He recited his long party piece, *The Raven* by Edgar Allan Poe, with so much feeling that Laura thought he had a performer's natural talent and might have been just as successful an actor as he was a painter. She was overwhelmed by his immense vitality and, by the end of the evening, she was completely captivated by him. 'I could not take my eyes off him,' she disclosed to her biographer, Janet Dunbar. 'He was the stable, the artist, the poet, the very land itself! I adored everything about him.'

The admiration was mutual although, on his part, it was for the painter more than for the woman: 'Here was a great artist who never ceased working,' read an equivalent entry in his autobiography. 'She possessed the energy of six; the studies for her larger pictures were wonderful. It was through her that I used china-clay canvases. Laura Knight could paint anything be it a small water-colour or a nine-foot canvas. Seeing is believing.'

What he failed to see was that, in many ways, they were counterparts of each other. They had similar volatile temperaments and immense vitality and vigour, sometimes expressed in high-spirited horseplay when it was not channelled into joyous, exuberant paintings of people and horses full of brilliant colour, celebrating an idyllic way of life in the sunlight of English summers. At times she could be as bawdy and vulgar as he.

Theirs was apparently a platonic friendship although, had they met before Laura's sterile marriage, it might have been different, for Laura found in 'A.J.' many of the fundamental qualities that were lacking in her cold introverted husband. She was an unfeminine type of woman, sometimes suspected of having lesbian tendencies. Her forthright masculine character, probably accentuated by a loveless marriage, relieved Munnings of any emotional pressure in their friendship. She made no sexual demands, which was a relief to him, because it seems he perhaps found it was impossible to respond to them with his peers. She was a year older than he and theirs was one of his few lasting friendships.

Laura's husband, however, disliked 'A.J.' intensely from the moment they met and always felt inadequate when he was around. He loathed his brashness, his love of practical jokes, his irrepressible high spirits, his foul language and his tolerance of blood sports which Harold, a strong pacifist, abhorred. In addition, he could hardly have been unaware of his wife's strong attraction to the newcomer.

Two or three days after their first meeting, Harold returned to Beer House from his studio to find 'A.J.' comfortably ensconced in his favourite armchair in the sitting room, with his legs sprawled wide apart. 'I've taken a bedroom here and Mrs. Beer says I can share your sitting room,' he announced amiably. Harold was horrified and the next few days were the most miserable he had known. He often left the room when Munnings entered, to dominate the fireside with his endless flow of anecdotes and his loud coarse laughter.

Laura continued to find her new friend amusing. Eventually, her husband concealed his feelings to the extent that the three of them sometimes went out on long country walks. They even indulged in a Beer House band; penny whistle, hair comb, drums on any old canvas, and sang. There was only a thin wall between their sitting room and Mrs Beer's bedroom but there was no need to worry about disturbing their landlady for, after some months, she assured them, 'I love music, me dears.'

Gradually, Munnings was completely accepted by the community so that no social gathering was considered a success without him, and he boasted that he 'organised more parties, picnics, outings and Christmas festivities than anyone in the country'. The arrival of his brown mare, The Duchess, and his Welsh terrier, Taffy, from Swainsthorpe, showed that he intended to be around for quite a time. He took a large converted sail loft for a studio with a stable below, and engaged a local lad, seventeen-year-old Ned Osborne, as his groom-cum-model in succession to Old Norman and Nobby Gray.

Osborne was far more active than either and made a fine figure posed in a scarlet coat and black cap for a spate of hunting studies with Cornish backgrounds of moors and woods or remembered Norfolk ones of flat fields and great skies. Munnings felt *The Huntsman* was his best painting of that period. It was a picture in tempera of Nobby taking his horse over a great jump. He was happy and his paintings reflected it. He had always been conscientious and accurate but at Lamorna his work became lighter and even brighter as if he had found new colours to express his mood.

He rode his brown mare with the local hunt, the Western Hounds, and enraged the Master, Colonel William Bolitho, by defying the Whip and saving the life of a fox which had given the hunt a good run. Finally, the animal leapt into the sea and swam for its life until it was washed up exhausted on to the cliffs. There, Munnings insisted it should be left alone to recover.

With shooting, like hunting, he took no part in the kill and never carried a gun, although he walked the fields as a spectator with several syndicates of his friends.

Such unexpected glimpses of gentleness occasionally penetrated the bluff and increasingly brash personality he showed to the world. One day, for instance, he decided to help two artists who were short of money, by selling their paintings to wealthy visitors in the Queen's Hotel, Penzance. He persuaded Mrs Dod Procter to go with him with the paintings in a hired dog-cart, to the hotel. He wore a red neckerchief instead of a collar and when the hotel commissionaire dismissed them with a sharp, 'Nothing today, thank you,' he marched into the vestibule with two pictures under each arm, scuffled with the commissionaire who fell and sprained an ankle, slipped into the hotel lounge and sold the paintings while the commissionaire was hopping about on one foot.

His own paintings differed markedly from those of the other Newlyn artists for he used Cornwall only as a background for his own ideas. He bought a handsome grey called Grey Tick, whom he painted for weeks on end, on grey days against grey walls, enjoying the challenge of expressing form in subtle tones. He also paid Mr Jory £14 for a black and white cow which had been trained to walk on a halter. Munnings loaned her to a local farmer, who fed her in return for her milk and calves and lent her back as a model whenever the painter wanted her. She proved a good investment because she soon made friends with the farmer's own cows and, when she was led down to a painting ground, one or two of the herd were sure to follow and group round her chewing the cud for hours on end while Munnings painted them all.

He was happy again and showed it in words as well as in pictures when he wrote he was 'painting to the sweet music of water running over stones and pebbles; the high sunlight piercing the foliage, flashing on leaf and stalk – throwing pools of light on transparent, rippling, sandy shallows. What colour there was in the running water, the reflections, the sunlit ripples; what subtle blue passages in the shadowed current.' As always, it seemed, a river inspired him and he transferred his emotions to canvas, primed with china clay as Laura Knight had shown him.

Whenever he left that close-knit community, with its shared interests and its exuberance in work as well as in play, depression tended to close in on him. In London on the way back from a short visit to Norfolk, he explained in a letter to Dod Procter, 'I tried to end my "blues" there, but couldn't, and they've followed me right through since leaving Cornwall and I have them now. Last Sunday in town was rotten .... I was simply withered up with the "blues".'

Back in Newlyn for his first Christmas there, he counteracted the blues with an almost unhealthy boisterousness. He, the Knights and the Gotches, decided to pool expenses and hold a Dickensian week of merrymaking at Gotch's studio for all their friends. However, the yule-tide celebrations started a fortnight earlier than planned because, as soon as the studio floor was polished and the walls festooned with holly, their friends could not keep away.

For three weeks the studio became a theatre where 'A.J.' played the starring role. He was in his element. Every day after tea he read aloud from Dickens's *A Christmas Carol* or the *Pickwick Papers*, oblivious that many of his audience slept through his performances, worn out by their long country walks over muddy ditches and stone walls in the afternoons.

'A.J.' was indefatigable. After the nightly ceremonial dinners, when the host took wine with each guest in turn, Munnings recited and sang, vamping out his own accompaniment on the grand piano until his friends fell asleep on the floor or went home.

He attended the Boxing Day Meet at Penzance where everyone who could find a mount followed the hounds and the others trailed behind on foot. 'A.J.' was so excited and ebullient after a fortnight's non-stop celebrations that he was called to order by the Master in no uncertain terms. No matter. The coming year would be a memorable one for him.

After Christmas the Gotch family moved into a new house they had had built and Harold Knight immediately rented their old home, delighted to leave Munnings to the company of Joey Carter Wood, a talented student at Forbes's school. His sister, Florence, occasionally stayed with him and also took painting lessons.

Their parents were wealthy. Their grandfather had made a fortune in the brewing industry and for several generations the Carter Woods had owned the Artillery Place Brewery in Westminster. They had a large house, Skinburness Towers, at Silloth on the Cumbrian coast, as well as a London home.

Florence and her brother were very friendly with a permanent resident at Cliff House, Gilbert Evans, a twenty-six-year-old Captain in the Monmouth Royal Engineers' Militia and one of the few non-painters included in the social life of the artists' colony. In 1909 he had been engaged as Land Agent by a brother officer, Colonel Thomas Paynter, who owned Boskenna, a large country house on an estate between Land's End and Penzance which included most of the farms in the parish. By the time 'The Bloat', as Florence was inexplicably nicknamed, had paid two or three visits to Cliff House, the good-looking Evans had grown very fond of her.

He was more practical than most of the artists and was the chief organizer of their hectic social life. Coffee parties took place nearly every evening in the students' lodgings or the artists' homes when high-minded conversation or childish paper and pencil games were the rule. Uproarious parties were given in the artists' studios with dancing to the music of a hired gramophone, solo acrobatic turns, singing and much laughter. On winter evenings there were play readings or rehearsals for amateur theatricals to be given in local halls.

Harold Knight painted Florence Carter Wood, or 'The Bloat', several times on her visits between 1909 and 1911. His life-sized oil, *Portrait of Florence*, showed her in profile sitting in a tall upright chair, her feet on a footstool. She looked elegant and aristocratic in an ankle-length gown, her fair hair in heavy coils above her long neck. Yet she seemed strangely vulnerable, despite her firm chin and rather patrician nose.

Florence looked magnificent on a horse. She was the perfect complement to the splendid creatures Munnings idolized. Moreover, the combination of an elegant young woman on a fine hunter afforded him immense satisfaction. At times perhaps, the woman, centaur-like in a flowing riding habit, seemed a very extension of the horse itself. Impetuously and perhaps because Florence was part of his Elysian world, he decided he must marry her. They had only two things in common: riding and painting.

He could hardly have chosen a less suitable bride than the carefully brought up daughter of very wealthy and devoutly religious parents. She came from a completely different class, had led an extremely sheltered youth and her parents, encouraged by the marriage of her father's sister, Kathleen, to the ninth earl of Harrington, were anxious that she and her younger sister, Helen, should marry well. So Joseph Carter Wood sold his brewery in order that both his daughters could be presented at Court – a privilege that, in those days, was closed to daughters of tradesmen.

Florence, however, had decided to be a painter and her parents probably felt that an art school in a remote part of Cornwall, where she could be chaperoned by her brother, was a safe place to protect her from undesirable contacts. They had reckoned without the fascination of a successful and handsome painter, outrageously different from any man she had ever met, who would have had little difficulty in sweeping her off her feet. If Munnings's contemporary, Laura Knight, had been captivated by him, an unworldly girl, some ten years younger, was even more vulnerable.

Joseph Carter Wood was horrified when Munnings approached

him for permission to marry his daughter. This was revealed in a letter from Geoffrey Garnier in which, unjustifiably, he described Munnings's family as 'of gutter extraction'. He revealed that Florence's father told Munnings: 'Go – and if at the end of twelve months you have made a clear £1,000 I will talk to you again.' Garnier, it seemed, had heard the inside story from his friend, Florence's brother, Joey. He added in his letter, 'A.J. made his thousand and so disaster came to The Bloat.'

To make £1,000 within the year, Munnings sold five pictures to the Royal Institute of Painters in Water Colours at an average price of £40 each, supplied dealers in Glasgow, Norwich and Newcastle and had three pictures in the 1911 Royal Academy. The best of them, *A Romany Boy*, was a study of a beautiful white mare standing with other horses on the top of a grassy bank in full sunlight. It was hung on the line and bought by the National Gallery of New Zealand.

One result of working hard and, in his free moments, participating in a hectic social life was that he had little time alone with 'The Bloat'; too little, perhaps, to make him suspect that the charming aloofness and sophisticated manner, suggested in her portraits by Harold Knight, might mask an impenetrable coldness to the opposite sex.

They were married on 19 January 1912 at The Church of St John the Evangelist in Westminster and spent their honeymoon in London, probably at the Artillery Mansions Temperance Hotel, Westminster which was owned by Florence's parents. For some reason that was never explained, Laura Knight was staying in the hotel at the same time.

She was the only outside witness when Florence became very upset and tried to commit suicide by taking cyanide. No-one seemed to know how she had obtained it or the reason for her suicide attempt. Conceivably, she may have been upset by the sexual side of marriage and, if so, it would have taken a far more sensitive and experienced man than Munnings to cope with her. Alternatively, she may have ceased to love A.J. by the time he had made his thousand pounds, but felt she must keep her side of the bargain.

He and Laura Knight managed to save her life and Munnings hurried back with her to Mrs Jory's hotel in Newlyn. There, his concern for his wife was obvious but no-one except the Knights knew why, and Laura made Florence promise never to attempt to take her life again. They remained close friends. Florence also formed a deep friendship with Joan Coulsen.

However, it was apparent to everyone that 'The Bloat' was living under a great strain. At times she was very depressed and when the wife of Munnings's friend, Charles Simpson, the bird and animal painter, had a baby, Florence visited her, questioned her closely about the birth and then ran from the room in tears crying, 'I couldn't stand it.'

Another day Jill Garnier passed Florence hurrying down the cliff path in tears crying, 'I hate him. I hate him.'

Eventually, Florence was found to have goitre, which might have caused her depression. She had an operation on her neck and afterwards took part, quite happily it seemed, in the flourishing social life of Newlyn. Munnings resumed his old life-style as if nothing unusual had happened. But he was a far from devoted husband.

CHAPTER VII

A Mysterious Tragedy

In the spring at Newlyn, picnics and barbecues superseded studio parties. One Sunday, at a barbecue in the woods, the fire was glowing steadily and the drink flowing nicely when it was discovered that no-one had remembered to bring the sausages. The barbecue seemed doomed until Gilbert Evans volunteered to knock up the local butcher and went off on his apparently futile mission. To everyone's surprise he returned in a short time, triumphantly brandishing a string of sausages. He had managed to obtain them, not from the local butcher but, by bribery or persuasion, from a less god-fearing one in Penzance.

Violin music mingled with mouth-watering sounds from the barbecue and the delighted painters each promised to reward Evans with a gift of their own works. A presentation supper was arranged for a few evenings later, on 6 April 1912 at Cliff House. The seating plan showed the twenty-two participants arranged ten down each side of a long table with Munnings at one end and Evans at the other. Laura Knight was there, but not Harold who was suffering from a mouth infection.

After the meal, Munnings proposed a satirical toast to Evans in which he recounted the barbecue episode, praised the 'bright and unsullied character' of its saviour and ended with a suitable verse from Longfellow. He then presented Evans with his promised picture which showed, appropriately, a man driving full-grown pigs to market. Laura Knight gave him a painting of a dancing girl and the others produced similar rewards.

That summer, Laura Knight enraged the locals by bringing professional models down from London and posing them nude on the rocks in the sunlight. Colonel Paynter, who owned the stretch of shoreline, was appealed to, but he replied that Mrs Knight was painting on private property and she and her models could do as they wished.The episode ended when Harold's mouth infection became so bad that he had to be admitted to a Plymouth hospital and Laura took lodgings nearby. She could not work and the doctor warned her that she was on the verge of a nervous breakdown and both she and Harold should have six months' complete rest.

While they were away Munnings made a series of paintings of his wife riding a brown horse below a bridle path known as 'Rocky Lane' in the Lamorna Valley. She rode in effortless command and looked elegant and relaxed in a light-coloured coat and a matching wide-brimmed hat, worn at a rakish angle. Her husband delighted in her on horseback and painted her four times in *The Morning Ride: Florence Munnings on Horseback* and twice in *The Morning Ride* showing two lady riders. Florence had modelled for both and also for *The Artist's Wife: The Morning Ride*. She wore the same outfit in all her portraits.

Visually, Florence was Munnings's ideal. Whatever the reality of their relationship, she inspired his first attempt to portray a sophisticated lady on horseback rather than the usual hunt servants. Her equestrian portraits prefigured his later remunerative society ones.

Practically, however, Florence seemed to take little part in Munnings's life. That summer he prepared for his first London exhibition to be held in the Leicester Galleries in March 1913. He also had three pictures in the Royal Academy; as well as *Shade* there was *A Norfolk Sandpit*, painted during his first summer in Cornwall, which he eventually gave to the City of Norwich. There was also *The Wind on the Heath*, a memory of Augereau in Norfolk.

While the Knights were away and Munnings was fully occupied with painting, Florence's friendship with the lesbian-inclined Joan Coulsen flourished. The first Christmas of their marriage was comparatively quiet, although Munnings did his best to brighten things up. At a New Year's Eve dinner at their hotel, attended by just locals – he and Florence, Joan Coulen and Gilbert Evans – he drew a picture of a church on the menu card. They had a splendid six course meal consisting of hors d'oeuvre, tomato soup, grilled plaice, roast turkey or roast goose, followed by plum

1. Artists at Page Brothers

Munnings was bound over, at a premium of £40, for six years as an apprentice to Page Brothers & Co., Norwich.

. A Stone-breaker in Cornwall

n the late summer of 1910 unnings made his first visit to ornwall. In 1911 he established imself with a studio at Lamorna ove.

3. Munnings's Brother, Charles

Charles Munnings was the youngest of the four brothers, and he died in his twenties in South Africa.

pudding with mince pies or stewed fruit and ending with savoury eggs.

His London Exhibition at the Leicester Galleries called *Horses, Hunting and Country Life*, was a great success. It consisted of fifty-six pictures and Munnings made £850. Moreover, it was significant because it showed that his unhappy married life had not affected his work. A leading art critic wrote:

> Vigour and sunlight and warmth and happiness permeate every one of Mr Munnings's pictures .... He is never a painter of sad scenes, he loves light and joyousness and because of this his efforts are very good to look at ....
>
> The studies at the exhibition show Mr Munnings at his best and they show him in a variety of moods – all gay merry ones.

Admittedly, the bulk of the pictures were East Anglian scenes, but there were several sketches of cows and pigs painted in Cornwall, while a selection of hunting pictures in the Cornish uplands was singled out as, 'accentuating even more the brilliance and sunniness of the collection'.

The exhibition was also significant because it marked the start of Munnings's life-long friendship with an early visitor, John Masefield, the future Poet Laureate, who struck up a conversation with the painter over a picture he particularly admired. It was a study of a man and a mare and Munnings told him the story behind it, thrilled no doubt to meet the man whose work he had always admired. Masefield, a natural storyteller, idolized artists whose pictures told a story in form and colour as Munnings's so often did. In a typical spontaneous gesture, the very next day, Munnings sent Masefield the picture as a gift.

It cemented a friendship founded on mutual admiration between a painter who loved to write ballads and a poet who liked to draw, and who, for many years, clung to the role of amateur art critic. In his effusive letter of thanks, Masefield wrote:

> There are few things that I shall value more than this most generous and charming present of yours. I shall look at it every day and think of the tales you have told me of the man and the mare in it. Thank you very much indeed, again and again ....

> I found in your work a sense of English country life which is very rare in English art, and a quality I always look for eagerly.

He promised to send Munnings a little book of his writings which would shortly be coming out.

When the exhibition closed Munnings was restless for a new painting ground and, leaving Florence to her own devices, he and Ned Osborne rode the brown and grey mares fifteen miles across the moors to the picturesque, primitive village of Zennor on the north coast of Cornwall near St Ives. His painting paraphernalia was driven over in the village waggonette by Mr Jory. He spent five weeks there, lodging with a Mrs Grigg for one guinea a week, while Ned had a bedroom and ate in the kitchen for fifteen shillings.

Everywhere he looked he saw country scenes he would like to paint, but he steeled himself to ignore the appeal of farm animals grouped against granite walls in the brown heather and concentrate instead on a series of Ned and the horses. He painted Ned in a scarlet coat and black velvet cap riding up the hill with the hounds; Ned as whipper-in mounted on one horse and holding another, like statues on the cliff top silhouetted against the grey sky, waiting apparently, while the huntsman went down the cliff after the fox; Ned riding bareback in shirt sleeves at a local fair....

The weather was fine and sometimes he left his pictures overnight in a granite cave at the top of the hill where the cool night air dried and hardened the paint and the dew slightly warped the staunch stretchers, but tightened the canvases. He found he painted more quickly there than on home ground and he allowed himself no more than three days to paint even the most ambitious composition. 'Leave a picture alone and let it finish itself,' was his new motto and some of the Zennor paintings were the basis for larger versions destined to set price records in the coming years.

After the Zennor trip he felt justified, on the success of his London Exhibition, in leaving Florence again and going to Ireland with his Norwich friend, Dick Bullard. He wanted to buy a grey to replace Grey Tick, who he had returned to the farmer from whom he had bought her. He was prepared to spend £150 on a fine replacement, but he left the two-day Irish horse fair the proud owner of a six year-old grey mare, which had cost just thirty-three guineas, and a four-year-old bay only two guineas more. He looked forward to painting his new models on the moors near Newlyn.

He was also eager to spend the late summer painting the gypsy hop-pickers in Hampshire. This had been suggested by an old friend, Olive Branson, who had been the best student of her time at the School of Animal Painting. He described her as 'the kindest, sweetest person' and regarded her as a generous and true Bohemian. 'The Lady', as the gypsies called her, always went to Hampshire to paint them at the end of the summer, travelling there in her magnificent carved and gilded caravan, drawn by two fine horses and accompanied by an assistant.

Munnings's East Anglian visits to country fairs with the Grays and his travels with Shrimp, were good preparations for his encounter with the gypsy tribe en masse who converged on the Hampshire hop fields – two or three hundred men, women and children, most of them true, or very near, Romany. 'Never in my life have I been so filled with a desire to work as I was then,' he wrote, and admitted that 'more glamour and excitement were packed into those six weeks than a painter could well contend with.'

Yet he did cope. His sense of form and colour helped him to choose well among the bewildering sea of brown faces and the black-haired impish children. He found it best to concentrate on painting certain sets of families: the Lees, Grays, Stevens and Loveridges, who were all inter-related. The lithe-figured, black-skirted women had great black hats with curling ostrich feathers to wear on gala days or when they went from door-to-door to sell brushes or clothes pegs. The stocky men owned lurchers and horses of all kinds.

Munnings paid his models the same rate as they made at hop-picking, although it was easier work. Because of his generosity, they called him 'Mr Money' and he received carefully written, badly spelt letters addressed to him by that name for many years. They contained the latest family news, invited him to drop in for a cup of tea if he was in the neighbourhood, wished him luck and asked him to write back – which he often did.

'What days! What models!' he exclaimed, as he painted fine pictures and made life-long staunch admirers, who responded to his easy country manner and his colourful vocabulary. A typical letter from an affectionate correspondent read:

> Dear Mr Money,
>
> Just a few lines hoping to find you well, as it leaves me the same at present.... I am married now and got a baby boy, but I never married a gispy though I am one myself. I am living in a house with my Mother Mrs Loveridge who you painted.... Dear Sir we was coming home one night and I saw me and my Mother drawings in a portright shop and we went in and the Gentleman gave us one of the little ones and your addres and I thought I would write to you, as I should very much like to hear from you.... Please ancer my letter back, I am not much good for writing, as I never had much scholing....

Apparently, he did answer, for her next letter ended:

> ... Thank you very much for the ten shillings and I baught myself a blose. In the remence of you its a orange coullour what you said allays suited mu coulour, as you now I am very dark, but I have not got my hair babbed, as the women now a days you cant tell from men. Dear Mr Money do you paint now, as if I ever go to London I should like to see your drawings as the collourings looks very nice on our little one.... With all good wishes and good Luck from your Friend
>
> Gispy Nell
> X
>
> Please excuse the kiss only thats my way.

The Knights returned to Newlyn, while he was in Hampshire, to find their Trewarveneth house had been taken over by Geoffrey Garnier, and Colonel Paynter had built them a fine new one from three old cottages knocked together. He had also built them two new studios on the beach and charged such a low rent that, at last, they could afford a car.

Florence had not been idle during her husband's absences. Her oil painting called *The Ruined Chapel* had sold for £109 in an autumn exhibition at the Walker Gallery, Liverpool and two of her pictures, *Chieca Bay* and *Water*, would be hung in the 1914 Royal Academy. Her friendship with Joan Coulsen deepened. She had also been entertained by Gilbert Evans, who took her for long walks and out for lunch or tea several times. They made a handsome couple; he unfailingly sensitive and gentlemanly, in contrast to her unpredictable husband and probably a much more understanding and relaxing companion.

Munnings seemed unaware of their close friendship or chose to attach no significance to it. He had plenty of distractions. That autumn he hunted his new grey with the Western Hounds where she earned the admiration of the Master. 'There was no doubt she was the sort they liked in Cornwall,' he noted with satisfaction. 'Not too large, strong, active and short in the leg.'

He painted her many times, never more effectively than in a picture of her ridden by a scarlet-coated whip through a fir wood, where the ground was carpeted by red pine needles and bright points of light penetrated the shade. 'It was a problem,' he wrote. 'The more subtle the problem the more absorbing, and so those days used to fly.'

Through his work he escaped from the trauma and bewilderment of an unhappy marriage.

Augustus John and his wife arrived at Mrs Jory's hotel and Munnings invited the Knights to meet them at dinner. John had decided that Newlyn was 'the only warm place north of the Pyramids in winter' and they proved a welcome addition to the colony.

John's party tricks outshone Munnings's and when it came to feats of strength he was very athletic. 'John would perform all manner of amazing tricks,' Laura Knight recalled. 'Opening bottles of wine, tenderly, without a corkscrew; flicking, from a great distance, pats of butter into people's mouths; dancing, on point in his hand-made shoes, upon the rickety table, and other astonishing feats, until dawn. Then, while the others collapsed into exhausted sleep, out he would go in search of Dorelia, and do little studies of her in various poses on the rocks. He never did anything better.'

Munnings and John went sketching together and Munnings complained about the difficulty of painting the way a horse's coat reflected the light. 'Why do you want to paint the shine on a horse?' John queried. 'If you see a brown horse why not paint it brown?'

Munnings could afford to ignore the advice of his contemporary. Perhaps he recalled it with satisfaction at his London Exhibition when an art critic commented, 'Everyone who is not blind can see the gold of the gorse; but not everyone can see the golden gleam in a horse's tail flicking in the sunlight. Mr Munnings can and reveals it daringly . . . .'

Munnings's fame was spreading and early in 1914 Barry Jackson, the wealthy theatrical impresario who had founded the Birmingham Repertory Theatre and the Malvern Festival, went to Newlyn for Munnings to paint his portrait on horseback. However 1914 was to prove a bad year for Munnings as well as for the country. In March Munnings's father died. His younger brother Fred and his wife took over the family farm and his mother moved to the Norfolk coastal village of Overstrand where his youngest brother Charlie, who suffered from tuberculosis, had a house. By the end of March, the threat of war hardly affected the Newlyn community, although Gilbert Evans was called to join his battalion in Nigeria. At his farewell party his friends presented him with a cheque 'to buy a little souvenir for our remembrance'. When he arrived in Nigeria a letter from Munnings written on 12 April 1914 showed that life in Newlyn continued much as usual:

> Yesterday was the last day of the hunt [he wrote]. A rather poor day. Big banks!! Damn big ones – met at Willy Bolitho's and had sloe gin . . . . Blote [sic] and Coulson [sic] been to tea at Trevelloe this afternoon and at present (8 o'clock) are upstairs dressing. Wonder what they'll have on. Dear me. How limited my ideas and wonderment are growing.
>
> The Ladies are here – Both of them *very* ordinary in blouses and skirts – Jennings* talking to them and asking them when the bluebells are coming out etc . . . .
>
> Now must go in to Dinner.
>
> A.J.M.
>
> Dinner over. Soup. Cold Mutton (Lamb) mint sauce. Very little mint in the sauce. Cold rhubarb and cream. Coulson [sic] just teaching them a hand at Auction Bridge.
>
> St Buryan Races tomorrow.
>
> There – now all this will sound very *dull* and very much in an old fusty groove and you will have had enough and so I wish you well in all you do and say *never* regret going away but look forward to the WORLD –
>
> Yours,
>
> Munnings

* Leonard Jennings, the sculptor.

That country race meeting at St Buryan inspired Munnings's first picture of *A Start*. It hung in the 1915 Royal Academy and was presented by the purchasers to the Walker Gallery, Liverpool.

The imminent war was not the only threat to the Arcadian life-style of the Newlyn painters. Every week Geoffrey Garnier gave a fancy dress dance at Trewarveneth and a men-only dinner. He described that last pre-war dance nearly fifty years later in a letter to Reginald Pound, author of a then recently published biography of Munnings. It was the one fancy dress dance no-one at Newlyn would ever forget:

> At about midnight [Garnier wrote to Pound] 'The Bloat' called to A.J. that she was tired and wanted to go home ('home' being the Cliff House or Jory's Hotel, Lamorna). A.J.'s answer, shouted across the studio, was 'All right, you bloody whore, buzz off!'
>
> I can see the scene now; all my guests in their fancy dresses suddenly spellbound. And then 'The Bloat' turning in tears to the door; Joan Coulsen, her great friend, hurrying to her support – and the disaster next morning. She was no more potty than I am – but she had married a man utterly unsuited to herself. So much for that.
>
> What a very odd thing it is that from time to time the fates will pour their most lavish gifts upon wildly unsuitable persons and get away with it! Turner for one; A.J. for another.
>
> With all his faults he was a very great artist, a wonderful person to make a party go – and the only genuine coward I have ever met.

'The disaster next morning' occurred on 24 July 1914. Florence breakfasted, as usual, downstairs with her husband and afterwards went to their bedroom. Half-an-hour later Munnings found her there, lying unconscious on the bed. There was a strong smell of prussic acid in the room.

He ran to fetch Mrs Jory and they tried to make Florence drink hot mustard and water, while a lodger cycled to fetch the Knights. When they arrived Laura tried artificial respiration for hours in an atmosphere she recalled as 'stinking of cyanide', while a crowd of helpless young people looked on. About noon Dr Miller arrived from Penzance, followed by a Dr Branwell, but Florence died soon afterwards.

That day a Norwich antique dealer, John ('Jack') Nurse, and his wife arrived for a holiday at the hotel, at Munnings's invitation. They found the place in turmoil, were told the news and met Munnings leaning on a gate nearby. He said, 'I don't know, Jack. Why did she do it? She thought I didn't love her but I really did.'

At the inquest, Munnings told the County Coroner, Mr Edward Boase, that he had always had a suspicion that he could smell cyanide in the room, but his wife insisted it was nothing. She had been depressed lately, but there had been no particular trouble, and he did not know the cause for the depression.

> The coroner: If the deceased carried the poison in the form of a powder, it is to be assumed that she would take it in water. Then one would expect to find some trace of a glass in the room: – I did not look.
>
> You have not the least idea what vessel she took it in – assuming she did take it: – No.
>
> Since the previous occasion some two years ago did she make any promises: – Yes.
>
> What was the cause of her doing it at that time: – I do not know.
>
> Didn't you ask her reasons: – It is a fearfully difficult question.
>
> There is always a motive in these cases, and I am trying to find out what it was: – She was terribly morbid and was in a fearful state at that time.
>
> Was there any particular reason or motive which might recur: – No. She imagined all sorts of things I suppose in her way.
>
> Concerning herself: – She was extraordinary at times and no one could understand her.
>
> You are referring to her being morbid: – Yes.

Mrs Jory in evidence said she did look around the room to see if there was a glass but she did not make a general search. She believed whatever Mrs Munnings had taken had come from her dressing case. She had opened the dressing case, but could see nothing there. The usual glass was in the room, but that was used to give the deceased stimulants.

Laura Knight gave evidence. She said she knew the deceased had made an attempt on her life in London some two years previously, but she had no reason to do so except that she was in a very low state of health. She (Laura Knight) was staying at the same hotel at the time. Florence said that she had tried to poison herself, but gave no reason. Recently, she had seemed depressed, but for no particular reason she knew of except she thought she had been a little anxious about her throat trouble. She thought suicide must have been a momentary decision for she had made plans for spending the next two days. She certainly did not know Florence had poison in her possession.

Medical evidence was given to the effect that it was a case of cyanide poisoning – possibly by cyanide of potassium, not something which could be administered to anyone without their knowledge or consent.

In summing up, the coroner said it would be more conclusive if the receptacle containing the cyanide could be found, but it had disappeared or else it was in something else which had been put aside and had not been recognized. Colonel Paynter, the foreman of the jury, announced that the deceased's death was due to poisoning by cyanide, self-administered during temporary insanity.

After the inquest Munnings went to stay with Ruth and Charles Simpson in their quiet home at Carbis Bay. 'It was not a marriage,' he told Charles. 'It was never consummated.'

Once again his tremendous courage took over. There were no signs of the bouts of depression when he had a real tragedy to face and his sorrow only showed when he read reports of women's suicides in the newspapers. They obviously caused him such pain that his friends tried to keep them away from him. Otherwise, outwardly he seemed able to put all memories of his tragic marriage behind him.

He gave his portrait of Florence on horseback to Gilbert Evans who had learned about her suicide when he was still in Nigeria waiting for the outbreak of war. 'He was very cut up,' a friend reported. After the war Evans returned to Lamorna to find Munnings gone and Florence's portrait waiting for him in the care of Joan Coulsen. He treasured it all his life and it always held pride of place in his home.

Many people in Newlyn felt that Joan Coulsen, as Florence's closest friend, should have been called to give evidence at the inquest on the girl whose grave is marked by a simple granite stone in Sancreed churchyard. The cause of her death would long remain one of the many unsolved mysteries of Cornwall.

CHAPTER VIII

'Wisps in the Wind'

It would be nearly three-quarters of a century before a likely reason for Florence's suicide would be revealed. Meanwhile Laura Knight felt she was the only person other than Munnings who knew the true cause. She indicated as much in two letters she wrote many years after the tragedy and after Munnings's death. One was to the author Reginald Pound who was writing Munnings's biography and had approached Laura, on the suggestion of Munnings's second wife, who did not want an account of the tragedy to be based on local gossip. Only a fragment of Laura's reply to Reginald Pound's letter remains. It reads:

> Possibly I am the only person who knows the actual reason for the suicide, which actually concerned her husband in no way, tho of which I was never able to tell him.
>
> Through no fault of her own she became involved in what might have proved to be a terrible scandal. This she related to me during the week she spent before the fatal outing. It was not evident to me that she had come to say goodbye.
>
> Had she not sworn to Harold, my husband, and myself by all that she and we held sacred that she would not repeat her former attempt at suicide from which I helped to save her ...

At the same time as she sent this letter to Pound, Laura received a letter from Munnings's second wife, expressing her fears in case the tragedy figured prominently in the biography Pound was writing. Laura Knight replied to her from Malvern on 22 August 1961. Her letter read:

> ... as you well know, I being so intimately concerned in that disaster and the forerunning incidents, not only laid no blame to A.J. himself but grieved for the whole wretched business he had to go through. And asked at the inquest to give what I considered

> a reason for her death, with utter conviction, answered: 'A mind temporarily deranged.'
>
> It was an impossible marriage that should never have taken place in any case, but both in my mind and in Harolds opinion whoever had married Bloat would have met with disaster, for Bloat, beautiful and fascinating as she was, had no stability of character or sense of responsibility either – call it madness of a kind, if you will. Even suicide was not denied to her in her crazy desire for experience. That she hurt others in such accomplishment of desire, never, I believe, occurred to her. There is a medical word describing this attitude of mind, a form, mild, of insanity.*
>
> I can only tell you that much as Harold and I loved Bloat, a year or two before she committed the final act we were obliged to see as little as possible of her follies and her refined cruelties to A.J. in so many ways to remain sane ourselves. How he stood it and still loved her, despite his outbursts of temper, I can never imagine. It was as if he were mesmerised not only by her great beauty but her imagination as well, which, augmented by events, reached beyond the normal in action – not only in its finality but in daily life.

Ultimately, Munnings's second wife insisted that only the briefest outline of Alfred's first marriage should be included in Pound's biography. Later she also refused Laura Knight's request to be allowed to 'clear up the whole matter with a certain beauty of understanding (I hope) in a further autobiography I am still at work on.† Would you trust me to do this?' she wrote. 'I swear you can.'

However, like Munnings himself who made no mention of his marriage to Florence in his three-volume autobiography, Violet chose to treat the whole affair as if it had never happened.

Not Gilbert Evans however, He married thirteen years after Florence's death and the younger of his two sons, David, recalls seeing a little silver match box engraved 'Ev', the name by which his father was sometimes known. Inside was a photograph of Florence. There were also his father's small leather diaries. His parents made no secret of the affair.

The diaries for 1912 and 1913 revealed the close relationship Gilbert Evans had had with Alfred and Florence when all three lived at Cliff House. They recorded the many times the three of them had

* Signs of an hysterical personality.

† *The Magic of a Line,* published 1965.

breakfasted and dined together and been to parties. Succeeding entries showed how his relationship with Bloat had deepened in the third year of her marriage.

In February 1914 he wrote:

> Sun 22. Had early lunch with Blote* in my room and then for a walk over the cliffs to Penberth where we had tea. Then back by road in the evening. A summer day to be remembered.

Reading the entry his son commented:

'If you can make a summer day in February you must be in love and all the evidence is that they were. I think my father felt that the situation was becoming impossible and, for one reason or another he decided to join a Sapper survey party that was going out to Nigeria in April 1914.'

Gilbert Evan's diary entry for March reads:

> Fri 27. Left Lamorna. Blote said goodbye to me in my sitting room.

In April, according to the diary they were meeting in London:

> Fri 24. Met Blote at Fullers. Had tea together.
> Sat 25. Met Blote at the Trocadero – 12. Went into the Park and sat and talked. Back to the Trocadero for lunch. She saw me off at Paddington. We parted at 3.15. I went to the train alone and sad.

Later he had added under this entry 'This was the last time I saw her alive'.

> Tues 28. Went to Liverpool from Cardiff.
> Wed 29. Thick fog. Sailed SS *Dakar* for West Africa soon after 3.0 pm

In August he wrote:

> Mon 7 Heard awful news of Blote's death.
> Tues 8 Went for a ride in the afternoon. Too miserable for words.
> Wed 19 Walked up to Kaduna in the evening. Felt very sad.
> Fri 21 Four years ago today.
> Sat 22 Dreamed last night it was all a nightmare and that Blote was alright.
> Sat 29 Last night I dreamed I was back at Lamorna. Blote met

* Evans's spelling of her nick-name.

> me on the stairs and asked me to forgive her for the letter she wrote. I said 'Of course' and that it was all my fault.

In 1987 another piece of evidence came to light: David Evans was helping his widowed mother to move house when, in the bottom of an old trunk, he found a scrap of lined paper:

'It might have been nothing at all,' he said, 'and I don't know why I unfolded it but inside was a lovely little jay's feather, bright blue, as brilliant as the day it was put there. I unfolded another little bit of paper and inside found two more little feathers and a tiny portrait of Florence. It was so moving and it brought the whole thing – their summer time romance – terribly close although it all happened so many years ago.

David Evans's mother never wanted publicity for the story which, all those years ago, could certainly have culminated in 'the terrible scandal' to which Laura Knight referred. Not until two years after her death in 1989 did David feel it 'was time to set the record straight' as he put it.

'It's all just wisps in the wind', he said, but the fact that Munnings told Charles Simpson that the marriage was never consummated could have made Florence quite desperate if, as has been suggested, at the time of her death she was pregnant by my father.

'Certainly there is no evidence of this but, if one looks at the diary dates and bears in mind that they were very much in love and he was going off to Africa and they did not know when they were going to see each other again – who knows, perhaps they did have a bit of a fling.

'A post mortem could have provided the answer but the coroner did not order one so it remains a question to which we shall probably never know the answer.'

Among the close friends to whom Munnings turned after the tragedy were the talented but little-known painter Frank Gascoigne Heath and his wife Jessica. The tall, good-looking Heath was always smartly dressed for painting, wearing a stiff collar, tweed coat, waistcoat and breeches. He was five years older than Munnings.

An indication of their friendship is a hand-written illustrated invitation from the newly-married Mr and Mrs Munnings, Miss Coulsen and Captain Evans to Mr and Mrs Heath to a New Year's Eve Party at Jory's Hotel on 31 December 1912. It reads:

The present year is drawing to its close
And when its last night comes we must be bright,
So we the undersigned ask leave to pose
As Hosts and Hostesses to you that night –
Come with warm heart and sprightly soul,
Come with good food and chirping mirth,
We'll follow Dinner with a merrie Bowl,
And ours will be the greatest night on earth.

R.S.V.P. to Mrs Munnings at once. No refusal. Food and wine all ordered.

The invitation reflects Munnings's courageous determination to lead a happy and normal life despite Florence's attempted suicide at the start of the year – or to pretend that it had never happened. In the meantime, while Munnings went off painting for days at a time, Jessica Heath was a great friend and supporter for Florence.

The Heaths and their four children lived at Menwinnion, meaning House of the Winds, which Jessica's father had given them as a belated wedding present. It was built on ten acres of scrub land at the top of the valley which Frank Heath had bought from Colonel Paynter. It had taken a year to build from granite, hand-drilled out of the ground and then split and shaped into the requisite sized blocks and had cost £1,000. Laura Knight's studio was at the bottom of the garden. Alfred and Florence Munnings were among the first visitors in 1913.

On 5 June 1914 Alfred presented Jessica Heath with an illustrated nine verse ballad describing his interpretation of her thoughts and feelings during her evening horse ride which, presumably, mirrored some of his own. Surrounding the verses were sketches of the horse and rider in various settings, an impression of the morning room at Menwinnion with Jessica standing at the bay window and one of a childrens' bedroom with twin cots. The verses read:

When in my home I can't abide
And when the mellow afternoon
Is drawing to a close outside
With shadows reaching far and wide
And sunset coming all too soon ...

Out there I find repose and rest
and riding on to Hill and Moor
A yearning dies within my breast
As watching long towards the West
I halt beneath some rocky Tor.

My many cares I then forget
In wide and peaceful eventide
When all is done with each regret
Long, long before the sun has set
and I continue on my ride.

My pony hears each little sound
However far, however near
and now with hurried step and bound
He bears me down a path newfound
His footsteps sure, dispelling fear.

By footways tortuous and slow
We reach the cliffs and springy turf
Where granite rocks are piled below
and so like savage castles grow
Arising from the sounding surf.

The sun has set, the air is still,
The West is gorgeous with its gold
A blackbird's song with flute and trill
Echoing from a farther hill
Is with the sound of surf enrolled.

The scent of gorse and heather sweet
the throbbing purple where the sea
and vast, long-stretching sky-line meet
and drowning surging 'neath my feet
Steal to the very heart of me.

Before I leave, to all around
For one short space, I give my heart –
. . . .
all filled with colour and with sound
The pulsing air – my heart spellbound
Is now both sad and loth to start
. . . .

I break the spell – I ride away –
and swiftly on my pony trots
Thro' twilit lanes of scented may
and home to where my babies lay
Asleep within their little cots.

A month later Florence committed suicide. 'A shadow has come over the valley' said Jessica Heath who was deeply affected. Afterwards the distraught Munnings frequently stayed with the Heaths enjoying a degree of comfort in the warm family home.

He was there for Christmas 1915 and, while riding his horse up Rocky Lane, was inspired to start composing his famous ballad *The Tale of Anthony Bell.* On the same visit he painted *The Huntsmen's Christmas Dinner* for their five-year-old daughter Aileen. It showed two scarlet-coated huntsmen dining with the fox and raising their tankards in a toast to him. There was a companion picture for the younger sister Nancy showing three scarlet-clad merry men carrying in a steaming Christmas dinner.

He also painted six tiny pictures for the girls' doll's house, all less than two inches square, showing hunting scenes from the ballad of Anthony Bell and two portraits. They were probably the forerunners of the miniatures he would one day paint for Queen Mary's doll's house at Windsor.

This was the warm, caring, vulnerable Munnings who loved children so that, one day, when he saw he was destined to remain childness, he would try and adopt a daughter. This was a very different Munnings from the aggressive foul-mouthed boor which was the public face he so often presented.

Whatever the cause of Florence's suicide and however Munnings felt about it, the tragedy apparently had no effect on his work. He still painted entirely to please himself. The results were assessed by Norman Garstin, an art teacher and the imposing intellectual mentor of the Newlyn painters, in *The Studio* magazine:

> The usual painter of horses [Garstin wrote] is more often occupied with transferring his client's views about his horse to canvas than he is with those eternal truths of nature, the perception of which is his own true claim to be considered an artist.
>
> For Mr Munnings, while knowing his horse well ... knows also that far subtler matter, the relation it is bearing to all the varying, changing moodiness of the atmosphere; to him it is not merely the horse but the horse in its environment that matters – there is the poetry and the harmony.

'The poetry and the harmony' of his work was inevitably threatened by the outbreak of World War I. In the first months of war, anyone seen sketching out-of-doors was regarded as a possible spy, but Munnings had no intention of putting himself to the test. Caught up in the first wave of patriotism, he hurried to London to volunteer.

At the Chelsea Arts Club, he found fellow members who had already joined the Artists' Rifles, solemnly drilling with broomsticks. He went to the nearest recruiting station with other volunteers from the club but, to his surprise, he was rejected by the Yeomanry because of his blind eye. Philosophically, he returned to Hampshire to paint the hop-pickers.

The rejection rankled, however, and a few weeks later he went with a friend to the headquarters of the Hampshire Yeomanry in Winchester and volunteered as a humble farrier. As an incentive, he offered to bring two horses with him and hoped he would be allowed to look after them. Again he was rejected but his horses were immediately commandeered and he received a telegram from Ned Osborne saying they had been taken to military stables at Penzance.

He rushed back to London, caught the Riviera Express to Penzance and pleaded with the recruiting officer there to release his horses because they were his models. If he could not get into the army he would have to go on painting them for a living, he said.

Fortunately, the recruiting officer was an old friend. In the dead of night Munnings took the animals home to Lamorna, riding the grey mare bareback through the driving rain, with Patrick, the bay, on a leading rein. Twenty-four hours later, he was back in Hampshire painting the gypsy hop-pickers again.

It was September and the golden sunlight cast the long shadows he liked because he found they helped his composition. For a short time he managed to forget the war and painted some of his favourite subjects. But once the hop-picking was over his determination to join the army returned. He made a third attempt to join up and volunteered at Bodmin but was graded C3 and again rejected.

Defeated, he went to Newlyn. The locals had no doubts about his patriotism and left him to paint out-of-doors wherever he wanted. Again work was a remedy for his sadness and frustration and animals offered an outlet for his affection. When one of his mares foaled, he behaved like a proud father and knocked up the village to announce the event; for days afterwards, he related the full obstetric details to anyone who would listen. When his nocturnal-minded bull terrier, Reggie, stayed out until the small hours he would sit reading Jane Austen and, like an anxious parent, wait up until Reggie returned.

Florence's death might have made him cynical towards women but, on the contrary, a new tenderness and romantic awareness was apparent in his study of *Evelyn,* an attractive young lady who was staying with her parents at Penzance. His drawing of the laughing-eyed, dark-haired girl, gazing at him tantalizingly and wistfully, was one of the most romantic he ever made.

He was thirty-seven and told her he was twenty-eight. He gave her riding lessons until her father discovered a letter from him saying 'the horses will be ready', assumed his daughter was planning to elope and recalled her from her visit to Newlyn. Munnings was left with the sketch of her sitting on a boulder, arms clasped round her knees, gazing at him from great dark eyes. Eventually, it formed the basis of an Academy painting.

Seely

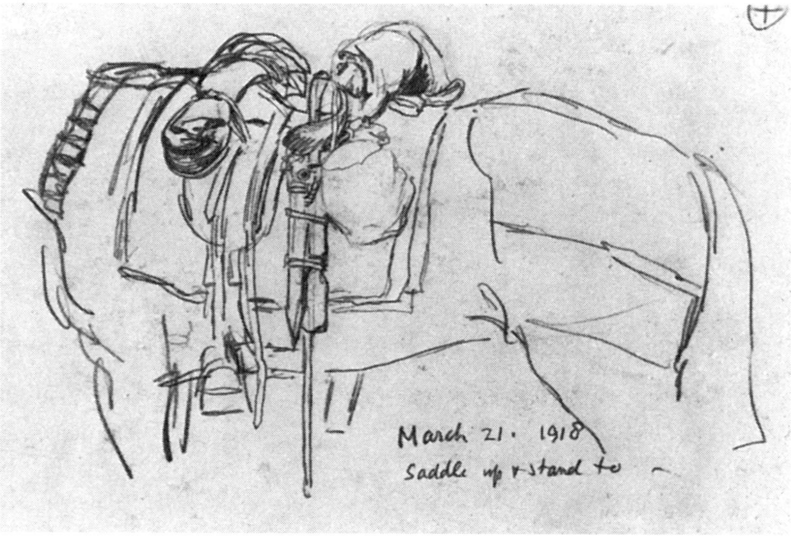
March 21. 1918
Saddle up & stand to

CHAPTER IX

A Painter at War

Whatever Munnings may have felt about the war it apparently had no effect on his work. In 1915 he met Father Bernard Walke, vicar of St Hilary, near Penzance, who, at first glance, thought he would dislike the man who showed an 'arrogant, almost insolent attitude' towards him. When, a few moments later, they were formally introduced Munnings threw back his head and smiled. It was a queer smile, Walke noted in his autobiography, and gave the impression of a face lit up from within. He saw two sides of a man who was both loved and loathed, just as Laura Knight had instantly recognized in Munnings's 'the stable and the artist'. 'What I saw then,' Walke wrote, 'and have seen many times since, was the invasion of a face by a vivid personality. At other times his is the face of a man who has spent his life with horses but, lit with that smile, it is the face of an ascetic saint.'

Munnings would have scoffed at that description and added a string of unsaintly expletives but, at that first meeting, the two men were soon in deep conversation about books. They discussed *Madame Bovary,* which Munnings had just read, and his favourite, *Pickwick Papers.* Walke recognized that the painter approached literature with the same fresh enthusiasm that he saw landscapes. 'Never before,' Walke wrote, 'had I met a man who gave so liberally of his personality to a friend of an afternoon. Wherever he loves or whatever company he keeps, he remains, at heart, a countryman.... He himself has never forsaken the land; he looks at it and loves it, its pastures and plough, its cattle and horses, its villages and old churches, as a countryman loves these things.' It was not surprising that a man who loved his country so much should long to fight for it.

The attraction Walke felt for Munnings was mutual. The painter introduced him to his Lamorna friends, firstly to Laura Knight who had broken her leg and found life tedious confined to her sitting room. 'A.J.'s evening visits to read aloud to her were virtually her only relief from boredom. He read Compton Mackenzie's *Carnival* and then Surtee's horsey adventures with Jorrocks, which allowed his dramatic ability full scope. It would have been hard to say who enjoyed the evenings most.

He was attentive and considerate to Laura and bought pieces of tasty fish for her supper whenever the local fishmonger had any. One night, he rolled an enormous tree trunk up the hill to her house for firewood. He had stolen it from a neighbour who lived at the bottom of the hill but Munnings knew it had been stolen in the first place so he felt fully entitled to administer poetic justice. He glowed in every sense as he watched the great log burn in the Knights' grate for three days and nights. Harold Knight was unimpressed.

Laura's admiration for 'A.J.' knew no bounds. She enjoyed his companionship, his immense vitality and his enthusiastic joy in work even in times of personal disaster which might have drained a lesser man. Above all, she admired his unflinching tenacity. 'He was a fighter,' she said. 'He fought the wind that shivered his easel and canvas. He fought the heat and the cold. He fought the shifting sun and the changing shadows.' Ironically, it seemed, there was no place for such a fighter in times of war.

The day came when even Ned Osborne was called up, although he had also been graded C3 because of a heart imperfection. When he left, Munnings took his two horses and three ponies, the very symbols of his existence, to a Penzance farmer to board until the end of the war. He believed, like many others, that it must come soon.

War had already destroyed his pattern of life at Lamorna and Newlyn, although many painting friends were still there. They were the Knights, Lamorna Birch, Ruth Simpson, Gert Harvey who painted flowers, still lifes and landscapes, Gladys Hynes, Robert and Eleanor Hughes and Parson Walke and his wife.

Bernard Walke was the first person to hear Munnings's famous ballad, *The Tale of Anthony Bell,* a hunting story in sixty verses. It was composed, like many of the painter's poems and songs, when he was out riding. In a lane in Lamorna, he hit upon the word 'boxes', as a rhyme for 'foxes', which had baffled him during the whole ride. After that it was easy:

Now, Anthony Bell, of whom I tell,
Was always hunting foxes,
He lived at a place called Highfield Hall
His horses were standing in every stall;
There were horses in all the boxes ...

He was so excited that he rode the twelve miles to St Hilary's Rectory on horseback and, over a bottle of claret, recited the sixty verses to his parson friend. They decided that the story, set about 1810 and telling a ghostly tale of an old squire who hunted six days a week, should have its first public performance at the local Christmas party. The audience heard how the family ghost came to the squire in a dream and foretold disaster if he rode at a certain wall the next day. He ignored the advice, had a bad, but not fatal, fall and recovered to rout the ghost with some surprising results. Guests at the Christmas party heard the ballad's first of many public renderings.

He had also composed a special song for the party called *In the Puddles with Julia,* a parody on Compton Mackenzie's novel, *Guy and Pauline.* At dinner he chose to sit next to the parson's wife, Annie Walke, 'a woman', he said provocatively, 'who won't mind what I say'. His enthusiasm for living, it seemed, was undiminished.

It showed in *The Piper,* the best of his three paintings in the 1916 Royal Academy. It was a watercolour of a kilted piper wearing the Black Watch tartan, playing his bagpipes outside the Bell Inn. Locals were dancing to the pipes, surrounded by onlookers with their dogs and horses. It was a nostalgic picture because, although the piper had posed in Munnings's Newlyn studio, the Inn, the country characters and their horses were painted from memories of his Norfolk days.

By that time, when painting in watercolour, he preferred to try it in oils first so that, with a laden brush, in a split second he could apply his image on to canvas, with a verve and assurance that gave him immense satisfaction. He had first painted the piper's figure in detail in oil and roughed in the background. He had then copied it in watercolour, drawing in the other figures in pencil and filled it in with colour washes. He considered it the best watercolour he had ever painted and sold it for £40 to a Mr Crittall, a steel window-frame manufacturer. That transaction led to a friendship, which had a material effect on his life.

Not all his paintings brought immediate returns. He had a running fight about money with the Norwich picture dealer and framemaker,

John Nurse, who, with his wife, had arrived for a holiday with Munnings on the day of Florence's suicide. He bought pictures from Munnings, who sold his fine frames to the Newlyn painters for less than £2 each.

> This is a hopeless business [Munnings wrote to him on 4 January 1916]. What the hell is going to come of it all I don't know. What I do know is that I got one or two bloody bills in today which I had forgotten about although the blighters who sent them hadn't.... I actually sold *3* drawings the other day, through a friend in Manchester. The first good sale I've ever made there. But it only helped to pay my horse corn for the last 6 months. Shit. And I must keep on *with* the horses as after this war there'll be no such thing as having any to paint I'm afraid, beside no money to keep 'em.

Apparently Nurse sent him £10 of the £25 he owed. Munnings was furious and refused to sell any more frames for him.

> ...I must say that you are a wily devil [he wrote]. Don't you tell me about my 20 quid stock. I want my price £25. I can remember each picture of that lot.... It isn't the fault of the pictures that you can't sell them, it's your moustache or some old coat you're wearing or your ways which haven't improved during this depression.
>
> You ask your Missus to take a good look at you with a fresh eye and see if you couldn't be brushed up a bit.

Six months later Nurse still had not sent the £15 he owed and Munnings wrote a strong letter to Mrs Nurse. He ended his letter with a spontaneous gesture which showed he was completely devoid of malice. The postscript read, 'I think you'd better bring him down for a holiday.

The suggestion perhaps also indicated an underlying homesickness and depression reflected in a letter to a one-time painting companion, an old school-friend, Mia Welham Clarke, who faithfully corresponded with him from Norfolk. On 25 September 1916, he replied to her:

> You seem full of words and able to write but I find as I get up in the tooth that I haven't the inclination to sit down and write long letters that I used to of yore – alas! All that glamour is gone and I just go on. You have been busier than we lately I expect with cutting and getting up the corn and getting ready for winter. The winter is coming on at a terrific pace isn't it – I never remember any month flying by so quickly as this....

> You seem to long for the rocks and the tides and the foam and breaking waves – I suppose as I live here I think less of them – I often long for the river and river scenes and if one is away from anything one can go on stringing fancy after fancy about it.
>
> I know just how the river is looking below your place now – the water moss along by the edge of the bank – the autumn colouring coming there amongst the growths. The willows and distances and all –
>
> Give me a walk by a river on a calm autumn day –

Once he had parted with his horses life was intolerable and he renewed his efforts to get an army job, however humble, as long as it involved horses. In 1917 he wrote to Cecil Aldin, an illustrator and specialist in black and white drawings of horses, dogs and old houses, whom he had known in peacetime as Master of the South Berkshire Hounds. In wartime, Major Aldin was in charge of the Remount Depot at Caldecott Park, near Reading. There, a thousand horses a week arrived, mostly from Canada, to be fed, treated for mange or lice if necessary, and restored to peak condition to be sent off to war – and probably to their deaths. 'Come at once,' the Major replied to Munnings.

He became a 'strapper' and for eleven months scratched the necks of thousands of horses to test them for mange. If they had it, he applied the appropriate foul-smelling ointment. He lodged at a local farm and sometimes rode to hounds on a fine Canadian charger with Major Aldin. In those few hours, he could forget his sickening distaste at the likely fate of most of the horses he was caring for, and his bitter frustration when Augustus John and William Orpen were appointed official British war artists with the rank of honorary majors.

His reprieve came suddenly. Paul Konody, art critic of the *Daily Mail* and the *Observer,* was asked to choose artists to go to France to illustrate typical scenes of every phase in Canada's war effort. Photography was relatively unreliable and there had been no photo-record of the Second Battle of Ypres. So Canadian-born Sir Max Aitken (later Lord Beaverbrook), Officer in Charge of Overseas War Records, started the Canadian War Memorials' Scheme for artists to provide a realistic pictorial collection. Their work was to conform to a prescribed scale so that it could, eventually, be shown together in one exhibition.

Konody invited Munnings, on behalf of the Canadian Government, to join the project and go to France as a civilian to paint their Cavalry Brigade in action. It was commanded by General 'Jack' Seely (later Lord Mottistone). Ironically, it meant Munnings would be meeting up again with many of the horses he had looked after in the Remount Depot.

He could have had no more exciting challenge. The Canadian Cavalry Brigade was something of an anachronism because barbed wire and machine guns had virtually eliminated cavalry on the battlefield. However, whenever the Brigade went into action – even as dismounted infantry – it covered itself in glory and, although the men usually dismounted and attacked with rifles and bayonets, it had, on the few occasions it had ridden into battle, received the highest percentage of honours and awards of any unit. Its success was largely due to its commander who handled his men with great dash and verve, reminiscent of the famous cavalry leaders in history.

Early in 1918 Munnings sailed to Boulogne with his hastily collected painting equipment packed in a light narrow box. He took an assortment of canvases cut to fit three stretchers, (one thirty by twenty-five inches and two twenty-four by twenty inches), sketching paper, oils, watercolours and brushes.

At Boulogne, he was met by a Canadian staff officer and driven in a Cadillac to the Canadian Cavalry Brigade's Headquarters. It was in Northern France in a section of the front line near the Omignon River called Small Foot Wood. Only charred tree stumps pierced the sea of mud over which criss-crossed duckboards led to the dug-outs.

Munnings arrived just as General Seely returned from his morning visit to the front on his famous horse, Warrior. The General was surprised to be met by an incongruously dressed civilian wearing a cloth cap, a check coat and box-cloth gaiters. For many months, no-one had been seen in anything but French, German, English or Canadian uniforms in that area.

Munnings asked the General if he could paint him, there and then, mounted on Warrior against the clear skyline in the direction of the German lines. In his memoirs, the General rated that sitting in full view of the enemy as:

> an almost unique occurrence on the Western Front! The Germans were husbanding their ammunition for their great attack of March 21st; although they would endeavour to demolish a battery that annoyed them and, of course, fire at any considerable

> bunch of men, one could play all sorts of tricks with them if there were only one or two together. So Munnings and Warrior survived several sittings, although a German artillery officer with a telescope must have been watching the whole proceedings, no doubt highly amused at the whole episode.

Seely and Munnings, it seemed, shared the same brand of courage that allowed them to ignore any personal danger for the sake of a worthwhile objective.

It was bitterly cold and, as Munnings painted, a thin crust of frost kept breaking under him and letting him through into the mud, until the General called for duckboards for him to stand on. Warrior also sank until the mud was over his fetlocks and he showed his disapproval by pawing and snorting.

The General could only spare an hour for the sitting. Afterwards, he was replaced by his batman wearing a spare beribboned uniform belonging to the General. Officers passing by, glanced at the uniformed figure on Warrior and saluted smartly. The batman alternated between gleefully acknowledging the salutes or pretending not to notice.

By four o'clock, when the light was fading, the rough sketch of the portrait, destined for a permanent place in the National Gallery at Ottawa, was finished. At dinner that night it earned the unanimous approval of the mess and the General opened one of his last bottles of good claret to celebrate. It marked the start of his long friendship with Munnings. 'It had never been the intention of the Canadian authorities that Munnings should join in the front line,' Seely recalled. 'But this whimsical and gallant soul thought that this was just the best place in which to be. And so it turned out, for by common consent, his paintings and drawings of the Canadian horses, close up against the front line, are some of the most brilliant things he has ever done.'

Munnings felt for those horses. He had nursed their counterparts back to health in an English depot, befriended them and, with great sadness, sent them off to war. It seemed appropriate he should be by their side to record them in action.

His odd clothes emphasized his civilian status but he was soon completely at home in that military elite which included Geoffrey Brooke, the Brigade-Major who was one of the British Army's great horsemen, and Prince Antoine d'Orleans, the General's French aide-de-camp, who had been appointed to the Canadians because, as a distant heir to the French throne, he could not serve in the French or English armies.

The painter's popularity was assured when one night after dinner Seely introduced him to the drink Irroy 'the champagne that makes you laugh'. Munnings reacted by singing his thirteen-verse ballad, *In the Puddles with Julia,* which he had composed for his last Christmas dinner at Newlyn. He had written both the words and music and the General accompanied him on the piano, while the Brigade staff joined in the choruses.

It was a gentle sentimental ballad, quite different from the bawdy songs the painter usually loved to sing in male company. It told of a twelve-month romance that climaxed in high summer:

> When the roses had finished their blooming
> And the petals all scattered did lie,
> We walked on the lawn in the gloaming:
> So I whiled away June and July.

The voices of the brigade staff took up the last words for the chorus:

> June and July with Julia.
> With Julia, with Julia,
> June and July with Julia,
> With Julia ages ago.

They led him into the next verse:

> There were long August days on the river,
> The river so hazy and blue.
> The reeds in the stream were a-quiver
> And round us the dragon-flies flew.

It seemed as if for Munnings, the war, coming hard upon his personal tragedy, had, for a time at any rate, revealed a softer side to his nature. His blustering temper, which usually exploded on the least provocation, had been replaced by resignation and a disarming frankness. When the Cavalry Corps Commander, Lt. General Sir Kavanagh, saw him in civilian clothes sketching near the front line and asked him, with a touch of arrogance, who and what he was, he replied disarmingly: 'I don't really know what I am. When they sent me out here they told me I was a genius.'

He sketched through all the hours of daylight in Small Foot Wood. In mid-March, when the Brigade was relieved by an infantry division, he was sent back with part of the staff and billeted in a doctor's house near Longchamp. This gave him a chance to transfer some sketches to paint and canvas.

Staff-Captain Torrance was so impressed by the portrait of his General that he helped Munnings all he could. He arranged for a troop in full marching kit to be sent out each morning to pose for a picture of men on the march watering their horses. It proved one of Munnings's finest war paintings.

Torrance also provided a batman and every morning Munnings was driven to his painting site in the doctor's gig, drawn by a Canadian Artillery horse, to meet the men by a stream at the bottom of the valley. Some held the horses while others fetched water in their canvas buckets, and they entered wholeheartedly into their roles as models which provided a welcome diversion. The warm, sunny weather lasted throughout March and, as the picture took shape, the men were thrilled to recognize themselves and their horses in paint.

Munnings's collection of finished paintings grew. As soon as one canvas was finished, it was taken off its stretcher, pinned to the mess room walls to dry and free the stretcher for another canvas. Studying the collection provided another diversion for the soldiers waiting for the great German attack to begin.

The brigade was frequently relocated in its role as a reserve and when it moved nearer to the Somme the painter, armed with a sketch book and pencils or a portable easel and a paint box, rode one of the brigade horses – sometimes Warrior. He usually rode with the signals' officer, not far behind General Seely, and handled his horse as well as any man in the brigade. 'All my command loved the man,' the General recalled.

They slept in abandoned dug-outs or Nissen huts except for a few memorable days when the brigade staff and Munnings were billeted in a magnificent chateau. Every evening the host dined with his uninvited guests at a large circular table in the main hall, while the brigade band played in the outer hall.

William Orpen arrived to paint the General's portrait and worked in a large upstairs room. Outside in the sunlight, Munnings painted Prince Antoine on his gleaming, black horse. He persuaded the Prince to sit all day, gradually circling the château as the sun moved round. This allowed Munnings to catch the ever-changing colours it reflected on the horse's coat.

The importance of this technique was later acknowledged by his friend, Charles Simpson, the bird and animal painter from Newlyn when, writing of Munnings's work, he emphasized how form was revealed by lighting:

> When painting a horse out of doors, it may seem an easy matter to paint just what is seen [he wrote]. But the slightest change of attitude, of effect, or hour of the day, will alter the shadow pattern or the sheen on the coat.... The horse used as a model must be shifted, if in sunlight, to accord with changed direction of light; but this is the simplest part of the problem. Changes of colour and the gloss on the coat are affected not only by a slight movement of the muscles, but by the reflection of the sky and anything in the surroundings on which a strong light falls.
>
> The more conventional horse painters of the past had a recipe for the pattern of this gloss, the high-lights, and the shadows; but this will not pass muster today. A painter like Munnings will take a horse out to get the colour of one shadow, or to study the infinite variations of light as it is reflected in the whorls of the hair, as the coat turns over with a sheen like silk on the modelling of the quarters.

Painting at the château, Munnings ran out of sable brushes. He said to Orpen, 'Do you mind if I ask you three questions?' The first was did Orpen have a car? Then, did he have any sable brushes and, if so, would he lend him some? Orpen replied, 'Yes' to the three questions and he lent Munnings all his sable brushes.

A week later the Germans occupied the château. Orpen just managed to escape with his unfinished portrait and, before he left, he asked Munnings to return his brushes. 'Don't you remember I asked you three questions?' Munnings replied. 'The first was "Have you got a car?"' 'What the hell has that to do with my brushes?' Orpen demanded. 'A great lot,' said Munnings. 'You can damn well drive to Paris and get some more for yourself. I haven't a car.

His portrait of Prince Antoine was too wet to travel and their host, the Marquis de Bargemont, no stranger to German occupation of his home, promised to take care of it.

The peaceful interlude was soon a memory and, with the start of the German offensive of March–April 1918, Munnings experienced his worst moments of the war. He lay awake at night listening to the sound of bombardment that heralded the beginning of the great attack. 'It became the background to all our doings,' he wrote. 'It went on, and on, and on.... I lay in bed trembling with fear.'

By day, however, he forgot his fear and sketched in the horse lines while the brigade band played nostalgic tunes. He made studies of individual horses standing patiently in the sunlight between the tattered camouflage that masked their improvised stables. Suddenly came the order to 'Saddle up and stand to!' Munnings hastily substituted an easel for his sketchbook and recorded an instant impression of a horse standing in full marching order ready to go.

He was interrupted by Staff-Captain Torrance, who told him to pack up his belongings and be ready to move. As an afterthought, he added, 'Can't you do something about your uniform?' Munnings managed to borrow a captain's tunic, a Sam Browne belt and a tin hat from the veterinary officer, and he rode a black Australian-bred horse from an Indian unit which had been caught running loose.

Riding back with the great British retreat, he eventually overtook some cavalry units and caught up with General Seely. The General, seeing Munnings in his false uniform, realized that if he were captured he would probably be put up against a wall and shot. That fear was nearly confirmed when Munnings stood on a bridge to watch the horses being watered:

> 'Qui est-il?' a French policeman asked the General.
>
> 'Il est un Boche,' Seely replied with a grin that satisfied the policeman.

Day after day, the painter, who had been rejected three times by the army, rode alongside front-line officers, often under enemy shell-fire. They travelled through shattered villages and overtook lines of French families pulling waggons piled high with household possessions. Often a rabbit in its hutch or a bird in a cage surmounted the pile.

They passed droves of cattle and a cavalry division in which some men had fowls or dead pigs hanging from their saddles. Some nights they slept out-of-doors in the forests and Munnings learned to use his saddle as a pillow. It was a luxury to spend a night in the loft of a deserted building, sleeping on a mattress stuffed with dried peas, even if he awoke several times to the sound of German air raids.

There was no longer time to sketch and Munnings saw that, as far as the Canadians were concerned, he was an added responsibility in his fancy dress of a uniform. That was confirmed on March 25th when orders came through for him to return to London. General Seely gave him some despatches to deliver to the Canadian headquarters in Paris-Plage en route. There he was surprised and delighted to find a few of his war pictures already hanging on the walls. Two colonels from the Canadian Forestry Commission so admired them, that they persuaded him to go with them to see their lumberjacks at work. 'They not only persuaded me,' Munnings recalled, 'they assured me … that they were going to kidnap me and all my paraphernalia.'

April 1st found him painting in the great Dreux Forest and living in one of the wooden huts surrounding a large log cabin that served as a mess. It was the beginning of a carefree adventure which led him to some of the most beautiful parts of France.

The Canadian Forestry Corps in France consisted of thirteen thousand men of all ranks. Their purpose was to provide the armies on the Western Front with all the timber they needed to move over the shell-devastated ground and shelter the men, animals and supplies, for it would have been impractical to ship the timber over from Canada.

The Corps was divided into companies, each with a team of one hundred and twenty fine horses. There was great rivalry as to which team was in the best condition and Munnings was thrilled to see such well-cared-for horses, after working among many destined to become cannon-fodder.

He painted all stages of the lumberjacks at work, at logging camps in the forests of Dreux, Conches and Bellême, from the moment when the first great oak was felled and pulled away by a team of horses, reminiscent of the Shires at his father's farm. A company's first task on taking over a forest was to make a clearing and build a saw mill.

Munnings recorded log hauling and loading, horses standing patiently in temporary stables while a permanent barn was built for them, forest views, horse portraits and a company tapping spruce forests for wood for aircraft production. His last painting was of a blue-uniformed French sentry sitting on a huge, felled oak with rifle and bayonet at the ready. He was guarding a scattering of German prisoners working in the flattened background, where only a few saplings had been left to grow.

Not all Munnings's paintings were military ones; he was enchanted by the local peasants and their animals and made time to paint them. One French farmer was so flattered by his attention that he offered him his daughter's hand in marriage.

4 & 5. Poster Work – Reclining Lady; Design for Colman's Mustard

Both these posters were designed by Munnings when he was working for Page Brothers.

6. Sketch of Girl for Tagg's Island

An early sketch of one of the subjects in the conversation piece portraying three of Munnings's artistic friends with four girl models at Tagg's Island on the Thames.

By mid-May the German offensive against the British front had failed. Munnings found himself touring the country of the Jura with a war correspondent and a Canadian officer in a chauffeur-driven car. Wherever they went they were welcomed enthusiastically by the locals. Driving past hill-side vineyards, misty blue lakes and tiny remote churches, the painter realized how much he had missed such peaceful scenes during the months of squalor and the years of uncertainty. He longed to return to that part of France to paint.

He visited the home of the novelist, Stendhal, and the Ornans birthplace of the painter, Courbet, who, every year, made a point of returning from Paris to his old home to paint his own landscape and his own people. Munnings perhaps realized how far he had travelled from his native painting grounds.

In those tranquil surroundings it was hard to remember that the war was not over until he was directed to return home through Paris. There, at the Folies Bérgère, the performance was interrupted by fire from Germany's latest secret weapon, the long-range Big Bertha gun. The next day he collected his forty-four canvases from the Canadian headquarters, some of which he found had been rolled up in a golf bag. He was then driven to Boulogne en route for Dover and London.

Only one painting was missing: the portrait of Prince Antoine, which had been left to dry in the great chateau on the Somme. Later, Munnings learned that the Prince had been killed and the Marquis who owned the chateau had lost everything and had fled to Paris, taking with him the portrait of the distant claimant to his country's throne. However, the picture arrived in London in time to be included in the most important art event of the year, the Canadian War Memorials' Exhibition held in January 1919 at Burlington House.

Forty-five pictures by Munnings dominated the Exhibition of three hundred and fifty paintings by nearly seventy British and Canadian artists. His pictures filled the Gem Room at the Academy and told their own story of the perfect wartime partnership between horse and man.

Great public interest centred round the dramatic, but by no means the best painting, his imaginary impression of a moment in the Battle of Moreuil Wood, described by General Seely as 'the greatest battle in history'. It occurred when the Canadian Cavalry Brigade took part in one of the successful counter-attacks which helped to secure Amiens and bring the German offensive finally to a halt. It was the stuff of

Kipling and Walter Scott interpreted by a painter who was steeped in the spirit of early twentieth-century England. By coincidence it also immortalized the name of a pupil from the painter's much-disliked old school, Framlingham College.

The *Charge of Flowerdew's Squadron* was a mêlée of horses and men in a furious battle charge reminiscent, on a small scale, of the Charge of the Light Brigade in the Crimean War. Leading it was Lt. Gordon Flowerdew, aged thirty-three, whose gallantry, according to General Seely, 'possibly deflected the whole course of history'.

He was one of the youngest of the ten Flowerdew brothers, who had been pupils at Framlingham College. Afterwards, he went to Canada and, on the outbreak of war, enlisted with Lord Strathconna's Horse and sailed with them to France. There he was soon commissioned and appointed to General Seely's staff.

The General once asked Flowerdew if he would like to have the V.C. and the young officer replied, 'That is my dream, but I shall never be brave enough to win it.'

By 30 March 1918, the Germans had captured Mézières, were advancing on Amiens and the whole British line was menaced by a million of them flung on to the English and French front. 'They had won the war completely, definitely and finally, but did not know it,' General Seely said in a post-war speech. 'An order had been given that they were to be stopped.'

Flowerdew's squadron was detailed to carry out an exercise 'as desperate as a man had ever been called upon to undertake,' he said. 'No human being would have accepted it with joy.' Because of the heavy casualties among senior officers Flowerdew was in command.

General Seely instructed him to take his men behind the Germans holding Moreuil Wood, while another party attacked from the front. He told Flowerdew, 'I know you will love to do it.' Flowerdew replied, 'Yes Sir. I shall love to do it, and I promise you I will not fail.'

The General said, that as he galloped through the wood, he heard a terrific fusillade on the German side, indicating that Flowerdew's squadron was going round and into the middle of the Germans. After three-quarters of an hour of desperate hand-to-hand fighting, they captured the enemy position. The victory claimed seventy-five per cent casualties and all but four of a hundred and fifty horses.

Lt. Flowerdew was not killed on the spot. He had one leg amputated in the Field Clearing Station and died two days later. Just before he died he learned that he would be awarded the V.C. It was the fulfilment of his lifetime's ambition according to the last entry in his diary, written on March 26th after an earlier encounter, four days before his final battle. 'It was a glorious battle,' he had written. 'I shall never forget it but I still cannot get that V.C.'

Whatever Munnings's feelings were as he illustrated the *Charge of Flowerdew's Squadron,* he afterwards gradually ceased to disassociate himself from his old school. Notes of his successes, presumably supplied by him, appeared in the School Magazine and he was the speaker at an Old Boys' dinner in London. After telling his audience how much he had hated 'the rotten place' he turned to the Secretary and asked, with a disarming smile, if he could join the Old Boys' Society. However, he never gave his old school one of his paintings.

The Canadian war paintings brought him only a small financial return but he would willingly have donated them to the Canadian Government. He felt that no artist had been given such a wonderful experience and been allowed a better chance to paint in such unforeseen circumstances.

Exhibitions of the Canadian war paintings in Burlington House and later in New York, Montreal and Toronto had two very significant effects on his life. First, within a few weeks of the Burlington House Exhibition, he was elected one of the thirty Associates of the Royal Academy. 'It was a stirring event,' admitted the countryman who, until then, had never considered such a possibility. From that moment his one ambition was to become a full Royal Academician and he rented a London studio with a bedroom and kitchen in Glebe Place for sixty-five pounds a year.

Secondly, his portraits of officers on horseback, particularly the fine study of General Seely, led to a spate of lucrative commissions from riders and sportsmen. Seely's portrait was admired by Princess Alice, wife of the Queen's brother, Major-General the Earl of Athlone, and she invited Munnings to paint her husband on his charger.

Sittings were held at Windsor Castle and Munnings was to arrive there on the afternoon prior to the first day's sitting. Before he left for Windsor, however, he attended a Royal Academy lunch given by Lord Leverhulme. There was excellent food and drink followed by many speeches and toasts.

He spent a pleasant afternoon and evening at Windsor with the Athlones and the next morning he was standing ready with his easel and canvas at the front door with Princess Alice, Lord Athlone in uniform and the butler when a groom led the chestnut charger round for the first sitting. Munnings instantly assessed the animal as 'the quietest horse ever foaled' and, at almost the same moment, realized he had left his paints in London.

There was panic until he remembered that the steward of his club, the Chelsea Arts Club, had a set of his studio keys and, after a telephone call, he sent them down by the afternoon train. Meanwhile, the delay had its benefit for Lord Athlone took Munnings to the stables to see the beautiful bays and greys used to draw the royal coaches in the Ascot Procession. They were the horses he longed to paint rather than the mild-mannered chestnut. He could never have foreseen that before very long they would be his models.

Meanwhile, his fine portrait of the handsome Earl astride a horse that looked eager to gallop off over the miles of open countryside stretching to a far horizon, hung on the line in the 1920 Royal Academy. It was one of six pictures which Munnings, as an A.R.A., was entitled to submit. All had been accepted. The Earl's portrait and one other proved that the year 1919 had been very important in the painter's life.

He commemorated it when a group of Canadian War Records artists gave a dinner in a large upstairs room of London's Café Royal to Paul Konody, the art critic who had selected them. Munnings composed some verses in his honour to be sung or read at the dinner:

I'm a judge of ancient and modern Art,
In Art I take the leading part.
Of a great concern I am the start;
For I am the brain, the mind, the heart
Of the great Konodian Army.

Men of genius great and small
Wield their brush at my beck and call.
I hire them up or I dash them down
With a friendly nod or haughty frown,
In my great Konodian Army.

I say the word and the thing is done.
I know the limits of everyone.
To all successful average men
I write a note with my fountain pen
To say their size is 12 by 10*
In my great Konodian Army.

In the case of a painter hard to beat
I tell him his size is 20 feet;
And major's rank and major's pay
Are granted him that very day.
And he goes to France for a pleasant stay
With my great Konodian Army.

Eventually, most of Munnings's Canadian War Memorial pictures were permanently housed in the National Gallery of Canada in Ottawa. Not all his war pictures, however, were included in that collection. He worked up some of his pencil, oil or watercolour sketches into finished oils, which the Canadians, possibly running short of cash for the Memorials scheme, chose to ignore; or perhaps they were unaware of their existence.

He kept a few for himself, *A Canadian Soldier, 1918* was bought by the New South Wales Art Gallery, and he copied some of his favourite paintings several times. He made four copies of his fine composition *Watering Horses on the March*. He and many others thought it was one of his best pictures. Two copies ended up in Alberta, one went to a private collector and Viscount Rothermere bought one, which he eventually presented to the Norwich Castle Museum.

The large oil, showing at a glance the bleak reality and urgency of war, hangs there in stark contrast to more than a dozen of Munnings's country scenes, gentle yet full of vitality, portraying the horses and people and customs men had fought to preserve – studies of the England the artist loved and was never happier and more successful than when painting.

* The various 'sizes' in the verse refer to the canvas sizes Konody imposed to ensure the painters conformed to a scale that allowed their pictures to be exhibited together effectively.

And he kissed the beautiful toe!
Was fixed on The Chef below!
The Chef

CHAPTER X

New Beginnings

On 11 November 1918, London blossomed with flags as seething crowds jostled through the streets demonstrating their joy at the Armistice. They waved Union Jacks from the tops of buses and the roofs and running boards of cars and taxis, and cheered and shouted and wept in their hundred thousands through a day that merged into night and again into day.

'The greatest day in the world's history,' Queen Mary wrote in her diary. She and King George V frequently appeared on the Palace balcony from eleven o'clock in the morning until well into the night, to be met by roars of approval from the solidly-packed crowds, whose voices drowned the popular tunes played by a military band in the Palace courtyard.

For Alfred Munnings, a successful painter with no domestic responsibilities, the day heralded the start of a period of London life that was stimulating and exciting. He still rented studios in Cornwall and Norfolk and owned five horses in Cornwall. He knew that, one day, he would have to collect all his possessions into one place. Meanwhile, his London studio in Glebe Place was home.

He used the nearby Chelsea Arts Club as a second home. Its rather Bohemian atmosphere delighted him and he ate most of his meals there, starting with a hearty breakfast and often ending the day in the smoky billiard room with a noisy crowd round the great open fire. He might find Harold and Laura Knight there, Augustus John and Orpen, swopping war stories, or John Sargent, Leonard Jennings or Sir John Lavery. Wilson Steer could sometimes be seen beating an opponent at the small round chess table, apparently unperturbed by clicking billiard balls or loud singing when Munnings or one of the others took a turn at the grand piano.

Munnings was popular in the club. Gradually, his East Anglian accent seemed more pronounced and his checked tweeds more aggressive, as if to emphasize his country origins. He had also acquired a vocabulary for swearing that enabled him, it was said, to curse in the foulest language for ten minutes without once repeating himself.

He celebrated the start of 1919 at the first Chelsea Arts Ball and booked a ground-floor box at the Albert Hall. Guests were forbidden to take alcohol into the building, but Munnings and his party cheerfully flouted that rule. They met beforehand, for drinks in his studio, and arrived at the hall with each man concealing under his coat or cape two bottles of champagne hanging from a cord around his neck.

Soon after midnight, Munnings and his party returned to his studio for another drinking session and Waters, a young sculptor, played his violin from the model's throne. He was in the fancy dress costume of a Regency buck and played 'After the Ball', a popular tune of the day.

The scene and the tune inspired Munnings's first picture of 1919 – *New Year's Morning after the Chelsea Arts Ball*. He painted it in David Jagger's studio, which was much larger than his own. Jagger posed in a pink Regency hunting coat, a sixty-year-old playboy from the original party sported a Dickensian costume, and Waters again played his violin, to an audience that included three professional girl models.

Munnings worked on the picture for several mornings while, from an overhead studio, another friend, H.M. Bateman, the *Punch* cartoonist, frequently communicated with bursts of tap-dancing, to Munnings's irritation. Nevertheless, during those few days, he often wished he had concentrated on more interiors with figures rather than so often battling with the weather, painting out-of-doors.

He had never spent so much time in London and, after a spell of work, he craved for fresh air and walked for hours with a friend in Richmond Park or visited Hampton Court or went to Brighton for the day. He saw the sights of London and attended his first race meetings at Sandown, Gatwick and Lingfield – not to bet on the horses, but to study those likely to run in the Grand National at Aintree in April. At a February meeting at Sandown, he particularly noticed a large, dark bay, Poethlyn, winner of the 1918 Grand National. Time would show that his interest in the horse was justified.

In the evenings he was happiest with friends, arguing, discussing or declaiming, over endless glasses of wine, as in his student days in Paris. The Chelsea Arts Club took the place of the village inns with their convivial atmosphere and predominantly all-male society. He admitted unashamedly: 'I was becoming all but a roisterer – in fact I may have been one.'

His suspicion was confirmed when he was first warned and then suspended from his beloved club, for using bad language in front of the staff. The suspension letter was delivered to his studio by the senior member of the club, Captain Adrian Jones, the sculptor of the bronze of a winged Peace in a chariot drawn by four horses, a memorial to King Edward VII, over the arch at Hyde Park Corner.

'It's a terrible thing to be suspended from a club,' Captain Jones told him. He seemed far more upset than Munnings who simply transferred his allegiance, for the time being, to the Café Royal. The popular restaurant near Piccadilly was a favourite haunt of actors, writers, musicians, painters and their models. 'Everyone in the artistic world was to be found there,' according to Laura Knight. 'Augustus John, Epstein, Betty May; every painter, sculptor and model, we all had our groups.'

Munnings felt completely at home and often rose from his seat on a red plush banquette in the ornate upstairs dining room hung with gilded cupids, called for silence and declaimed one of his ballads, to the amusement, boredom or embarrassment of a usually tolerant audience. He subjected them to his sixty-verse *Ballad of Anthony Bell* but stopped short at reciting more than two verses of his shorter composition, the *Ballad of the Café Royal*. It was so crude that, even he admitted, most of it was unsuitable for mixed company.

Sometimes, he and his friends moved on from the Café Royal to Paul Konody's rooms in the nearby Albany and argued the night away. The critic approved of futurist paintings and he and his friends damned Reynolds, Gainsborough and other eighteenth-century traditionalists. Their views, so dramatically opposed to Munnings's own, provided a convenient excuse for his sporadic outbursts of aggression.

Much to his surprise after his suspension from the Chelsea Arts Club, he was accepted as a member of the Arts Club in Dover Street, off Piccadilly. It was more elegant and far more expensive than his old club and occupied one of the finest Georgian houses in London, furnished with priceless antiques. The upstairs drawing room so impressed him that he conceded it was 'a room to live up to'.

Its great chandelier glittered against crimson damask curtains and crimson walls hung with fine pictures. The room's dignity was only disturbed when a newly-elected Royal Academician held a celebratory champagne party there. So Munnings confined his blunt talk and earthy humour to the dining room where the main table was reserved for members of the Royal Academy. There, the conversation, like the wine, flowed freely, long after dinner was over.

He also joined the Royal Academy Dining Club, founded in the days of Turner. It had no permanent home but met four times a year in a private room in various large restaurants where there was a piano and an accompanist. The traditional toast was 'Honour and Glory to the next Exhibition'. Munnings was a strong advocate for holding the dinners in the Academy.

Soon after his suspension from the Chelsea Arts Club, Sir Edwin Lutyens invited him to dine at 'the Club of all Clubs', as Munnings described the Garrick. A fellow guest was the Earl of Oxford and Asquith, the former Prime Minister, who afterwards wrote in his diary, 'Conversationally the situation was saved by Munnings, the artist, who recited us two ballads on hunting and steeple-chasing. I thought they were unpublished works of our Jan [John Masefield] but it turned out that Munnings himself was the author. He delivered them with marvellous *brio*.'

Apparently, other diners had enjoyed Munnings's performance. The next time Lutyens asked him to dine there the members requested him to recite his *Ballad of Anthony Bell*. It so impressed a keen hunting man present, that he suggested Lutyens should propose the painter for membership. To Munnings's delighted amazement, he was accepted. Soon afterwards, the Chelsea Arts Club reinstated him, but he no longer felt it was very important.

Asquith could have been forgiven for confusing Munnings's

ballad with one by Masefield. Its vigour, zest, freshness and jaunty rhymes were characteristic of the poet's work. Moreover, the two men had other things in common: both were countrymen at heart, took pleasure in the thrill of hunting but loathed the kill, and relished the subtle relationship between horses and riders. Both also possessed a definite coarseness and an unexpected gentleness.

Their friendship, which dated from the painter's London exhibition, was renewed while Munnings was painting his first portrait of a famous racehorse, Poethlyn, the dark bay he had noticed at Sandown. Two months later it had won the Grand National.

He had watched the race standing by the formidable Chair Jump. Afterwards, he had studied the winner in the paddock with its jockey, Ernest Piggott, grandfather of Lester Piggott, and the owner Mrs Hugh Peel. A few weeks later, Mrs Peel invited him to her home in Flintshire to paint Poethlyn.

He was staying there when a registered parcel arrived for him, containing John Masefield's long narrative poem, *Reynard the Fox*. It told the story of a great chase seen through the eyes of the hunted animal and Masefield had sent it for Munnings to make sure there were no hunting inaccuracies.

The painter was flattered. He was delighted when Mrs Peel suggested he should read it to her house party after dinner. Her guests were mostly hunting people and, that evening, they gathered round the fire for the poem's first public hearing. It was six times longer than the *Ballad of Anthony Bell* and Munnings, after several private rehearsals, delivered it with great gusto and revelled, as usual, in holding the centre of the stage. His audience was enthralled. They offered one or two suggestions about hunting technicalities, which he passed on to Masefield. Meanwhile, his own reputation as an entertaining house guest as well as an equestrian portrait painter soared.

It was May and the chestnuts were in bloom. He made several studies of Poethlyn in the stable yard and on the grey, stone terrace outside the house, with Major and Mrs Peel and their stud groom. But he expressed his happiest impression of the great horse, which he recognized as 'one of the vivid memories of a lifetime', in words, rather than in paint. It was the moment after a painting session when the animal was released into the railed paddock. Munnings felt the horse's joy.

> The glorious morning; sunlight on trees and grass; the flash of the horse's heels as he bounded in the air again and again; the anxious men watching. Like a statue the horse stood, head and tail in air. Then three, loud ear-splitting snorts; more acrobatics to show us again what a horse could really do. Then he turned round and round and lay down and rolled and rolled in sheer joy.

Such love and understanding of horses as characters was reflected in his paintings and was an unchallenged quality explaining his superiority over other equestrian painters. He disliked portraying horses against a conventional background of earth and sky, but preferred to show them reacting to their environment, as in two of his three pictures in the 1919 Royal Academy. Both featured the mare Grey Tick ridden by Ned Osborne. In *Zennor Hill, Cornwall*, she was coming up the hill with the huntsmen and hounds and she was among them again in *Drawing for an April Fox*. Munnings's third Academy painting was an appealing study of *Evelyn*, the dark-haired girl from Cornwall.

Just before the Summer Exhibition he had collected all his pictures from Cornwall. His election as an A.R.A., immediately before the exhibition, had left him no time to use its attendant privilege and submit six pictures for consideration instead of three. All three were bought on Private View Day by two Scottish brothers, Tom and Jim Connell, the owners of Connell's Gallery in Bond Street.

A few mornings later, both brothers arrived at Munnings's studio before he was even up. They looked through all his Cornish paintings and were particularly impressed by his studies of the gypsies, conveying their colourful, eventful but relaxed life-style. The brothers immediately decided to hold a one-man exhibition of his work.

The bemused painter, who had only had a few hours' sleep after a heavy night, was more dazed when the brothers came up with an even better idea. They offered to buy outright all the pictures they had chosen for the exhibition and asked him to name his price. They left when Munnings had accepted what he considered was a very generous offer, amounting to several thousand pounds.

He arranged to meet them for dinner that night, at the Savoy Hotel, to receive the cheque. It was his first visit to the Savoy and the cheque represented a nest egg beyond his wildest dreams. 'I was a millionaire!' was his first reaction. 'I was an A.R.A! I could now buy the house of my dreams . . . a house somewhere in Suffolk, with a river. . . . I must have a river . . . and, more important than all, meadows and stables. . . . Stables to house the five horses down in Cornwall, whose keep was mounting into vast sums of money which I was afraid to think of. . . . In such a place, with A.R.A. after my name, I'd care for nobody.'

That sentence, from his autobiography, indicates an insecurity and a sense of inferiority that could well have accounted for much of his showing off, rudery and blustering. If so, those feelings would have been severely aggravated by his failed marriage.

Where his work was concerned he certainly cared deeply what people thought – of his writing as well as his painting. The reception given to Masefield's *Reynard the Fox* probably encouraged him to think of having his *Ballad of Anthony Bell* published, and he sent a proof to Masefield for his comments. The poet's reply, written on a sheet of his favourite tiny notepaper, measuring just four-and-a-half inches by three-and-a-half, was most encouraging:

> I have read it through with huge delight [he wrote]. It is excellent and I would not alter a word. It will be a joy to people in the land for generations to come. I am asking the *Manchester Guardian* people if I may write about it in their paper when it is published.
>
> It is a first rate work and you must Neglect Everything and do the illustrations for it and have it out as a book.

The ballad was published in *The Field* on 13 December 1919 and Masefield's flattering review appeared in the *Manchester Guardian* six days later, declaring publicly that it was 'one of the best ballads of modern times'. He added:

> If he were not so good a painter, one could wish that Mr Munnings would take permanently to the writing of poetry, for none but a born poet could have written this tale, and all who read it will want more. . . . We hope that Mr Munnings will write some more ballads.

His hope was realized but Munnings was far too busy painting to take the advice in his letter to 'Neglect Everything'. He also refused a subsequent invitation to illustrate a deluxe edition of *Reynard the Fox*.

He had met his gypsy friends again at the Epsom Spring Meeting and had sketched the women in their traditional costumes which, he thought, 'surpassed all dreams'. He agreed to meet them again in Hampshire at hop-picking time and there he worked up his Epsom sketches into two of his finest works, *Gypsy Life* and *Epsom Downs: City and Suburban Day* which, together, earned him £1,650.

He usually paid the gypsies half-a-crown a sitting and he was terrified that they might discover how much money he made from their pictures. He also took care to conceal from them the flask of whisky he kept in his hip pocket. He nipped behind a bush to have a swig from it when they were not looking, because he hoped to hide from them his growing addiction.

He realized that, at long last, he was free from financial worries. He was free to buy a house 'somewhere in Suffolk, with a river'. He and three artist friends searched the county, sometimes using as their base the Chelmsford home of his friend, Mr Crittall, the steel-window manufacturer who in 1916 had bought *The Piper*.

One weekend, Mr Crittall took them round the district in his large chauffeur-driven car. They were armed with a handful of estate agents' leaflets and in the car boot was a wicker hamper packed with cold food, wine and cigars.

They worked their way through most of the houses shown in the leaflets which led them to the pretty village of Dedham, on the Suffolk-Essex border. At the end of the village they picnicked on the lawn of an empty house which was for sale. It was an elegant white Georgian house, built within the courtyard of an original Tudor one, and set in forty acres of grounds. It was surrounded by fine old trees, paddocks and meadows with grazing cows. Through the trees were glimpses of the Stour Valley and its river flowing through Constable country.

The chauffeur fetched the house keys from the village and the party wandered through beautifully proportioned rooms leading into one another. There was an elegant dining room with Regency bow windows, three other reception rooms, seven bedrooms, kitchens, servants' quarters and two cellars. 'The day was beautiful; so was the food; so was the wine,' Munnings recalled. His friends and Mr Crittall were enthusiastic. Munnings had found 'the house of my dreams'.

He bought it for £1,800 and later discovered the price included two village cottages where a groom and a gardener lived rent free and worked for thirty shillings a week. Both agreed to stay on and the groom offered to move into the main house with his family so that his wife could do the cooking and the cleaning. Munnings felt that, at last, he was a man of property.

His misgivings came later. His five horses arrived from Cornwall and his furniture and possessions from Swainsthorpe, with the sectional studio which was lengthened slightly and erected in the meadow. By then, Munnings heartily wished he had never set eyes on the place and he was terrified that, burdened by so much responsibility, he would never paint again.

Work, as usual, was the palliative. Sir Edwin Lutyens, who had been instrumental in reinstating him in London's club life, was again his mentor. The architect had been commissioned by his friends, Sir John and Lady Horner, to design a memorial to their second son Edward, a young cavalry officer who had been killed in the War. It was to stand in a small side chapel at Mells Church, Somerset, adjoining their home. Lutyens invited Munnings to sculpt a bronze statuette of the officer on horseback to surmount the pedestal he had designed.

His choice of sculptor was a daring one but he recognized, like Charles Simpson, Munnings's life-long artist friend from Newlyn, that the painter's horse pictures showed 'a sculptor's grasp of essential form'. Munnings's work, Simpson once said, 'represented the furthest limits to which a picture can go in approaching the art of the sculptor'.

Munnings, despite his limited experience in the medium, accepted the challenge. It was his first work in his resited studio and, perhaps as a safeguard, he asked the sculptor, Waters, who had played his violin after the Chelsea Arts Ball, to assist him.

Lutyens sent a sketch showing the height of the statue and the width of the base – the horse would be the size of a small deer – and Munnings modelled two rough impressions of the rider's head for Lady Horner's approval. One showed the young hussar looking straight ahead, the other with head bowed. Lady Horner chose the one looking ahead, to face the east, and sent photographs of her son for Munnings to work from.

He modelled the horse and rider in his studio from his bay mare, ridden by his groom wearing military uniform. The painter's life-long 'feel' for horses plus his supreme knowledge of anatomy and his mastery of form carried him through. Waters was allowed to sculpt the details including the boots and stirrups.

Edward Horner's head caused Munnings more difficulty. One day, while he was away, Waters tried his hand at it. When Munnings saw the result he sliced it from the body with a piece of wire, put it on a stand, obliterated Waters's work and started again. Eventually, Lady Horner approved the bronze of her son, looking like a handsome young Spartan, riding into the east. It was the focal point of one of Lutyens's most moving memorials.

By the time the statuette was finished Munnings had grown reconciled to his new responsibilities. But there were more to come. In July 1919, at the Richmond Horse Show in the Old Deer Park, his attention was caught – and held, by an immaculately-dressed horsewoman on a fine chestnut at the head of the procession of entries in the Ladies' Hack Class.

He first saw her and the horse waiting to enter the arena, motionless, the focus of all eyes. She rode side-saddle and the full skirt of her habit draped over the horse's back gave the illusion they were one. She sat poised for a moment and he took in every detail; her dark hair, magnolia complexion and the white gardenia in her buttonhole in sharp contrast to her dark habit. The sheen on her black top hat was echoed in the silky tail and mane of the horse. Then, at her imperceptible signal, horse and rider moved towards him as one.

* * *

The horsewoman was Mrs Violet McBride, who was born in 1885 at 18 Park Road, off Regent's Park in London. She had two half-brothers and a half-sister who were so much older than she was that she was brought up like an only child and was her father's closest companion. He was Francis Goldby Haines, a riding master, and Violet's earliest memories, like Alfred Munnings's, were of horses, but from a different and more sophisticated viewpoint;

from a seat in a brougham, phaeton or landau, or else riding in the best part of London.

Her father ran a riding school from a rented house and meadow at Temple Fortune, near Golders Green, where he also kept a pack of drag hounds for Saturday hunts. Two of Violet's earliest memories, recorded in pencil in a blue exercise book of memoirs, described her excitement when her father took her for moonlight drives in a phaeton from Temple Fortune, and when she rode with her mother in a landau in Regent's Park and saw the Princess of Wales drive past.

Gypsies fired her imagination. When she was little more than a baby, her father carried her in his arms to a gypsy encampment at Temple Fortune and she described in her exercise book a picture that Munnings might have painted. 'The caravan, tethered horses and dogs, lots of children and dark-skinned women in bright-coloured handkys [sic] and earrings, the smoke going up from the fires and a lovely smell of cookings [sic]. (I was always fond of food . . .).'

She remembered that, when she was three-years-old, she pressed her nose to the sitting-room window to watch her mother set out for her daily ride on a fat, pretty bay cob. When she was six, her father taught her to ride side-saddle, until her nurse pulled her off her pony so roughly that she bruised her knee on the pommel and refused to get on a horse again for a year.

When her fear of riding disappeared she had an hour-and-a-half lesson every day at her father's riding school. At eight she was allowed off the leading rein outside the school and she hunted, for the first time, with the Brighton Harriers on the annual family holiday.

By then the family had moved to Oakley House at Marylebone. It was a gracious home, which the actress Sarah Bernhardt had rented for several London seasons and had kept a tame tiger in the stables, which Goldby Haines used for his riding school.

The house was set in three acres of grounds and was rumoured to be haunted. Haines had sold his Park Road House and the lease of Temple Fortune to buy it for £4,000, which he considered 'a good spec' for he had learned that the railways would soon want the land for their new line to Manchester.

Violet loved the house, ghost and all. She also loved the family coaching holidays, particularly one when the whole family and two grooms drove to Langland Bay in Wales where her father was to judge a horse show. It took a week to get there, staying at inns and post houses on the way. She wrote in her notebook:

> Oh how well I remember the sound of the horses trotting along, the jingle of the harness, the grind of the iron-tyred wheels on the sandy roads, the horn blowing when we arrived and left any place. The climbing up and down over the wheel, admiring the way Daddy flourished his long whip to tickle up one of the leaders, loading up after stopping the night at one of the posting houses. When the brake was released the coach slightly lurched, the leaders pricked up their ears and the wheeler's backs seemed to broaden as they started forward, straining at the traces. Kenneth blew a blast on the horn and, amid grins and nods from the landlord and his wife and the servants, waiter and ostler, we were off.

Annual holidays, however, were usually spent at Brighton in a furnished house with stabling nearby. Her father drove the family there in a roomy carriage drawn by a pair of bays and they stayed at Reigate for a night, on the way. Their two grooms went by train with two hacks, Violet's pony and the luggage.

Violet wrote in her notebook that she paraded along the promenade, wearing a blue serge sailor suit and a despised sailor hat with the name *The Neptune* embroidered in gold on the ribbon. Her black wool socks and high-buttoned boots were 'soon to be changed for stockings,' she added ruefully, 'as people were supposed to look at my legs'.

She went down to the sea in a horse-drawn bathing machine, but was only allowed to paddle. Her sister took dips in the water, wearing a low-necked bathing costume with short sleeves and thick blue serge knickers that covered her knees. Violet was so jealous that, one day, she lay down in the sea, fully clothed.

She was a plain child. The boys called her 'Old Ugly Mug', her father nicknamed her 'The Badger' and her mother was sorry for her, but said she was glad she was ugly because she would be no trouble when she grew up. Not surprisingly, she was a self-conscious and secretive little girl, with an inferiority complex. Like Munnings, she regarded dogs and horses as her only true friends.

Her education was left to a series of governesses, apart from a short period, when she drove a pony and trap to and from Miss Sutton's Select Academy for Young Ladies in Finchley Road. She was not used to mixing with children her own age and the others teased and kicked her, pulled her hair and bullied her unmercifully. Every morning, she cried bitterly before going to school and, after ten days, her parents allowed her to leave.

Horses and riding were her salvation and her father taught her all he knew. She was his greatest admirer, 'No hacks were broken like his, and none had that proud air of distinction that he seemed able to implant after he had broken them,' she wrote in her exercise book. She, too, was given an air of distinction by him as he impressed on her that she must sit straight and control her mount with a light touch.

She was ten-years-old when the Railway Company bought Oakley House and the family moved to 70, Seymour Place, a tall Georgian house overlooking a large meadow that occupied more than half of Seymour Place. There was a row of stables where Goldby Haines ran 'The Largest and Most Select Riding School in London. Patronised by Royalty', as his advertisements read.

The ground floor of the house consisted of a sitting room called the Gallery because its large windows looked down on the partly-walled riding school. A large dressing room, full of riding habits, led off it. The family and two servants occupied the two upstairs floors. 'In spite of no garden, no freedom and no trees I loved all the horses and was fairly happy at the sudden change in my life from a lovely home and luxury to the muddly existence,' Violet wrote. Her half-brothers and half-sister left home and Violet's life centred round horses.

Every morning at quarter to eight, before breakfast, she rode in the Park with her father. After breakfast and two hours of lessons with her governess, she rode again from twelve to one. In the afternoon she drove round the Park with her mother in the brougham and, after tea, went with her to the shops and stores in the Edgware Road.

It was a thrilling day when she rode her black pony, Tommy Tittlemouse, at the Crystal Palace Horse Show. She was the only child in her class because no children or ladies, other than professional riders, competed at horse shows. The pony won a prize and Violet was given a little gold bracelet with a horseshoe and hunting crop fastened to it, as a souvenir.

When she grew too big for the pony it was sent to Marlborough House for the young Prince Albert and Prince George (later King George V) to ride. Eventually, Goldby Haines sold it to the Duke of Portland for his son but, when the Duke learned how upset Violet was at parting from her pony, he refused to buy it. So, for the rest of Tommy Tittlemouse's life, he pulled Violet about in her little basket tub cart with yellow wheels.

Violet delighted in making coloured brow-bands for the bridles of her father's horses, by plaiting together two bright ribbons and a strip of leather. They were the fashion of the day and she described how she made her father a special 'Good Luck' one, in bright cerise, when he rode off to Marlborough House to show a horse to the Prince of Wales. Violet saw him off, a fine figure in braided trousers, top hat and box spurs, and the horse's brilliant brow-band added the final touch, she thought.

At Marlborough House, however, Lord Suffield, the Master of the Horse, ordered him to remove it immediately, before the Prince saw it. It seemed it was in the royal colours and was, therefore, in very poor taste. 'Take off my browband indeed,' Haines replied. He was intensely proud, his daughter wrote, and was prepared to take offence on the slightest pretext. 'I certainly won't remove the browband. In fact I won't show the horse at all,' he said and turned the animal round and rode away.

The trouble was soon resolved when Lord Beresford took Violet to Marlborough House to show the Princess of Wales a beautiful black mare. 'You may be sure I plaited no pretty browband for that occasion,' Violet recalled.

She was still shy but was completely confident on a horse and trotted up and down and cantered before the Princess and her younger daughter, Princess Victoria. Princess Alexandra bought the mare, asked the name of the young horsewoman and said she would call the horse, Violet, after her. She invited Violet to ride wherever she liked in the grounds. Violet was particularly moved by the little cluster of dog's graves under the trees.

Her namesake, the black mare, went to Sandringham but was brought back to London the following summer, when the Court returned. Every day it was saddled up and sent to Seymour Place for Violet to exercise but she found it difficult to ride. Princess Alexandra was a fine horsewoman but had to adjust how she rode side-saddle because a severe thrombosis after the birth of her third child, Princess Louise, had left her lame in her right leg. Her horse was trained to be ridden with an offside side-saddle, so that when Violet rode it, she had to turn the skirt of her habit round and felt most insecure.

She was exercising it in the Park one afternoon when Princess Alexandra passed by in her carriage, stopped and asked Violet to canter her horse alongside. Violet was terrified that, at any moment, she might fall off and be crushed by the mass of carriages that converged in the Park every afternoon at five o'clock.

Normally, however, she was a fearless rider and every summer Goldby Haines took her round the horse shows and, over the years, she won many prizes including the Gold Cup at Olympia. Accidents did not deter her and she once spent six months on her back with an injured spine but, almost as soon as she was on her feet, she was back in the saddle again.

Gradually, with success and the confidence that came from it and from mixing with high society, she acquired poise and elegance. Imperceptibly, the ugly child developed into a handsome woman who was very popular with London's horsey set.

She saw Queen Victoria's Diamond Jubilee procession in 1897, from the Home Secretary's (Lord Ridley's) stand in Carlton House Terrace. Four years later, she married an Irish veterinary surgeon, William McBride. However, the event remains shrouded in mystery and by 1907 Violet had returned to the house in Seymour Place where she lived with her parents for the next thirteen years. She perpetuated the rumour that she was a widow but, in fact, her marriage had ended in divorce.

* * *

When Alfred Munnings saw Violet McBride ride into the arena at Richmond Horse Show he felt a strange affinity, as if he, too, knew every movement of her horse. It was no illusion. A glance at his programme showed the horse was Dandy II which, many years before, its owner, Francis Goldby Haines, had commissioned him to paint. At the time he had been intrigued, he remembered, by the owner's young daughter riding her piebald pony. She rode well and he had asked if she would sit for him one day. 'Not likely,' she had replied. 'I once sat for an artist in Chelsea. It was a non-stop job and I gave it up.'

This time, he promised himself, she would sit for him. He found Goldby Haines and asked to be reintroduced to his daughter. Again, he asked her to sit for him and she still refused. Again, as with Florence, he was completely captivated by the sight of an elegant horsewoman riding a magnificent horse and looking as if they were one.

A few days later, Violet McBride was riding in the Row with Sir George Holford and certain members of the Royal Circle known as 'The Liver Brigade' because, even after a heavy night, they rode at eight o'clock every morning. Her companions included Lord Charles Beresford, a Lord of the Admiralty and a great ladies' man, Lord Ribbesdale and Sir Theodore Brinckman. Sir George Holford was a knowledgeable art collector and Violet asked him if the name 'Munnings' meant anything to him. He conceded it was 'of some account in the art world', and added, as an afterthought, that he would like to see a picture of her on a horse, painted by him. Violet, a one-time ugly duckling, warmed to the idea.

A. J. Munnings's portrait of her riding side-saddle, proudly poised on a beautiful horse, hung in the 1920 Royal Academy, but the painter rated it the poorest of his six paintings there, although it was certainly the most significant. Perhaps he had been too preoccupied with his subject to pay his usual attention to the background, which was roughly sketched in. The only one of his six paintings mentioned by the critics was his gypsy study *Epsom Downs: City and Suburban Day*, which *The Times* described as 'gay and amusing' and which the *East Anglian Daily Times* said 'typifies a direct vision and a robust handling that tell as much at the Academy as elsewhere'. As for the portraits, the national and provincial critics were so obsessed by the first Academy portrait of a lady daring to smoke a cigarette within those sacred precincts – Philip Connard's *Fanny Fillipi Dowson* – to notice the implication of Violet's portrait.

It was called *The Painter's Wife*. Two months before the Summer Academy, Violet McBride and Alfred Munnings had been married quietly at Chelsea Registry Office and had left in a chauffeur-driven car for a week's honeymoon at the Lygon Arms in Broadway. The bridegroom was forty-two, seven years older than his bride although she entered her age on the marriage certificate as thirty-two.

Most of their honeymoon outings were to Alfred's first Cheltenham Race Meeting, which made a pleasant start to a practical and convenient marriage between two people whose main and virtually only interest in common, once again, was a passionate love of horses. During that week the sun shone every day.

A. J. MUNNINGS
51.

CHAPTER XI

The High Life

Alfred and Violet Munnings each approached their second marriage with no romantic illusions. Violet was far more business-like and worldly than Alfred and had become extremely self-reliant. She once explained in his defence to a friend that he was a genius and was, therefore, entitled to be different from other men. That might have been her excuse for their childless and, seemingly, sexually unsatisfactory marriage.

She saw the purpose of her marriage was to relieve 'Munnings', as she always called him, from all domestic and financial worries so that he could devote himself entirely to art. From their wedding day she paid all the bills, ran their homes and dealt with their correspondence. Alfred was delighted to be rid of those irritating distractions and gave her power of attorney so that he need never go into a bank again. He asked her for money when he needed it, but he maintained a childish illusion of independence by hiding pound notes from her between the leaves of books on his library shelves.

Surprisingly, Violet never attempted to alter or intrude on his life-style outside their homes. He still frequented his beloved clubs, and usually went alone to stay with famous people in their stately homes to do portraits of their families and horses. He periodically disappeared into the country on solitary painting expeditions to paint the gypsies or landscapes with horses. However, as his self-appointed business manager, Violet insisted on accepting an escalating flow of commissions for him for equestrian portraits from wealthy society people, although she knew how much he disliked painting such pictures.

'It meant painting for money,' she admitted. 'He had establishments to keep up, more expenses to meet. He was never such a good artist after he married me.' He rarely acknowledged that truth, although in time he realized it. He conceded to her common sense and consoled himself that better men than he had spent their lives painting commissions: men like Sir Joshua Reynolds, who had more than a hundred sitters in a busy year. '... but for all that,' he wrote, 'I wanted to be painting the English scene'.

His frustration could be detected in letters to Violet for, whenever they were apart, he wrote to her nearly every day. Occasionally, he rebelled at her arrangements for him, and showed this in a letter written from Hampshire six months after their marriage. He was painting the gypsies there when Violet arranged for him to do a portrait of the stallion, Rich Gift, owned by Eleanor, Viscountess Torrington.

She sent wires and express letters to the inn where he was staying, to say the thoroughbred had arrived at Dedham. He replied like a rebellious schoolboy: 'I *must* and *will* finish here,' he wrote. 'During these three weeks I have done better work than ever before, and now have it in hand .... No doubts now ... I have the loveliest idea! An old, pale blue, open trolly-waggon and boys and children and all – such colour .... Art cannot be managed. The best should and might be done as I'm doing it – now.'

Nevertheless, when he eventually returned to Castle House to paint Rich Gift, he was wildly enthusiastic about the handsome, dark brown horse and found him 'an inspiration'. The gypsies were forgotten as, with an innate ability to live for the present, he painted the horse, day after day, in the October sunlight. The painter had retained the modesty of his student days, as well as the enthusiasm, and granted he learned much from painting Rich Gift: '... from mixing the rich, dark, bluey tones of quarters, back and shoulders – painting the turn of the neck – always so difficult – the three-quarter view of his head, the perspective across the forehead from the eye to the shape of the orbital bone on the other side, the nostril – passage by passage.'

But when he saw the finished painting, after a few years' interval, he was disappointed. It was not as good as he had thought and, as with so many of his unspontaneous commissioned portraits, he longed to improve on it.

He redeemed his first unsatisfactory portrait of Violet time and again. She posed for him on a grassy bank, elegant and relaxed wearing a trim riding habit and slouched hat; he showed her, equally relaxed, riding a young grey on a grey day and, less characteristically, as a prim housewife darning his socks in a deck chair in their garden. She looked quite beautiful in his portrait of her in a dark riding habit and silk top hat, standing in profile beside the grey, one hand resting casually on her hip, the other holding the horse's reins.

Wearing the silk hat and dark riding habit, she was the centre of one of his finest equestrian compositions called *Changing Horses*. She held two horses, a grey one fresh and ready to go as soon as a horseman had tightened the girths, the black sweating with nostrils blowing. Perhaps the black head with its dilated nostrils reminded Munnings of the model of the horse's head from the Parthenon and he tried to recapture his student's vision. Time and again, he made Violet gallop a horse round and round a field and only pull up and dismount when its nostrils were really blowing, so he could copy them for the nostrils of the black in his painting. Such meticulous attention to detail paid off when the painting was bought by the Carnegie Institute in America for £1,000 and won a gold medal in the 1920 Paris Salon.

He had painted *Changing Horses* while he and Violet stayed with the Master of the Belvoir Hunt, Major Tommy Bouch, near Grantham. The Major was an old admirer of Munnings's work and he commissioned him to make a series of behind-the-hunt pictures of horses at exercise, hounds in their kennels and horses being ridden and groomed. They were inspired, as far as the Major was concerned, by the series of Canadian war paintings of men preparing their horses for battle.

Violet left and Munnings painted from dawn to dusk, occasionally taking a day off to hunt and, every evening, he went to a party given by one of the hunting crowd. He should have been in his element, but a recurring phrase in his letters to Violet was 'Life is sad', a sentiment he often reiterated when he wrote to her from other stately homes where he stayed for weeks on end to fulfil those lucrative equestrian commissions.

The results of that visit to Major Bouch were seen in *Pictures of the Belvoir Hunt and Other Scenes of English Country Life*, the title of his exhibition of forty-one paintings in London's Alpine Club Gallery, in April 1921. The public attended in their thousands and Munnings was besieged with commissions and invitations from many of the most sought after society hostesses. After the Exhibition, Frost and Reed, the print publishers and art dealers of King Street, St James's, bought a set of four paintings of the Belvoir Hunt, for reproduction, and so began their life-long association in buying and selling hundreds of Munnings's paintings and reproducing many others. 'He frequently complained that we and other dealers were paying a tithe of what they were really worth,' said Stanley Wade, a director of Frost and Reed. 'Munnings predicted his original works would one day make enormous sums. Today, I realize how right he was in his judgement.'

Dominating the Exhibition was Munnings's accolade as a successful equestrian portrait painter. It was a large study of the Prince of Wales (later the Duke of Windsor) on his hunter, Forest Witch, a picture presented to the Prince by *The Field* magazine to commemorate his season with the Pytchley. Its presence justified the astute manager of the Alpine Gallery, Orpen's brother-in-law, Mr Knewstub, raising the Exhibition's admission price to half-a-crown. Within a few days, however, Knewstub was accused of exploiting the painting to benefit his gallery; King George V was approached and his son's portrait was removed to the top of the staircase at the Royal Academy where it served Munnings, if not the Gallery, equally well.

The Prince had sat for Munnings in his London studio. He drove himself there every morning and arrived bareheaded, wearing white breeches and a check coat to change into his pink coat and top hat and pose on the wooden saddle horse. Before he arrived, Sir Theodore Cook, the editor of *The Field*, invariably turned up with a bottle of vintage port, glasses and two handsomely-bound volumes of Surtees's novels from which he read aloud to the Prince, to Munnings's constant distraction. The painter noticed that, periodically, the handsome sitter studied himself in the mirror and often gave his silk hat a slight tweak.

Munnings and the Prince were both dissatisfied with the picture. The Prince thought it made him look like his younger brother and the painter, for once, had overstretched himself. 'It was no easy business,' he said, 'to paint this young man, whose name at that time was on every lip, and who had the greatest press of any man living. I felt I was up against it.'

He over-reacted by choosing a six-foot canvas – far larger than was expected – and filling in one side with a symbolic British oak. He chose the tree from every hoary old oak in the region but, eventually, he thought its gnarled trunk dominated the picture. Afterwards, whenever he saw the painting reproduced, he longed to repaint the tree.

Despite Munnings's obvious anxiety during the sittings, he made a rare but typically impulsive and selfless gesture. He invited his neighbour, the sculptor McMillan, to bring a pair of small bronzes into the studio and place them where the Prince could see them. They had been rejected in a competition for a memorial to the Machine Gun Corps, but Munnings thought they were works of genius and preferred them to the winning entry.

The Prince noticed them. He sat astride the saddle horse, smoking his pipe, and thought deeply as he held the smaller one in his hand. It showed an exhausted, mud-spattered Tommy, sitting on a bank, his legs outstretched, his head bowed, done to the world but not beaten. 'Poor bugger!' the Prince said, as he studied the bronze. Afterwards, Munnings took him to meet the sculptor and he bought both works.

Even without the royal portrait the Exhibition consolidated Munnings's reputation. The critics enthused:

> The paintings breathe the spirit of life that goes on horseback over wind-swept hills and plains....
>
> An epic story of the real life of the English countryside.... Better than a tonic. It is meat and drink to the hungry and thirsty....
>
> A lyric poet who writes his ballads of the English countryside with a brush and a box of paints....

The Times's critic could have added 'and also with a pen', because copies of Munnings's *Ballad of Anthony Bell* were on sale at a shilling each at the Exhibition. Its staunchest professional admirer, John Masefield, had written a long and enthusiastic foreword to the Exhibition Catalogue which revealed his affinity with the painter. He wrote:

> The beauty of the horses and the scarlet of their riders and the pied rhythm of the hounds and their excitement, among the sombreness of the leafless times ... are kindling to the

> soul. And who, of all our many painters who have loved such scenes, has painted them so movingly as Mr Munnings? Who has caught the rhythm of the hounds going to covert, and the quickening of the soul in the hunter and the unmatchable beauty of the English horse?
>
> I love the chequered light of the wood with the grey hunter, dappled light and dappled horse, both lovely. I love the raw February scene of the hounds going out in the snow. Somebody ought to have put all these scenes into poems, and now Mr Munnings has beaten us.

The modest, future Poet Laureate seemed to have forgotten how often he had expressed such sentiments in his own medium.

In childhood, Munnings had been nurtured on poems and literature; later, encouraged by Masefield's effusive criticism, he was lured into believing that, if he ever applied himself, he could paint in words as successfully as he painted visually. He was not the first poet or painter to try to express himself in two art forms, and he probably recalled his idol Browning's words:

> Rafael made a century of sonnets . . .
> Dante once prepared to paint an angel.

Masefield, likewise, loved to display his slight artistic ability. One of his first Christmas greetings to Violet and Alfred was a copy of his poem, 'The Racer', illustrated by three bravely-drawn horses and jockeys, carefully initialled.

Truly, 'Munnings could write with the pen of a poet', according to his author friend, James Wentworth Day, but he was referring to the painter's prose rather than to his ballads, which he described as 'of a rollicking, rumbustious sort'. Those 'rhyming digressions' as Munnings, in justifiable modesty, called them, nevertheless showed a mastery of rhythm, rhyme and rhetoric and a sense of humour which their creator rarely, if ever, displayed in real life.

Typical was his seven-verse ballad extolling Violet's hunting prowess, which was eventually published in a slim book of verses dedicated to her. The ballad began:

> My wife in the West never takes any rest;
> She hunts in the wind and the rain.
> Though sodden her vest, so strong is her chest,
> She goes out and does it again.

The tempest may blow, like arrow from bow,
Her steed's on a loosely held rein,
Up hill and down dale, twelve miles in a gale,
They scorn the steep slope and the strain.

It concluded:

It rains and it pours, the river it roars!
It rose to such height in the night,
The hunting was stopped and the horses all popped
Their heads out to look at the sight!!

'Ha, ha!' they all neighed. 'It's the end of our trade!'
And the woman sat working so glum
At the seat of her breeks, which for five or six weeks
Had shown a small glimpse of her – !

The reference to 'my wife in the West' referred to Violet's Exmoor hunting retreat, a cottage at Withypool adjoining the blacksmith's forge, where she spent many months each year riding and hunting her three horses. Often, Munnings joined her.

His more ribald verses, some too filthy for publication, were usually composed during nights out with 'the boys'. So were the harmless, outrageously personal ones. Ralph Potter, a Norwich journalist, recalls meeting him in the Red Lion public house at Stoke Holy Cross, a couple of miles from Norwich. Potter would play well-known tunes, such as 'Do ye ken John Peel', on the piano to accompany 'A.J.'s wickedly appropriate verses about his fellow drinkers, which the painter composed and sang spontaneously.

He was once accused of composing his verses at home, Potter said, but Munnings denied this in his earthiest language. To prove his case, he approached a complete stranger, who was drinking in the bar, learned a few details about him, and immediately sat down at the piano and incorporated them in a raucous song. The stranger was so impressed, Potter said, that he went away with a signed copy of the verses.

Of all Munnings's outpouring, however, *Anthony Bell* remained his party piece. He often revised it and it 'brought the house down', he wrote to Violet from Kirby Hall, Melton Mowbray, where he was painting a wealthy American sportsman, Robert Strawbridge, a Master of the Cottesmore. He had recited it at a local charity concert before all the élite in their scarlet evening coats and, afterwards, he had gone on to a huge champagne supper party. 'Everyone there, all in scarlet. What a go!' he wrote. 'Next day, Strawbridge insisted on me riding to the first draw on a hack. Saw all the fun and rode like the devil, trousers and all. Both the Princes out. Then, that night, I'm blessed if they didn't dine here!! Prince of Wales, Prince Henry and only Mr and Mrs Strawbridge and myself to meet them. And then I'm blessed if I didn't have to do *Anthony Bell* after dinner for them.'

A letter to Violet from Anthony de Rothschild's Southcourt Stud, near Leighton Buzzard, written soon after their first wedding anniversary, shows him in his element. As a result of Munnings's portrait of Rothschild's Galloper Light, he had been commissioned to paint a series of brood mares, foals and stallions in their paddocks and his host had invited him to stay for several months and 'paint whatever you like'. '... these days of work among the *dear*, *dear* horses and country soak into me,' he wrote. 'Each mare is an unconscious friend. Each goes on eating grass and cares nothing for me, but I love them, and as for their children, they are too wonderful for words. So long as I'm with horses and people I'm at peace ... I could do some great things here.'

He did and he went to the Rothschild bank in the city to collect 'the largest and most generous cheque' he had ever received. Apparently, it never occurred to him to offer to use some of it to defray the cost of repapering his bedroom at the Rothschilds' home. He had knocked over a bottle of ink when he was trying to swat a May beetle, and it had gone all over the pink rosebud wallpaper.

> What a go! [he wrote to Violet]. You never saw such a pattern as it made in all your life. The ink had run down in six long black marks to the skirting board. I seized a sponge and rubbed it off and the pattern too – Lord, *how* funny. I laughed till I cried. I think I'll paint some more rosebuds on the wall.
>
> Bless me, I forgot about everything else for the moment. Very good for one, these things: take [sic] one out of oneself for awhile. My word they do.

11. Cassie Jeweller, 1909, 58″ x 28″

12. Tagg's Island, 1919, 34½″ x 50″

Artists and models at Tagg's Island on the Thames. They were all personal friends of Munnings.

13. Oxen at Chantilly, c. 1922, 24″ x 20″

aron Robert de Rothschild, great grandson of the founder of the banking dynasty, invited Munnings
) stay at his country home in France and paint the family, the Hunt at Chantilly and anything he
ked. 'Stay with us for a year' was the Baron's open invitation.

14. Studies of Cherrybounce and Anarchist, 1944, 16″ x 20″

Munnings bred Cherrybounce, a big outstanding bay, sixteen and a half hands, with a white star on her forehead. He once said 'I've used her hard and often and never known her lame'. Anarchist however was probably his favourite.

15. Rich Gift, a Bay Racehorse held by a Groom, 1921, 26½″ x 30″

Rich Gift was owned by Eleanor, Viscountess Torrington, and Munnings found the horse an 'inspiration' and was his 'first aristocratic visitor at Castle House'.

16. My Garden in Winter, c. 1930, 32″ x 41½″

An unusual subject for Munnings which demonstrates his versatility and ability to capture atmosphere.

17. In the Unsaddling Enclosure at Epsom, c. 1948, 26″ x 33″

Iunnings returned again and again to courses such as Epsom and Sandown. For him 'Epsom xpresses the true meaning of the words "The Races"'.

18. Under Starters Orders, c. 1956, 44″ x 70″

19. Study of a Start at Newmarket, 1951, 18″ x 26″

The scene that had the most fascination for Munnings was undoubtedly the start of a race. They carec about him at Newmarket. Lads riding by on The Heath called out 'Mornin' Sir Halfred' and the Jockey Club loaned him an old horse-rubbing box on the course as a studio.

There was plenty of time for letter-writing in those stately homes where he enjoyed prodigious hospitality at weekends, when his hosts were in residence, but when they returned to London in the week he was often left to his own devices. Writing to Violet helped to fill the lonely hours when introspection and sad thoughts crowded in on him. The letters to her were indulgences not duties. 'I've done it for years,' he wrote to her of his lonely life-style. 'Sad world!' He never felt that way when he was with the gypsies, the untameables with whom he was completely at home.

He wrote long and affectionate letters to Violet. One ended, from 'Your most loving husband whose one certain comfort is that he has you somewhere in the background of his most miserable existence'. Another time he wrote: 'Getting married to you makes up for *All* other mistakes. You're my one and only stand-by.'

He wrote to her from Blenheim Palace where he was painting the Duke of Marlborough and his son, Lord Ivor Spencer-Churchill: '. . . a palace beyond all dreams. Faded flags, trophies of victories and pictures by Reynolds and Sargent . . . noble court-yards . . . . *Such* oaks and elms – my Lord, such elms . . . .'

Perhaps his longing to paint the elms came between him and his subject, master-minded by the ninth Duke who insisted 'We must have a signpost in the picture . . . and why not have a stonebreaker? Changing horses, four greys with a second horseman in full rig . . . . Mind you put me on the best horse . . . .'

The painter hoped the picture would 'reach the heights' but confessed to Violet that 'it fell far below'.

He wrote disconsolately from Eaton, the Duke of Westminster's great house near Chester:

> I can't tell you what a business this is – all the time wishing one was home and out of it and not having to paint anyone who doesn't want a real portrait.
>
> I can't paint under such conditions . . . . Another job of this sort would send me mad. Never again . . . . Being so business-like yourself, you don't overlook my failings. My failings aren't criminal. All I know is that my life is all work and that it is done against difficulties all the time . . . . It's a sad world, my masters.

'I'm sure you will like me better if I get to work and write less,' he wrote to her during his three weeks' stay in Richmond,

Yorkshire, with Herbert Straker, Master of the Zetland, and then continued to write to her nearly every day. 'Awful!' he wrote. 'Sitting over the fire in the hall here, feeling doleful.... It is dismal alone after 5 o'clock.' A walk in the woods after a rook-shoot accentuated his melancholy: 'Those dead rooks looked dismal and made me pessimistic – well – about things everywhere.' Violet wrote to him about a stray calf that had turned up in her garden at Withypool and he commented, 'Animals are far better than ourselves. We're all damned awful.'

He was enthusiastic again, however, when his series of paintings for Anthony de Rothschild at Southcourt Stud led to an invitation from Baron Robert de Rothschild, great-grandson of the founder of the banking dynasty, to stay at his country home in France, the Chateau de Laversine, and paint the family, the Hunt at Chantilly and anything he liked. 'Stay with us for a year,' was the Baron's open invitation.

He met Munnings in his magnificent Paris mansion, 23 Avenue de Marigny, set in acres of gardens opposite the Elysée Palace. It was a treasure house of priceless furniture, *objets d'art* and magnificent paintings including several Van Eycks and Rembrandts. They drove to the Baron's palatial château on the summit of a steep, wooded slope, rising from the river Oise. There Munnings found himself in another world.

The Baron's beautiful wife, Nelly, was one of the great hostesses of the day. There was a dinner party nearly every evening and, at weekends, the château was filled with guests including artists, writers and musicians. At one house-party he met the Duke and Duchess of Alva, Prince Murat, Master of the Chantilly Hunt, and his Princess, Field Marshal Earl Haig and 'all the nobility for miles around'. At a great Hunt dinner party, liveried Hunt servants played hunting tunes in the outer hall on their round brass hunting horns. He told Violet that 'Beautiful women glittered with diamonds, the dining table reached the length of the salon and Samuel, the white-haired butler, and footmen passed slowly round, quietly giving the year of the wine they were serving.' He took his wine carefully, he reported, otherwise 'tomorrow I should not be any good at work. What a life.'

He slept in an ornate bed with a plumed and curtained top and, every morning, before leaving for Paris, the Baron, wearing a cerise patterned dressing gown, came to the bedroom to enquire what he would like to paint that day – Frank (the stud groom), the horses, the children, the dogs or himself? Looking at the weather, Munnings would decide.

He worked every day either on pictures of the family or, pre ferably, on the peaceful country scenes such as he had longed to paint in wartime France, less than four years ago. He painted the yoked, cream-coloured oxen driven by a peasant carrying a long hazel-stick and a labourer riding one white horse and leading another against a background of flat farm land. They were subjects he had loved painting in England, seen in new settings. 'Don't tell folk I'm making a fortune,' he cautioned Violet, adding, 'I tell you I find painting *very* difficult – don't like portraits.... Always thinking of you and how extraordinary it is that nobody else matters except you.'

A vivid memory was of St Hubert's Day, celebrated at Chantilly when two liveried Hunt servants led pairs of hounds up the church aisle to be blessed, along with the Hunt, by the priest. Afterwards, he rode with members of the Hunt in a cavalcade from the great stables, down the ride and into the forest. Once again, it was a picture he recalled in words not paint. 'I was riding through the forest,' he remembered, 'hearing the melancholy, strange notes of the great brass horns sounding through the trees.... Somewhere in the depth of the forest, more hounds with the Hunt servants were waiting.... Blue liveries, the sun lighting on circular brass horns and yellow foliage, the tufters giving tongue ... hollow notes of horns in far-away drives....'

He stayed in France for Christmas and Violet never complained. 'Make hay while the sun shines,' she wrote to him at the luxury villa in the Pyrenées, where he was painting the smart American wife of Harry la Montagne, a wealthy horseman. On Boxing Night, his host took him to a stag dinner given by Frederick Prince, Master of the Pau Foxhounds. Most of the sixty male guests wore scarlet coats and the host later showed Munnings his sixty horses standing in his stables. The painter's Christmas was in marked contrast to Violet's English one, with only her dogs, including a little black Pekinese, for company.

For a time it seemed that the luxurious conditions Munnings experienced in France made him dissatisfied. He complained to

Violet that his Dedham studio was in the *wrong* place: 'I've known it for ages. I *was* a fool,' he wrote. 'I could never have done these pictures there. I'm glad of parks and large houses as much as I *hate* leaving home, simply because I've not got a good painting spot of my own. Before I die I will leave an explanation to the world that if I had bought the *right* place, I should have done great work.'

So much for his demonstration fifteen years previously, when he drew in chalk on the billiard room blinds in the Norwich City Club to refute the suggestion that an artist needed the right atmosphere of a studio in which to paint. So much, too, for the 'house of my dreams'.

Occasional severe bouts of gout made him irritable. Evidently, there had been sleepless nights because, he told Violet, French beds enabled him to sleep flat and cured the pain in his back and neck that kept him awake. He was sure the pain was caused by their dipped beds at home.

It seemed there were other reasons for his sleeplessness: 'I know too much about *long sleepless nights*,' he was to write some twenty years later, to Lady Wentworth, Lord Byron's granddaughter, when he stayed at her magnificent home, Crabbet Park, in Sussex to see her two hundred Arab horses. Meanwhile, he complained to Violet from France: 'Do you know, the longer I'm away from London, the less I want to go back there. Beastly hole.'

The lease of his London studio at Glebe Place was running out and Violet bought a corner site in Chelsea Park Gardens and had a house and studio built to their design. The living room, dining room and bedroom were on the ground floor. The first floor was mainly given over to a huge, grey-painted studio overlooking a small, walled garden where he planted three sapling plane trees. He called it Beldon House after Beldon Hall in one of his beloved Surtees's novels, but he regretted having to spend time there, painting portraits, instead of living at Castle House. As he grew older, it seemed that, for various reasons, happiness and contentment so often eluded him.

There were mood swings and other letters to Violet showed him childishly contrite and appreciative: 'I like your butter better than the Club's butter and my bed better than the Club's beds – and *our* house better than the Club,' he wrote to her from the Arts

Club after the Private View of the 1923 Royal Academy. The letter showed he was far more delighted because his six paintings occupied 'the most feet in line space', than disappointed because he had been defeated for election as a full Academician by Glyn Philpot.

When he found life good he could hardly contain his enthusiasm. Lunching at the Garrick, he sat next to the Irish playwright, Sean O'Casey. 'Such a nice fellow. I like him,' he told Violet and, in the same letter, assured her that a domestic help who looked after him at his Chelsea studio was 'the nicest person going – *Perfect*' he wrote, 'she is so quiet and kind'.

In contrast, his own explosive irritability was becoming all too apparent. An admirer, meeting him for the first time at Brighton racecourse, was disconcerted to be told to 'Look at that dreadful creature over there and that still more horrible b— beside him.' They were a bookmaker and his clerk and Munnings asked his new acquaintance, 'Now do you wonder why I paint horses?'

There were endless commissions to paint horses with or without their riders: Mrs Leopold de Rothschild with her beloved grey hunter; Steve Donoghue on his Derby winner, Humorist, owned by Jack Joel: Lord D'Abernon's famous racehorse, Diadem; *The Drummer of H.M. First Life Guards*, with his gold-bedecked uniform and glittering silver drums on a crested horse, representing a touch of pageantry that fired the painter's imagination. In sombre contrast there was *Isaac Bell and his Foxhounds, Kilkenny.*

The brief visit to Ireland to paint the famous hunting personality had coincided with atrocious weather, some Sinn Fein activity and a crisis in Bell's domestic affairs which, eventually, resulted in the loss of his house, his lands, his stable of fine horses and his pack of hounds, rated as the finest in Ireland. It rained so hard that Munnings was reduced to painting the hounds, one at a time, in the dining room.

He saw Kilkenny Horse Fair as a sea of mud with shivering horses and his painting caught the bleakness of the beautiful, forlorn, stone-walled country, scarcely touched by time. Dominating his picture was a magnificent grey – probably one of Bell's horses. The painting was first exhibited in the 1923 Royal Academy and, although it had been painted in a far from exuberant atmosphere, it was destined to make one of Munnings's dreams come true when it was accepted as his Diploma Work on his becoming an RA.

It proved more significant than any of his works created amid the colour and social glamour of France, an atmosphere which, at times, had tended to make him discontented, perhaps because it was so far removed from his inborn country values. He had turned to words, not paint, to record some of his impressions of France, and wrote a seventeen-verse poem telling of a French chef who committed suicide when he lost his sense of taste and smell. He started to write this in France but finished it on board *S.S. Berengaria* on his way to America and he recited it, on the least provocation, throughout that trip.

It typified his 'total lack of intellectual pretension', an appealing quality according to the American art connoisseur, Joseph Baillio. This feature caused a wealthy American clientele to respond to him and to 'his amusing eccentricities, his crusty wit and brusque manner,' Baillio said. The Americans took to him spontaneously and enjoyed his company while he, in contrast to his apparently soul-searching period in France, had 'a gloriously mad time'.

CHAPTER XII

The New World and the Old

Munnings revelled in his only trip to America. In the spring of 1924 he was invited to be a judge at the twenty-third annual picture exhibition at the Carnegie Institute in Pittsburgh, with his fare paid and a generous expense allowance. Violet was not included in the invitation.

It was a fierce nine-day crossing in the *Berengaria* and the gales terrified him at times. He was most afraid at night. He could not sleep and went on deck to watch the huge seas breaking over the bows of the ship. However, in retrospect, thanks to his fellow travellers, he pronounced it 'a wonderful voyage'.

The passengers included another judge at the Pittsburgh Exhibition, the famous French painter, Albert Besnard, the Strawbridges, in whose home at Melton Mowbray Munnings had recited the *Ballad of Anthony Bell* to the Prince of Wales after dinner, and Frederick Prince, one of his French hosts and Master of the Pau Foxhounds. Parties were held nearly every night and indicated the social life ahead for the painter in America.

By the time the ship docked he had been persuaded to visit Mr Prince's Massachusetts estate to paint the polo-playing millionaire, his wife and his son. The one stipulation Munnings made, however, was that Prince must ride a grey or have a grey in the picture. Prince agreed, although it meant buying a new horse because all his greys were at his French stud.

A few days after the ship docked, Munnings was taken to visit the Pittsburgh Hunt and saw a good-looking grey mare which her owner was willing to sell. He wired Prince who authorized him to buy her for £250. She was waiting for Munnings to ride when he arrived at Prince's palatial home, Princemere, near Boston, an imitation castle complete with towers and battlements and connected to a fine parkland by a stone bridge. The presence of the grey horse suggested that, within the wealthy hunting set, the painter's every whim would be indulged.

'Al', as he was known, was lionized in America. Handsome men and lovely women, who owned strings of magnificent horses, queued up to be painted and a few, who had already sat for him in England, wanted to be painted again in their native settings. One lady threatened to follow him to England with her famous steeplechaser and sit for him there if he would not paint her in America. He refused to paint her at all.

The first in the queue of sitters was waiting when he arrived at Pittsburgh Exhibition Hall to meet the Hanging Committee. The meeting had to wait while the Director of the Carnegie Institute introduced him to a pretty young lady eager to be painted on horseback, there and then. Munnings protested that it was too cold to paint out-of-doors, but the Director suggested he should start work in one of the last galleries to be hung. The head carpenter built a wooden saddle horse to his specifications and, within a few hours, his first sitter was posing for him. A few days later he painted her handsome grey horse at the Country Club.

For Munnings it was the start of a six months' 'trail of labour', which took him to New England and Long Island, New York, Buffalo, Niagara, the Genesee Valley and across into Canada by way of a bewildering number of commissions. He received lavish hospitality, ate and drank too much – in spite of the strictly-enforced prohibition – had gout and too little sleep. Yet his tremendous stamina and energy kept him going, reinforced perhaps because the eccentric in him was stimulated by the eccentricities of his wealthy hosts.

Although he had gout the only record of his characteristic rudeness and love to shock was at a big race meeting, when a rider on a good-looking chestnut passed by. Munnings's friends told him, in hushed tones, that the rider was the famous Herbert Hoover. Munnings snorted derisively and pronounced loudly and clearly, 'He rides like a butcher.'

At Princemere, Mrs Prince sat for him on a wooden saddle horse in the billiard room under new lighting specially installed by an electrician from the Boston Theatre. Later, the painter explored the grounds and found a disused, large, two-storey stone building.

At lunch, he mentioned to his host that the upper storey would make a marvellous studio. Prince confessed that he had quite forgotten the building existed, immediately had a large north light let into the roof and, a few days later, posed for Munnings on the saddle horse in the newly improvised studio.

Another improvised studio was the impressive glass-covered ride surrounding the Long Island racing stables, the home of fifty-six ponies used by the American polo team. There Munnings painted handsome polo players and members of the local hunting and racing fraternity and their families on horseback.

He was amazed because some of his sitters quibbled over the £500 or so he charged for a portrait but, mindful of Violet's instructions, he was no longer prepared to bargain. He felt his attitude was justified when one millionaire argued fiercely before agreeing the price, and then pulled a large case out from under the settee where he and Munnings were sitting. It contained two violins, one a Stradivarius, for which the owner boasted he had paid eleven thousand pounds, and the other a Guarnerius, which had cost him ten thousand.

At another lavishly-furnished home Munnings's hostess had just returned from Paris with several Picassos as souvenirs. They were propped up on the drawing-room floor against the legs of Queen Anne chairs. 'Nobody liked them,' Munnings reported gleefully, 'not even our host and hostess; but they could not return from Paris without a Picasso or two. Never mind the cost! At best they were making some fun, helped by the cocktails. The noise increased a hundredfold at the sight of the "masterpieces".'

The non-stop hospitality he enjoyed was more to his liking than the dreary weekdays he had spent in the great homes of England, with only equestrian models for company until his hosts returned at the weekends. He rated his American hosts as 'the most hospitable folk whose way of life on well-wooded estates adjoining each other was, without doubt, beyond description'.

The new attitudes and standards he encountered among wealthy and often extremely cultured Americans, buoyed him up when he was 'worked to death'. Even Violet could not have faulted the stoicism with which he accepted commission after commission. Often, when he painted a successful portrait of a lady on horseback, her husband wanted a companion one, and their friends were not to be outdone.

Harry La Montagne, whose wife Munnings had painted in France, was asked how long the painter took for a portrait. He replied shrewdly, 'I guess it depends on how good the boarding house is!'

The 'boarding house' was customarily excellent and, although Munnings could usually paint his riders in two or three sittings and their horses in another two, the distractions were irresistible. He was taken to vist the English Derby winner, Papyrus, at Belmont Park, to a dinner at the Boston Traveller's Club where he sat next to one of his idols, John Singer Sargent, who was painting frescoes in the Boston Library, and he went sailing with Starling Burgess, the yacht designer responsible for many winning boats in the America's Cup races.

Munnings considered Burgess the most outstanding personality he met in the States, not because of the bottle of home-distilled gin, eighteen inches high, kept in his studio in defiance of prohibition, but because he entertained his guests by reading long passages from Browning and Swinburne to them in a style that Munnings himself could not have bettered.

Munnings sailed with him to an island occupied entirely by rats and, more to the painter's liking, to a deserted stretch of sands inhabited only by hundreds of seals. Often, the painter returned there in a chauffeur-driven car, and lay on the sand to listen to the cries of gulls and watch the white surf break steadily on the beach. He found it was the best way to recuperate after a long painting spell and a period of high living.

Alone on the beach, he perhaps ruminated on the difficulty of painting equestrian portraits, compared to ordinary likenesses where the artist could pose his sitters in a studio and arrange the lighting to suit them. He had to capture not only the likeness of the sitter but also his or her seat on a horse, the horse itself and whether it was on the move or standing still, always against an ever-changing background of light and sky.

He was disappointed by many of his commissioned equestrian portraits. He felt he was wasting his talent painting them instead of scenes of his own choosing, which involved 'the tone of a day, the light – grey or sun – on things, on horses – people. Worse than that,' he complained, 'I long always to sit by a river and paint....'

He sailed home from Montreal in early October and his most vivid memory of the hectic six-months' trip was the seal-inhabited island where he had spent hours on his own. He also recalled with delight, the paintings in the Boston Art Gallery by Monet, Sargent, and the American, Winslow Homer, and he remembered the long-dead port of Old Salem where magnolia trees bloomed in the walled gardens of Georgian-style white wooden houses. As for the ladies, his impressions of the many elegant and exquisite beauties who had lionized him and sat for him, blurred by comparison with his affectionate memory of a fat, benevolent-looking, old negress cook in the home of a sitter, the young polo-player, Bobby Strawbridge. 'She must have been the broadest-bosomed, the most sympathetic soul in Long Island,' he recalled. 'I shall never forget my first sight of her when she entered the breakfast-room one morning.... She just shone!'

If it was sympathy he needed, he found it when his ship docked at Plymouth and he caught sight of Violet, standing on the quayside beside a new car, a 1917 Buick complete with brass radiator and headlamps. She drove him home through the golden autumn landscape and, after six months' absence from the countryside he loved, he found the long-shadowed sunlight beyond all his expectations. At Dedham, a beautiful new Irish mare was waiting, another sign of Violet's approval. She had exchanged her for one of his paintings and appropriately renamed her Dollar Princess.

His small stud was growing, due to the addition of three of Violet's horses and a little dealing and breeding. Eventually, he had thirty-four horses to ride, hunt or paint as the light and his moods dictated. But his mental struggle as to whether to ride or paint was only a preliminary contention. If he decided to paint, he argued with himself whether he should fulfil one of the endless stream of lucrative commissions for equestrian portraits or work quietly and contentedly at home, painting his own models in the settings he loved.

He also questioned whether he should continue to paint in watercolours. During the post-war boom, he had sold about six watercolours a year through the Royal Water Colour Society alone. They ranged in price from £200 to £450. Gradually, however, he found it disturbing to change from one medium to another, particularly when the demanding immediacy of watercolour interrupted his work on a large oil painting and disturbed its flow. Gradually and deliberately, after his return from America, he abandoned watercolours. However, he reluctantly decided to accept the equestrian commissions because, he acknowledged, it was through them that he could afford to keep a stable full of horses to paint – even if he never seemed to have enough time to paint them!

He sought other consolations: 'An artist meets with so many frustrations and setbacks that no feasting or falling under a table is too good a reward for his labours,' he wrote. 'His is the life of laughter and tears.'

However, one June morning in 1925 all his misgivings about commissions were forgotten, Violet returned to their Chelsea studio from riding in the Row with his 'chance of a lifetime'. It was an invitation from Queen Mary to paint the Ascot Procession.

He remembered a day, some six years previously, when Lord Athlone had taken him to the royal stables at Windsor to see the beautiful Cleveland bays and greys used for drawing the royal coaches. How he had longed to paint them instead of his host's docile chestnut. Now they were his to portray amid the pageantry and glittering scarlet and gold of a royal occasion in the grandest of English settings. What equestrian painter could ask for more!

Ascot was less than a week ahead. Every morning for four days, a royal Daimler arrived at his studio to take him and Violet to Windsor Castle. In the stables there, he made preliminary sketches of the horses, the ten carriages and the splendid livery of the outriders and the white-wigged postillions.

Every day during the Ascot meeting, the Royal Family and their guests were driven across the Park in Daimlers to Duke's Lane, before the Golden Gates where they transferred to the carriages. This allowed the horses to be fresh and full of action when they trotted down the course.

Every day, Munnings was driven to the first of his chosen positions on the route, before the empty carriages separated by pairs of scarlet-coated outriders on fine white or grey horses moved off to the rendezvous at Duke's Lane. From his first position, he viewed the long glittering line of scarlet and gold as it moved between clumps of trees, across the smooth parkland.

The chauffeur then manoeuvred the car so that the painter could see the Procession from several other vantage points. He watched it drive down the course, arrive at the stands where the royal party alighted and after the meeting, he watched the party return in the carriages to Windsor Castle and a welcome from the local people.

The ladies in the royal party wore different outfits every day. Munnings chose to paint the Queen holding a pink parasol over her powder-blue silk cape with a chinchilla collar and a blue hat trimmed with fluttering blue and pink ostrich feathers.

He assimilated and refined his impressions over the four days of the meeting. He gloried in the colours of the livery – dark blue, gold, scarlet and white and, just as he had been thrilled as a seven-year-old boy at the horses and their white rosettes at his aunt's wedding, his imagination was again fired by rosettes – large red ones on either side of the royal horses' heads. He expressed himself equally well in words as in paint:

> These lovely rosettes gave an indescribable beauty to the whole Procession. 'Red rosettes, red rosettes!' I repeated to myself all the time as I sat in the car, speeding away ... to where the chauffeur ... advised me to go and wait again....
>
> I recall the wide-stretching vista of the Park, the sound of hoofs on the turf, the swinging movement of the horses' shoulders against their collars, the glitter of gold braid, of silver mounting on the harness, the rise and fall of postilions and out-riders as they rode along the sunlit landscape.... My mind became so full of all this brilliance, glitter and activity that it was difficult to decide which, out of all that I had seen, would be the best arrangement for a picture.

He decided, during the eight weeks he lived in an old hotel at Windsor, and received all the royal cooperation he could have wished, for he lacked the mental power to recall everything he wanted to paint, an ability acquired and developed by many painters. Every detail, therefore, had to be there for him to copy.

On fine days, he was driven in a wagonette to his chosen spot with a distant view of the Castle. The elegant curved landeau was brought for him to paint, and grooms held the individual horses for him against the trees. At other times, he worked in the Castle

Mews and painted the magnificent silver-and-gilt-mounted harness or the red rosettes in their glass cases and the uniforms and portraits of the leading postilions.

Violet posed for him, seated in the landeau dressed in the Queen's clothes and carrying her pink parasol, while the Queen herself was photographed, for Munnings to copy in a comparable position, on the terrace of Buckingham Palace. The King's likeness was chosen from dozens of press photographs, while a friend in a grey top hat modelled his position in the coach. The Prince of Wales, who had sat facing the Queen with the Duke of York, was painted from a bust sculpted by Jennings and given a top hat and collar and tie. The Duke of York was barely visible.

Munnings could not resist painting a companion picture showing the Ascot Procession returning to the Castle, with the low afternoon sun casting the long shadows he loved to paint. Both remarkable paintings were documents of historical value but quite divorced from the natural freedom of the best of Munnings.

He celebrated their completion by joining the gypsies in Hampshire at hop-picking time. For six blissful weeks he was rejuvenated by painting his dark-skinned friends with their hordes of children, dogs, chickens and horses. He worked from dawn until the blue smoke rose from the fires at dusk and signalled him to make his way to the White Horse at Holybourne, where he was staying, for an evening's drinking.

Freed from royal restraint, he felt he was painting far and away his best gypsy pictures. He completed the fine study, *Gypsies on Epsom Downs, Derby Week*, for the 1926 Royal Academy and celebrated a particularly good day's painting by opening a bottle or two of champagne.

Eventually, the 'heartbreaking setback' of sunless days and continuous rain stopped him painting out-of-doors and sent him home to Dedham. He arrived there with a quaint little rough-haired terrier, Bob, he had bought, and more than twenty canvases he had painted. 'Well done, you clever little man!' was Violet's greeting. But he needed no-one to endorse his achievements for he knew himself that, as usual, he had painted his best pictures during a time of sheer pleasure that had left no room for depression.

Both his Ascot pictures were shown in the 1926 Royal Academy and, on the Private View Day, the King and Queen congratulated him. 'The horses are moving,' said the King. *The Ascot Procession* was bought for the Royal Collection while the companion painting was purchased by the Tate Gallery for £850. It hung in the Royal Pavilion during several Ascot weeks and was eventually loaned to Windsor Castle.

Munnings showed another Ascot picture among his six Academy exhibits that year. It was *The Royal Carriage waiting for Their Majesties at Duke's Lane, Windsor Park, on Ascot Gold Cup Day.* However, none of the three royal pictures in the Academy that year brought Munnings as much satisfaction as a more modest little painting hung for a second time. It was *Kilkenny Horse Fair*, first accepted for the 1923 Academy but which was shown there again, as his Diploma picture, and achieved for him his highest ambition: on Derby Day, 1926, he was elected an RA. The election was a dead heat between him and Sir Walter Russell and Munnings received the President's casting vote.

He went to Spain to celebrate and, for once, travelled without his painting equipment. His companions were two Australians: the artist and art critic, Lionel (later Sir Lionel) Lindsay, who had persuaded him to make the trip, and the architect, Bertrand Waterhouse, who found Munnings 'a mercurial and unpredictable travelling companion'. They visited Madrid to see paintings by Munnings's favourite artist Velasquez, Toledo to see the El Grecos, and back to Madrid. There in the Prado, Munnings was lost in admiration before a Goya which, he considered, was the best painting of a nude in the world.

Then he saw his first bullfight, which upset him for the rest of his trip: 'Oh, little white horse! Little white horse!' he repeated in anguish after he had seen a white horse blindfolded for the fight, its ears stuffed with tow, its neck impaled on a bull's horn, dragged slowly round the ring while blood poured down its white jaw and neck. Finally, it was detached from the bull and beaten until it staggered to its feet again:

> It was stamping on its own entrails, which stretched and split like pink tissue paper [he wrote to Violet].
>
> Poor little once-useful horse, glad to work for only what it was given to eat – which had helped a human earn his food too: and this was its end – a victim to a roaring holiday crowd.

He was sickened again at the sight of a bay horse waiting to enter the ring, 'its teeth chattering with fear, having been in the ring before'. It was thrown by the bull but whipped to its feet again by the attendants. 'There, from the under-part of its belly,' he wrote, 'hung a large protuberance of bowels.... Not a soul cared, excepting ourselves. That I'll swear.'

The passionate horse-lover was revolted and bewildered by such sights. Nevertheless, his holiday from painting had served its purpose according to a letter to Violet, written on his birthday:

> Dear Violet,
>
> You will get this just after I have lived 48 years – awful ... I shall feel like work after all this. It only needs a change like this to make me realise that I shall always paint. But I want now to do *the* work – out of doors.
>
> Toledo was wonderful. So is Wharfedale in Yorkshire, or anywhere – if it comes to that.
>
> Love, much of it.
>
> A.J.

Confirmation, that he was at his best when he was left to paint exactly where he liked, came in an authoritative book of reproductions of one hundred and thirty-five of his finest paintings. It contained a perceptive appreciation by his friend and travelling companion in Spain, Lionel Lindsay. 'His imagination will not work confined to the four walls of a room,' Lindsay stated. 'It demands sky and meadows, the clouds moving, trees and water, and the magic of light.'

The book was published in 1927 and brought Munnings flattering recognition. In it, he was described as 'a portraitist of horses, plainly without rival'. Lindsay continued:

> The gypsy series must be appreciated with the best of modern masterpieces.... His truth is that finer aspect of realism which is dominated by a prevailing sky; those chanceful and mysterious effects of lighting which come swiftly to the artist only after long years of observation and practice.... To have found one's art in the texture of one's life, and embroidered upon it, in technical mastery, fresh and original design, is tantamount to a definition of genius.

'*The* work out of doors', which he had intended to do in the country, was not to be. Thanks to Violet, he was soon involved in a string of lucrative commissions and, as a result of the Royal Ascot pictures, he was invited to paint another big royal occasion, *The Presentation of New Standards to the Household Cavalry by H.M. King George V*. The ceremony was in June. He described it as 'a sight for the gods . . . . Black horses, burnished steel cuirasses, plumed helmets and swords, glittering in the morning sun. The bright light with the strains of martial music glorifying the pompous ceremony – the blazonary [sic] of colour; and, beyond all, the march up the Mall to the Palace of the massed bands of the Life and Horse Guards, on grey horses, leading the way with music which smote the soul.'

He caught the mood of the occasion in words but found it a far more tortuous process to grasp in paint. Despite his slight visual memory, he usually made little use of sketchbook notes. His practice was to paint from life – putting his own interpretation on everything he saw. Therefore, to paint a grand identifiable spectacle was a complicated process.

After the Presentation of New Standards ceremony, he persuaded the Admiralty to fly flags from their windows, similar to the half-a-dozen or so flown from Buckingham Palace, for him to copy. He went to the Barracks, day after day, to make studies of the horses, the standard-bearers, the colours, and the band and their instruments, although the latter were barely discernible in his picture. An officer, wearing a uniform similar to the King's, posed on the King's chestnut charger.

His racing pictures came more naturally for every movement of any type of horse was indelibly engraved on his mind. For many of his larger racing pictures, he arranged for his three grooms each to have a day at the races so that they became as imbued with the subject as he. At the race meetings, he made rough sketches of the scenes he wanted to paint and afterwards used his own horses as models, supplemented by ones he borrowed from friendly trainers along with their jockeys wearing sets of colours. He returned, again and again, to courses such as Epsom and Sandown to paint, as backgrounds, the appropriate stretch of course, the stands and even the old number boards. Such composite pictures were given a unity and freshness by his inimitable sweeps of wide skies and brightly shadowed turf.

Similarly, he painted Princess Mary, Countess of Harewood, and the Earl of Harewood in his London studio, and afterwards added the horses, the Bramham Moor Hounds and the wild Yorkshire countryside.

His studies of hunters and famous racehorses, with or without their equally famous owners, were endless. As a result, the pattern of his life-style changed dramatically and although, now and again, a river scene intruded, for nearly three decades, no studies of gypsies hung in the Academy.

Occasionally there were compensations when he relished life to the full. Without exception, this reflected to advantage in his painting. For instance, he rated his portrait of the Earl of Birkenhead (F. E. Smith), a Lord Chancellor of England, as probably his best portrait of a man on horseback. This was possibly because he took so much pleasure in his stay at Birkenhead's country home, Charlton Manor, Oxfordshire. 'The conditions were right, the family right, three times over. A wonderful circle,' he enthused.

There was a long-term sequel to his fine study of the dark-haired Birkenhead, wearing a yellow jersey and white breeches, astride a large roan-coloured war veteran. The sitter made him a member of the small exclusive dining society known as 'The Other Club', which he and Winston Churchill had founded in 1911. Membership was confined to fifty, only half of whom could be Members of Parliament.

Dinners were held in a private room at the Savoy Hotel where Munnings, after an initial welcome from Churchill, found himself from time to time in the company of Sir Edwin Lutyens, H. G. Wells, Lord Gort, Duff Cooper, A. E. W. Mason, Gordon Selfridge and his wartime friend, General 'Jack' Seely. He soon made his mark. E. V. Lucas described him as 'a vivid devil' and Arnold Bennett noted in his diary that he was a very considerable reader and a reader of verse and talked well.

Munnings still kept in touch with his Lamorna friends to whom he was always 'A.J.', and when Lamorna Birch was elected an Associate of the Royal Academy, he gave a dinner for him at the Garrick Club. It was a happy reunion for 'A.J.' had invited all Birch's friends from Cornwall. Unfortunately he had forgotten to send an invitation to the guest of honour until it was too late and Birch had gone to a dinner at the Chelsea Arts Club. However, his friends at the Garrick drank his health until the small hours.

Harold and Laura Knight were among the guests. For several years Munnings had, unsuccessfully, put Laura's name forward as an Associate of the Royal Academy. In 1927, when she was in rather low spirits, she was elected and was only the second woman ARA. Munnings telephoned her the news before her official notification and invited her and Harold to join him at a party at the Whitney-Smiths that evening.

They arrived to find Munnings already installed in his favourite role of court jester, standing in the centre of the room, reciting his own poems and telling stories about Laura in their Newlyn days. 'A.J. was in his best form,' Laura recalled. 'He had a performer's talent; he might have made a success on platform or stage, even as he had made in the painting world.'

Harold had not then been made an Associate. No doubt he found it hard to conceal his humiliation at being surpassed by a wife who, as a fifteen-year-old girl, had stood behind him at art school and copied his every line and brush stroke.

Now it was Munnings who helped Laura's work. He took her to the circus at Olympia and introduced her to Bertram Mills, whose wife had been a childhood friend of his. Mills invited Laura to paint there and her circus pictures were among the most popular of her paintings. She joined Munnings's party at Epsom Races and, although she was not interested in painting racehorses, she returned to Epsom several times to paint the gypsies. They fascinated her almost as much as they did Munnings. Munnings was completely relaxed in her company. He introduced her to Orpen and later, discussing the meeting with her, said Orpen had thought she was lovely. 'That was funny,' 'A.J.' said, 'I never thought you were lovely.'

As far as Alfred Munnings RA was concerned, half a century of life was a good time for stock-taking and there could be no better place to trace the development of his work than in Norwich, the city of his adoption. In 1928 nearly three hundred of his pictures, representing all stages of his career, were shown in a loan exhibition at the Castle Museum. It proved the most popular art occasion in England since 1911, when 100,000 people had queued in London to see Rembrandt's *Mill*. In Norwich, 86,000 visited the Munnings Exhibition in six weeks.

It was the largest Exhibition the Castle Museum had ever had and it took three weeks to prepare. The walls of the galleries were distempered Munnings's favourite shade of grey. Eighty-five-year-old Eddie Martin, then little more than a boy, helped his father to hang the pictures and recalled how everyone, including Frank Leney, the curator, was shocked by the way the painter cleaned a picture which had arrived in a dirty condition. 'The experts would have dabbed it with a little of this and a little of that,' he said, 'and we should have given it special treatment. Munnings just picked it up, went into the kitchen and found a pail and scrub brush and a piece of carbolic soap and set to. I remember he didn't like the way one of the pictures was hung and said to Leney, "Never do that. Never put two pictures together so that one horse is smelling the other's arse."'

The Exhibition contained nearly two hundred oils compared to thirty-seven watercolours, but the following year Munnings was made a full member of the Royal Society of Painters in Water Colours.

Before the civic opening, a lunch was given at the Maid's Head Hotel; among the guests were several of Munnings's friends including Sir Edwin Lutyens, Mr Arnesby Brown and Mr Locker-Lampson. Munnings's speech of thanks was uncharacteristically grateful, and characteristically modest, and was very different from the next speech he would make in the city on a civic occasion.

'The only fortunate thing was that they were varied,' he said of the kaleidoscope of landscapes, gypsy paintings, racehorses with jockeys in glowing silks, portraits of the famous on horseback and – to show how it all began – cracker-box lids, advertisements and two pictures done at Mendham when he was twelve-years-old. He expressed his gratitude to the city by presenting the Museum with a large version of Augereau in *The Gravel Pit*.

The critics eulogized about his works: they traced the influence of Cotman and Crome in his untutored freshness of vision; of Gainsborough and Constable with whom, they said, he shared the great East Anglian 'nursery of Art'; of Stubbs and Sargent whom he so admired; and the early influence of La Thangue, the close communicator with nature, in the many ways he recorded light breaking across shadows. His mastery of line and colour was compared to that of Degas.

The pictures had been assembled with great difficulty from civic and private collections in England and overseas. The Birmingham Corporation were reluctant to lend the *Arrival at Epsom Downs for Derby Week* during a holiday season, and the Duchess of Westminster only allowed the portrait of her riding with the harriers to leave her home providing the artist lent her another of his pictures to take its place.

Munnings had mixed memories about that painting. He had painted the well-built Duchess in the ballroom at Eaton where, every few minutes, she had got down from the saddle horse and made suggestions about the painting. She complained that Munnings was making her too stout. He disagreed but altered the picture several times to please her, allowed her to change her bowler for a velvet cap and, when she could not decide whether to wear a crimson coat or a pale blue one, painted two versions of the picture. He did not demur when she said her eyelashes were not dark enough and drew them in herself with a soft, dark pencil. He was always vulnerable where handsome women who handled fine horses well were concerned.

The Duke was highly discerning: 'Mr Stubbs,' he said when he saw the picture, 'the women have been getting at you.'

The art critic of the *Eastern Daily Press* selected the painting as 'one of the greatest gems of the exhibition,' and noted, 'The influence of George Stubbs on the artist is here to be distinctly noticed. This picture has probably more poetry and grace in it than any other work in the collection.'

A frequent visitor to the exhibition was a tall pale eighteen-year-old local boy who was too delicate to go to school and whose only motive in life was to paint. Edward Seago, the youngest disciple of 'the East Anglian nursery' of painters, was virtually self-taught and until then had never studied the work of an artist who had achieved fame and financial reward in his own lifetime. The effect on him was overwhelming. Eighteen months later at his first London exhibition, several critics detected the influence of Munnings in his choice of subjects and in his technique. 'See, he's even put in Mr Munnings's buttercups,' was a scathing comment from one visitor.

As soon as the exhibition closed, Seago contrived an introduction to Munnings, and drove over regularly to Dedham for practical advice from the man who had hitherto been a name for him to conjure with and whose hard-riding life-style was a local legend.

When, soon afterwards, 'the promising young painter', as the local press described Seago, had a picture of children and ponies accepted by the Royal Academy, Munnings felt impelled to try and cut him down to size. He was disgusted because Seago had had no formal training in drawing or painting:

> Walk right into the Academy (on Varnishing Day) with your ticket and don't faint when you see how awful your picture looks .... You are already getting beyond the youthful years when the young brain absorbs easily and learns quickly. Begin to be a serious student and let all business of *young* Seago and young genius go and during years to come you'll possibly make a hit.
>
> Don't be misled even by having this picture here in the R.A. It was out and only got in by the smallest chance and then only allowed to go up there because I pleaded for it.

He urged Seago to take art lessons and reminded him of the long studentship and years of learning of Velasquez, Rubens and Rembrandt and of the Italian artists.

> You have now to begin and learn something and from now until the end of this term you ought to go in to Norwich School and work there ... for God's sake go and do some real study and shake the dust of utter ignorance off your feet .... If your father thinks you ought to be making a few pounds, show him my letter .... Let him understand that he has to make a student of you for a while and not a young pot boiler [sic].

The postscript carried an extra warning, perhaps to forestall any local adulation that might mitigate the advice of the wily letter writer. It read: 'Don't regard what folk in Norfolk say at all. They know *nothing* of art. They think they do.'

Seago took Munnings's advice to the extent of going to one term of evening classes at Norwich School of Art. Then, with a headstrong independence equal to Munnings's own, he followed in the older man's footsteps and painted many of the same equestrian portraits, including Lord Derby's winner, Hyperion, and Princess Mary at Newmarket, but at half the price.

He even contrived to become friendly with John Masefield and collaborated with him on several books of poems and pictures. The influence of Munnings was so strong that it took Edward Seago many years to discover his own painting identity.

Meanwhile, at his half century, Munnings himself received a salutary warning from Violet. A birthday greeting on his breakfast table read:

> *Half a century* hath thy flesh and bones lived and partaken of the joys and ills of this life. BE THOU CAREFUL that thou abuseth not the good health the Blessed Lord hath given thee!
>
> Go thou unto thy Club seven times seven, but be not carried away by thy *generous* heart. Thou orderest wine in abundance to pour down the gullets of thy guests, but, oh, Alfred, I pray thee pour it not down thine own gullet.
>
> . . . Were I to pass to another world, where the cares of an artist are unknown, who would then take care of thee – thy finance, thy household, thy health and thy belongings? Go thee more to the country to inhale God's pure air . . . .
>
> Yet your wife, who married thee for companionship, raileth not at thee; for life is full of compensations. Therefore, O husband, I am content to come second to thy Art and work and revelry upon this earth, and while there is time *Take Heed!*

Munnings probably accepted the truth of her words, but the conflict between painting for money and painting the things he loved was insurmountable. Drink eased the frustration and kept at bay the underlying depression. His gout worsened and he grew irritable and careless of what Violet and the world thought about him, as distinct from his paintings, although he was momentarily cheered by reports of the success of the first American exhibition of his paintings in the Howard Young Galleries in New York.

Violet confided her thoughts to her blue notebook and wrote her advice on marriage 'for the daughter I have not'. The sad and bitter writing in pencil was headed: 'The Thoughts of a Woman of No Importance – Yet, in a way, In Touch with King Solomon':

> Be thou, my daughter, careful whom thou chooseth for thy life's partner, for a loser can he never remain. A party to thy household must he always be. A man about thee, be he good or bad, is he better than no man about thee?

Shouldst thou obtain a husband who riseth and eateth his breakfast in peace, read thee items from the morning paper, walk the dog (and if wet weather dry his feet) or tell the hour of his returneth to his house for luncheon and dineth only at his club 4 times in the week and returneth before 3 or 4 a.m., thou art lucky.

And who at Xmas will taketh thee to a theatre, and admire or even notice, the dress thou hath taken hours at night (while thou waitest up to count the cuckoo [clock] notes on his return), to fashion, and at times of dire concern wilt honour thee by taking thee to the dullest restaurant, per chance Scotts, where he enjoys the food and readest the evening paper between courses. Then thou art indeed blessed, who always letteth thee know his movements, who giveth thee the privilege to pay the bills with his money, keep his accounts, run his house and at times of stress, cook and wait upon his guests, drive his car and generally make thyself useful, then again thou art a lucky woman.

But supposeth thou findest thyself with a made man who giveth not these privileges. Then do, I say unto thee, part with him not, for at all times he hath his uses. His hat alone in the hall giveth thee a degree of standing to all callers, impresseth the gasman, enchanteth the canvasser and enthraleth all thy rogue friends. And, my daughter, what thou hast shalt thou hold, for when thou reachest the years of blessed experience, thou wilt fold thy hands and say unto thyself 'Life is full of compensations.'

CHAPTER XIII

Art and Domesticity

'They had daily battles, she wanting her way and he wanting his,' said an honest naive, unbiased witness to life in the Munnings household in the early thirties. She was the housekeeper's surprisingly articulate and intelligent daughter, a sixteen-year-old parlourmaid, Marjorie Coppin, who Munnings, eventually, wanted to adopt.

'At first I tried to please Mrs Munnings,' she wrote in her unpublished memoirs, 'but he got so annoyed and would keep on about it that, slowly and surely, he got his own way which made her cross with me.... He often shielded me from his wife and I began to realize that he was not the bully I thought at first, but kind and generous.' Munnings taught Marjorie to wait at table and instructed her even during dinner parties. He made her feel important, she said, by telling the guests: 'Marjorie is going to wait on us this evening,' and they all looked on and smiled.

The dinner parties he gave were always particularly pleasant, in her opinion, when Mrs Munnings was away at their Exmoor cottage for three months. 'At one dinner party,' she recalled, 'Mr Munnings suddenly exclaimed: "I wonder whose arses will be sitting on these chairs when I am gone." There was a moment's silence and I, being young, felt quite embarrassed for him, nearly dropping the dish in my hand.'

At that dinner, she recalled, they had an especially good juicy melon for dessert. After the guests had retired to the drawing room Mr Munnings came back and told her to take the rest of the melon out to the kitchen and have as much as she liked, but just leave him a small piece for breakfast. She was busy and did not take it to the kitchen immediately. He came back again, saying "You take that melon out and have some." There was no peace,' she wrote, 'until we had that melon. He had a very strong determined manner and what he wanted done had to be done.'

> Both the Munnings were very strong-willed people with clashing opinions, [she wrote] never in agreement. He was domineering and must have his own way in everything. He was in charge of the management and running of the house and those working there relied on him to say what should be done. When Mrs Munnings gave orders to Mother she nearly always began by saying: 'Mr Munnings wants . . .' He did the shopping in Dedham Village on horseback and delighted in giving everybody orders from the saddle.
>
> I had a good deal of running about to do answering their bells. His wife would ring for something and he would enjoy contradicting her. This often happened at a dinner party to the amusement of the guests. Once, she called for a lemon, cut and squeezed, but he said, 'No, we want it whole.' So it continued, with contradictions all through the dinner, making the meal quite farcical.

Marjorie recalled Mrs Munnings's frequent outbursts of temper with everyone in the house. Munnings, then, was always on the alert in case Marjorie and her mother were upset, and often shielded them from such eruptions. 'When they had an argument he rushed through the house, slamming doors behind him. . . . Fundamentally, he was kind-hearted, generous and thoughtful towards us. When he wanted something done personally, he would ask in a quiet, charming manner, sometimes winking his eye and would end up saying: "There's a dear," especially when wanting a really hot bottle put in his bed and expecting it to be hot when he came in late.'

Marjorie recognized that Violet Munnings's three little dogs were permanent causes of contention because he did not like them soiling the carpets or leaving their hairs on the chairs. Violet liked to have the dogs in her room at night so she and Munnings had separate bedrooms. 'I sensed he had protective, parental qualities,' Marjorie wrote. 'He liked children, particularly girls. With his love of life, of animals and people, he gave the impression he would have been a happy family man.' Perhaps the young housemaid had hit at the root of one of Munnings's many frustrations.

Mrs Coppin, in the end, gave notice and she and Marjorie were about to leave when Mrs Munnings went into the kitchen one morning and told them Mr Munnings wanted to adopt Marjorie. He was going to make all the necessary arrangements, for he thought he could give the child a better life than she would have with her mother, who had separated from her father, a solicitor's clerk.

> Mother was very taken aback.... Mrs Munnings told me that I would have the room next to her bedroom and described some of the clothes I would have.
>
> This was the way of Munnings; he swept the ground from under your feet with his swift decisions, without consulting anyone. He thought to help us, but he had given us no previous hint.
>
> However, Mother did not want to have me adopted and we eventually left their employment for good. I sometimes look back with nostalgia on that period of my young life and wonder what it would have been like had Munnings adopted me.

In her memoirs, Marjorie Coppin also looked back on musical evenings, when Munnings entertained his guests by firelight and played the piano in the drawing room or the gramophone in the library.

However, her unique insight into the home life of Violet and Alfred Munnings made scant reference to the main interest they had in common, their love of horses. Alfred, perhaps subconsciously, stressed it when he named a self-portrait, with Violet on horseback, *Our Mutual Friend*. It showed the painter standing nonchalantly by the front door of Castle House, watching Violet on a horse he had bred called Master Munn. In the 1935 Royal Academy, the picture's original name was changed to *My Wife, My Horse and Myself*. He painted several versions of it over the next twenty years, for it probably appealed to his ego to be seen in such an elegant ambience. The version in the 1953 Academy was shown as *Our Mutual Friend the Horse*, with Violet on a different horse, Rufus. Two years later another version was there as *The Bay Horse and Ourselves*. The paintings displayed to the world a satisfactory and affluent life-style.

Meanwhile, as Munnings worked on preliminary studies for *Our Mutual Friend*, his 'best equestrian open-air portrait', as he described it, hung in the 1931 Royal Academy. It showed Princess

Mary, Countess of Harewood, on a grey horse, given to her as a wedding present by the Women of Ireland. The painting was probably successful because the conditions were ideal. The horse – of his favourite grey colour – and the rider were painted together, in the open air, in perfect weather.

He stayed at Egerton House, the Newmarket home of the Earl and Countess of Harewood, during a Spring Meeting, and every morning, after breakfast, the Princess rode the grey to the spot the painter had chosen in a woodland ride and posed for him against a leafy background. The portrait was completed in three sittings, on three consecutive mornings. There had been no question of using a saddle horse or painting horse and rider separately. 'No horse could have stood better – no sitter was more patient,' Munnings commented. His satisfaction soon turned to unhappiness on a Spanish visit to paint the American ambassador, the Hon. Irwin Laughlin, and his son and daughter. The glare of the Spanish sunlight hurt his eye and he worked only on grey days; the 'wonderful dry sherry' and liberal draughts of champagne and brandy brought on a bad attack of gout and he was literally sickened by the side effects of the antidote colchicum. He was also mentally sickened by bull fighting tales at dinner. Eventually, he caught a chill and spent five days in bed. 'Never was I so tired of work,' he wrote to Violet. 'Those pictures got on my nerves.'

He was happier when he moved to Biarritz to spend a week with Edward Baron, of Carreras fame, in a rented luxury villa. Baron had invited Munnings to stay when the artist painted his two daughters in England, earlier in the summer. In Biarritz, Munnings ran into his old friend, Frederick Prince, the American millionaire, whose equestrian portrait and a companion one of his wife, he had painted in New England.

He told Prince he was exhausted and the exuberant American managed to bolster him up. 'He says there is nothing I can't do – that I'm *the* man,' Alfred wrote to Violet, his enthusiasm renewed. Prince had suggested that as Munnings had spent his life messing about trying to paint people on horses he might, for a change, before he died, try to paint people *off* horses and invited him to start with him and his wife. A few days later, Munnings moved into the Hôtel du Palais as Prince's guest.

'It is like an Arabian Nights' tale,' he wrote to Violet, 'whatever

I ask for I can have.' He asked for a large room on the third floor for a studio and a model's 'throne' made from four, empty, whisky cases, covered with a green baize table-top. He was given a new easel, canvases, brushes and oil and varnish. Mrs Prince, meanwhile, had boxes of dresses sent from Paris for him to choose what she should wear.

He planned a full-length, Zoffany-style portrait of the 'dear, dilettante, well-preserved lady' nearing seventy, and suggested she should be painted in a champagne-coloured silk gown shot with grey, 'quite thirty yards round the hem'.

Her first sitting set the pattern: she arrived two hours late, followed by her maid carrying a basket of purple figs and a cup of chocolate on a silver tray. Munnings told her, in no uncertain terms, that she must arrive in time for her sittings. She was quite unperturbed. 'There could only be one Mrs Prince in the world,' he wrote resignedly. '. . . I lived on purple figs!'

After four sittings they all moved to the Ritz in Paris: 'What wealth can do is surprising to me,' he wrote to Violet after travelling in a railway compartment which Mrs Prince's maid had lined with white sheets to protect her mistress's clothes from being soiled.

He toured the Ritz with the *mâitre d'hôtel*, but could not find a room with a northern light for a studio. 'Munnings, go anywhere – to the Meurice – to the Chatham, so long as you get your good north light,' his host told him. He finally chose a ground-floor reception room in the magnificent old-world Hôtel D'Orsay, with two north-facing windows overlooking the Seine.

He finished the portrait of Mrs Prince there and started one of her husband sitting in an old French chair, his black cape thrown over the arm. Both portraits had an imaginary background of a colonnaded terrace. More impressive than either, however, was a study of husband and wife playing patience at a card table under a glittering chandelier. It was unfinished when the Princes left for a ten-day visit to America, and it was arranged that Prince's brother, Charles, would sit in Prince's place, while a Worth mannequin would deputize for Mrs Prince. Munnings could not resist using the young girl's beautiful arms in the picture instead of Mrs Prince's.

'My most hearty congratulations on your masterpiece, my dear Munnings – not for a long time have I seen a picture that gave me such pleasure,' wrote Sir John Lavery after the conversation piece had been reproduced in the *Sporting and Dramatic*.

> ... for a subtle piece of portraiture it would be hard to match his conversation piece [wrote the Australian etcher, water-colourist and critic, Norman Lindsay]. Both sitters are perfectly revealed: Mr Prince, handsome, dignified, capable and altogether a gentleman; Mrs Prince, a Narcissus self-absorbent; an American millionaire's wife, so petted that she is able to gratify her every whim, whose progress through life is rather more regal than that of a Royal princess.

Munnings had found it a pleasant exercise but he preferred to stick to horses as subjects to paint.

He returned to England to find an invitation waiting from Lord Mottistone, formerly General Seely, to illustrate his book, *My Horse Warrior*, the story of his twenty-six-year-old charger. The painter stayed at Mottistone's Isle of Wight home, Mottistone Manor, for several weeks and produced eighteen illustrations. His host wrote of the study of Warrior's head: 'The likeness is so striking, the expression so true, that I confess it moves me deeply.'

When Munnings, fresh from Prince's impressive generosity, raised the question of payment, Mottistone was taken aback. 'I made you,' he reminded him bluntly. 'I started you off on royal equestrian portraits with the work you did with the Canadians.' Munnings dropped the matter.

Later, Mottistone described the book to a friend and was genuinely amazed to learn that Munnings's fee, at that time, could have been enormous. He took the first opportunity to rectify matters. He was dining at The Other Club one night, sitting opposite to Munnings and Lord Moyne, who were commiserating with each other about their gout. Munnings was in the throes of a particularly bad attack and Mottistone invited him, then and there, to be his guest at Bad Ems Spa where he went regularly for treatment for his bronchitis.

In mid-August, Munnings joined Mottistone and his youngest daughter, Louise, at the Romerbad Hotel on the banks of the narrow River Lahn, before it joins the Rhine. Every afternoon, Mottistone booked the only available sailing dinghy. Once, it got out of control in a half gale and ploughed up the soft bank on to a meadow, reminding Munnings of his boyhood days on the River

Waveney. 'Lord M. is a wonder,' he wrote to Violet. 'He makes something happen every day.'

Every morning both men took the cure and, in the evenings, counteracted any benefit by drinking under the trees in Coblenz village square and listened to the music of the band dressed in their national costume, on the bandstand.

> My father gave the impression of being a very wealthy man, which he wasn't [Louise, later the Hon. Mrs Charles Fletcher, explained]. He felt obliged to treat Munnings to this fantastically expensive trip. They were put on a diet and told not to drink, but every evening we dined at wonderful restaurants on the banks of the Rhine.
>
> Munnings was very sentimental. He and my father were so moved by a German singer that they both sat there with tears running down their cheeks. While Munnings was with us, he heard that his dog had died and he went to his room and cried.

Munnings wrote to Violet: 'I feel so utterly sad to think I shan't see that dear dog again that I can't keep from tears. I can hardly see to read the paper. It was all because you said there is more room in the car now without him. What a fool I am....' That letter contained his only reference to the death of Florence: 'I went through a hundred times worse happenings than that and it still stops me dead in what I'm doing when I remember it all. Terrible.' He tried to console Violet about the dog's death: 'We must make the best of it and carry on and there it is. You might have had children who might have gone wrong or died even.!' Did he realize that the assortment of dogs with which Violet surrounded herself could have been her substitute for children?

The thermal baths gave Munnings time to reflect. He forgot the fun of the afternoons and, at times, was submerged in gloom. In another letter to Violet he wrote:

> This accursed gout upsets all my life. Nobody has gone on longer at such work than I have.... No more of those jobs. *Never* again. I'm ready to live simply and do as I wish. My sight isn't anything like so good as it was and *well* I know it.
>
> I detest all the surroundings of Castle House – I do indeed. It's alright [sic] on a late night in July with a moon....
>
> The two pretty watercolours are good and I don't want to sell them – the last time I was happy when painting. [Violet

> was disposing of some of his pictures.] The sound of the water, the lovely spot and all about it gave me pleasant hours. I used to sit there and paint quietly with the hours fleeting by and I loved it ....
>
> My *best* days have been painting quiet landscapes and motoring with you and seeing places .... You said you didn't think you'd been much of a success as a wife. Think how you've looked after one thing – the money side .... I'm *thankful* for all you've done. Your good influence and sweet kindness have been an endless source of wonder to me. I can't be good.

Suddenly there was a mood swing. His gout was better, the sun shone and he was ready to go home. He wrote to Violet: 'My feet are right down. I feel *very* well – never better and no exaggeration ....' He added he was so glad he had a good home to go to. There would be more visits to Bad Ems; his doctor was 'the nicest and kindest of men' and Mottistone was 'far nicer and kinder than I had dreamt any man could be'. He had paid the doctor's bill, as well as the hotel one, and had also paid for a box of cigars for Munnings. His daughter was the 'nicest sweetest child'.

Twenty-one-year-old Louise thought Munnings 'inspiring company'. So did many women. The country lad had become something of a ladies' man, happy in the company of attractive women, who responded to his charisma with a warmth the matter-of-fact Violet never showed.

Alfred Munnings returned from Germany to face a new and exciting challenge; an invitation from Sir Harold Wernher to make a bronze statuette of his illustrious racehorse, Brown Jack. The horse was one of the most famous stayers in English racing history. He had won the Queen Alexandra Stakes at Ascot six years running and his owner decided to present a bronze of him and his jockey, Steve Donoghue, to Ascot. Sir Harold discussed the idea with Lord Hamilton of Dalzell, the King's representative at Ascot and a former Senior Steward of the Jockey Club, who consulted the Newmarket trainer, George Lambton, about the best sculptor for the job. He was advised to see the Edward Horner Memorial in Mells Church. They looked no further than Munnings's bronze statuette of horse and rider.

Brown Jack arrived at Castle House for a six weeks' stay, long

7. Canadian Cavalry Brigade on the March

Early in 1918 Munnings was sent to France as an official war artist attached to the Canadian Cavalry Brigade. Lord Mottistone described his paintings, close to the front line, as 'some of the most brilliant things he has ever done'.

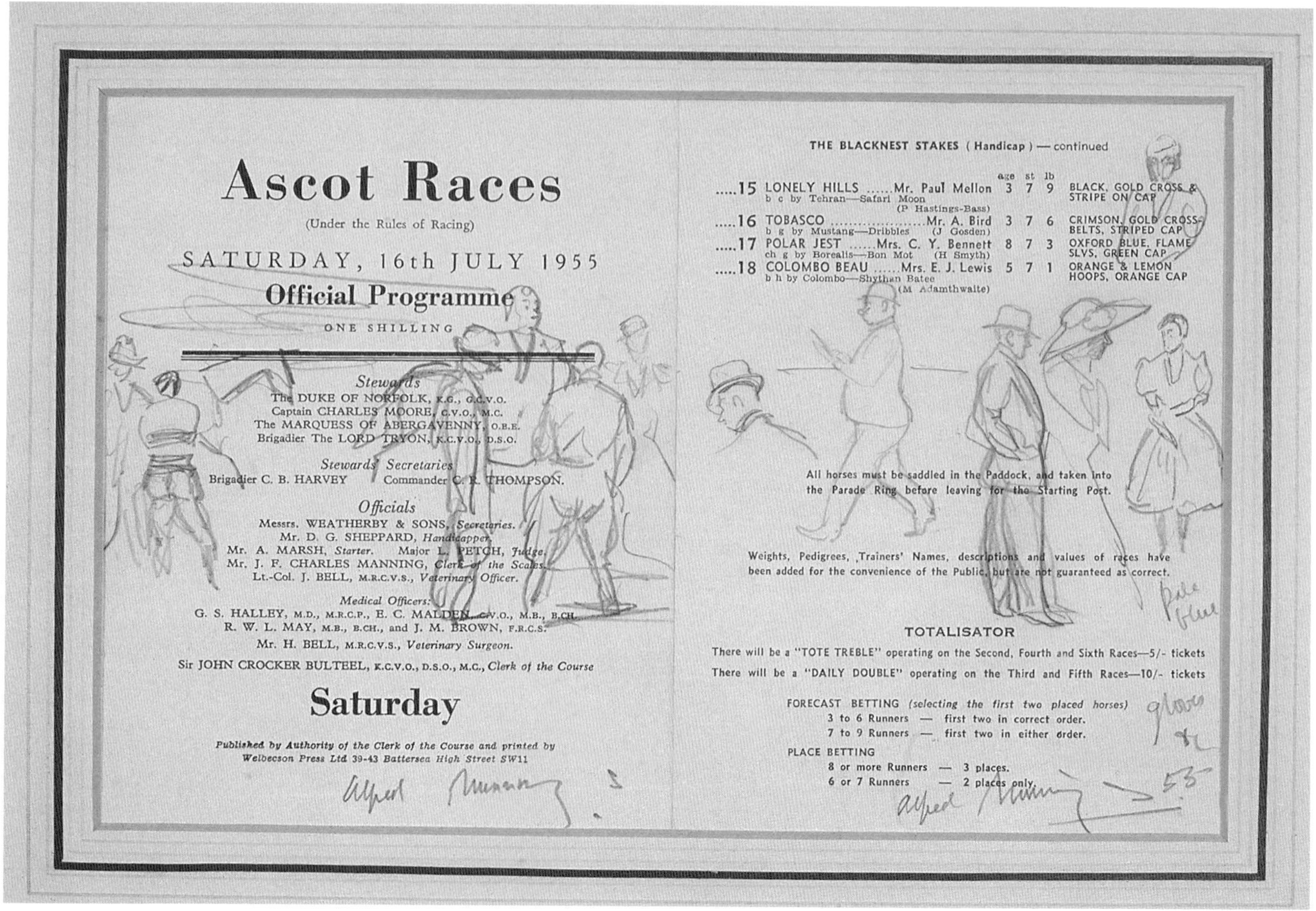

Ascot Races

(Under the Rules of Racing)

SATURDAY, 16th JULY 1955

Official Programme

ONE SHILLING

Stewards

The DUKE OF NORFOLK, K.G., G.C.V.O.
Captain CHARLES MOORE, C.V.O., M.C.
The MARQUESS OF ABERGAVENNY, O.B.E.
Brigadier The LORD TRYON, K.C.V.O., D.S.O.

Stewards' Secretaries

Brigadier C. B. HARVEY Commander C. R. THOMPSON.

Officials

Messrs. WEATHERBY & SONS, *Secretaries.*
Mr. D. G. SHEPPARD, *Handicapper.*
Mr. A. MARSH, *Starter.* Major L. PETCH, *Judge.*
Mr. J. F. CHARLES MANNING, *Clerk of the Scales.*
Lt.-Col. J. BELL, M.R.C.V.S., *Veterinary Officer.*

Medical Officers:

G. S. HALLEY, M.D., M.R.C.P., E. C. MALDEN, C.V.O., M.B., B.CH.
R. W. L. MAY, M.B., B.CH., and J. M. BROWN, F.R.C.S.
Mr. H. BELL, M.R.C.V.S., *Veterinary Surgeon.*

Sir JOHN CROCKER BULTEEL, K.C.V.O., D.S.O., M.C., *Clerk of the Course*

Saturday

Published by Authority of the Clerk of the Course and printed by Welbecson Press Ltd 39-43 Battersea High Street SW11

THE BLACKNEST STAKES (Handicap) — continued

			age	st	lb	
.....15	LONELY HILLS ......Mr. Paul Mellon b c by Tehran—Safari Moon (P Hastings-Bass)		3	7	9	BLACK, GOLD CROSS & STRIPE ON CAP
.....16	TOBASCO ....Mr. A. Bird b g by Mustang—Dribbles (J Gosden)		3	7	6	CRIMSON, GOLD CROSS-BELTS, STRIPED CAP
.....17	POLAR JEST ......Mrs. C. Y. Bennett ch g by Borealis—Bon Mot (H Smyth)		8	7	3	OXFORD BLUE, FLAME SLVS, GREEN CAP
.....18	COLOMBO BEAU ......Mrs. E. J. Lewis b h by Colombo—Shythan Batee (M Adamthwaite)		5	7	1	ORANGE & LEMON HOOPS, ORANGE CAP

All horses must be saddled in the Paddock, and taken into the Parade Ring before leaving for the Starting Post.

Weights, Pedigrees, Trainers' Names, descriptions and values of races have been added for the convenience of the Public, but are not guaranteed as correct.

TOTALISATOR

There will be a "TOTE TREBLE" operating on the Second, Fourth and Sixth Races—5/- tickets

There will be a "DAILY DOUBLE" operating on the Third and Fifth Races—10/- tickets

FORECAST BETTING *(selecting the first two placed horses)*
3 to 6 Runners — first two in correct order.
7 to 9 Runners — first two in either order.

PLACE BETTING
8 or more Runners — 3 places.
6 or 7 Runners — 2 places only.

8. Ascot Race Card

Whenever Munnings saw a fine example of a racing scene, he would sketch it on whatever paper was to hand.

enough for Munnings to get to love him as well as sculpt him. 'What a horse was this!' Munnings wrote. 'Wise head, kind eyes, large ears, magnificent shoulders – quite the most difficult problem I have ever tackled.' In tackling it, Munnings made a detailed study of the horse's anatomy, did many drawings, and discovered and portrayed the 'most unassuming, kind and modest horse-character' that ever lived.

Throughout his stay Brown Jack had early morning gallops round a forty-acre field to keep him in trim for the portrait. Munnings also did a painting for his owner and, when Brown Jack went home, the artist complained that no human being could have left such a gap as the horse left at Dedham.

The statuette was so true to life that Sir Harold abandoned his original idea of adding the jockey. Brown Jack, standing alone, should speak for himself. Every June the statuette* stands in the Royal Enclosure on the Friday of Ascot week, when the Queen Alexandra Stakes is run, and at the July Meeting, for the Brown Jack Stakes. It shows the character of a champion, and knowledgeable horse-lovers can learn more from it about the unique animal than experts at the Natural History Museum learned when they examined his skeleton after his death. That showed nothing out of the ordinary.

The Ascot Meetings held nothing like the attraction for Munnings that Epsom, with the gypsies, did or the smaller and more intimate meetings at Newmarket, Sandown or Hurst Park. 'Week after silly Ascot', he headed a letter to Violet from Cliveden, where he was painting an equestrian portrait of Lord Astor. The first sitting had to be abandoned because it poured with rain. Lord Astor arrived for the second sitting wearing a different coat, without a slit at the back, but Munnings could not be bothered to tell him. 'All you had to do,' said Lady Astor when she heard about it, 'was to take the big scissors from the harness-room and cut a slit there and then, right up the back of his coat.'

Munnings admired Nancy Astor tremendously. The first woman MP crowded as many celebrities round her dining table, at

* Five bronzes of Brown Jack were cast. Munnings kept two, one of which is on loan to the National Horse Museum at Newmarket and the other is at Castle House. Sir Harold Wernher kept one and gave one to Ascot. The fifth was sold by Munnings to a Scottish art dealer and later changed hands.

weekends, as possible. 'Thirty dishes served,' remarked Winston Churchill, 'and no damned room to eat one.'

Munnings finished the portrait in his Chelsea studio and wrote to Violet at Exmoor: 'It's all a b . . . r and makes me sure I'll *never* do it again. It reminds me of Ireland and years of such things.' How often had he threatened never to do another commissioned equestrian portrait!

Meanwhile, at Dedham he bought the Old Grammar School schoolroom and converted it into a studio measuring sixty feet by forty. 'The Dedham brook ran past it, lime trees stood about it. No man ever had a finer country studio,' he claimed.

He delighted, too, in the unspoilt view from the windows of his house. However, while he was abroad a builder received planning permission to erect a row of cottages there on a large plot of land and Munnings returned to see from his windows the new red-brick walls rising in the heart of Constable country. He bought the land and the partially-built cottages, irrespective of price, and had them pulled down.

In January 1936 King George V died and, soon afterwards, Munnings painted a posthumous portrait of him – the only posthumous portrait he ever made. It was commissioned by the Hon. Douglas Tollemache to give to the town of Ipswich. Munnings portrayed the late King on his white Highland garron, Jock, in Sandringham Park, with a view of Sandringham Church in the background. The King had been riding the pony there only six days before his death.

The painter stayed with a Norfolk farmer friend at Heacham and swore him to secrecy about the picture he was working on, as he did twenty-year-old Gerald Tealing, a local man, who drove him to and from Sandringham. He was afraid the press would make a big story if they found out.

The pony was ridden for the painting by French, the King's groom, dressed in his late master's homespun shooting suit, white spats and trilby. The devoted groom was determined the picture should be right and, at intervals, he dismounted to study it and then, resuming his pose, might tell Munnings, 'Look now, Sir; this is how His Majesty used to sit; his shoulders a little hunched; so.'

News of the painting leaked out. One day Tealing saw a newspaper reporter and cameraman climb a wall and photograph

Munnings at work. The painter grabbed the camera, smashed it and saw the intruders off with some choice language. Later, he accused Tealing, in no uncertain terms, of telling them he was there. Tealing had a hard job to convince him he was innocent. 'In the late afternoons, when I went to collect him,' Tealing said, 'while I waited for him to finish painting, I dare not even read a newspaper for fear it might rustle and infuriate him.'

He was surprised, therefore, when one day a Mr Barber called at his house and asked if he could go along with him when he collected Munnings from Sandringham. Tealing demurred but Barber insisted and said he was a great friend of the painter.

> When we approached the stable yard I switched off the engine and coasted to a standstill, as I always did [Tealing said]. Mr Barber got out with a swagger. I just caught the door before it slammed shut. He strode over to the artist and looked over his shoulder at his work.
>
> The things Munnings called Barber are unrepeatable and he rounded on me for taking the nosey old so-and-so. Then he collected up his painting things and asked me to drive them both to Dersingham Marshes. There he invited Mr Barber to walk back with him to Heacham along the beach, a distance of about seven miles. This was nothing to Munnings but when I saw them again, at Heacham, Mr Barber could hardly hobble because of the blisters.
>
> Munnings told me, 'That'll teach the old bugger to poke his snout into things that don't concern him.'

Tealing usually drove Munnings in a 1925 Vauxhall, but one day he took a comparatively new Ford V8 along because he thought his passenger would enjoy riding in a nearly new car. 'Nearly new, nearly new,' Munnings exploded. 'I need a shoe-horn to get into it; mind your bloody ear when you shut the door and if the man in the back wants a piss the one in the front has to get out. If you wish to take me out in future, bring the old car,' he admonished Tealing.

The posthumous portrait of King George V was shown in the 1937 Royal Academy and the print publishers, Frost and Reed, wanted to reproduce it. Stanley Wade, their young director, went with Munnings to Marlborough House to get Queen Mary's permission. They waited in a small, downstairs room. Suddenly, Munnings said to Wade in a hoarse whisper, 'I have a feeling that someone is watching us.' Wade had exactly the same feeling. Looking up, they both noticed a small hole in the ceiling.

Eventually, they were taken to an upstairs drawing room where they placed the picture on an easel. Queen Mary entered and studied it critically. Wade asked if he could have permission to reproduce it and the reply was 'certainly not'. He then asked if he might know the reason for the refusal and Queen Mary answered, 'You may not, but I will nevertheless tell you. The fact is that the painting is very good, but it illustrates my husband with his back bent and as more of a country gentleman than a King. It may be, and I believe it is, a perfectly accurate representation, but it is not appropriate that my people should see him thus.'

Later, Queen Mary allowed Frost and Reed to make a limited reproduction for private issue. But when Munnings saw the original hung in Ipswich Art Gallery, he was disappointed because the cream walls made it look cold and blue.

He was often critical about the settings for his pictures. Once, after the long-suffering Stanley Wade had finished hanging an exhibition of his paintings in the Frost and Reed galleries, Munnings arrived, at five in the afternoon, and said that everything must be rehung on a background of white muslin. Wade had just time to buy up the entire stock of white muslin in an Oxford Street store.

He and his assistants finished rehanging the exhibition at ten o'clock at night, when Munnings returned from the Arts Club after a long drinking session. He criticized the way the muslin had been draped and illustrated his meaning by climbing a ladder, somewhat gingerly, taking a stretch of muslin and attempting to nail it to the wall. His hammer missed, hit his finger, and his string of oaths was so colourful that a tired young assistant gave notice on the spot.

Strangely, his behaviour was usually more controlled in the company of writers. It seemed as if they understood him better than painters did and he responded to them better than to his fellow artists with whom he might be in competition or at cross-purposes. The farmer-writer, Adrian Bell, lived with his young family about ten miles from Dedham. Munnings had read and enjoyed his books, particularly his trilogy of fictionalized autobiography: *Corduroy*, *Silver Ley* and *The Cherry Tree*, but he did not know the author lived at Wiston, just along the Suffolk–Essex border. They were introduced at a local dinner party. 'Mr Bell?' Munnings said to the good-looking young writer, 'I wish you were Adrian Bell!'

Bell, twenty-three years younger than Munnings, was highly amused. He thought the remark was naive but sincere and he had a strange feeling that he was face-to-face with a character from his own trilogy; Mr Colville, the down-to-earth, well-to-do farmer, who spoke broad Suffolk and was dapper in a county-horsey sort of way. Munnings continued to amuse and interest him. The interest was mutual. Munnings probably admired Bell for throwing up his London job to take a small farm in Suffolk and write. He often took Bell on outings in the old-fashioned Buick, 'the Yellow Peril', driven by Mr Dines, the local carrier wearing a chauffeur's hat, for Munnings himself had never learnt to drive.

They toured the local countryside, stopping at interesting houses that caught the painter's eye. He loved houses and often contrived to meet the owners and bluff his way inside. They looked round ancient little churches and, sometimes, the painter mounted the pulpit of an empty one and declaimed on life and art, in a manner his father might have used.

In Brundish Church he reflected on the brevity of life. 'What is it all for?' he asked Bell. 'All our struggle in paint and to write?' 'Only a sparrow in the roof answered,' Bell recalled.

The acutely perceptive and sensitive writer saw beyond his extrovert companion's boisterousness and recognized a deep modesty, particularly in the presence of one of nature's manifestations. 'Thus,' Bell wrote, 'the supremely successful artist could be humbled and brought to a fit of inspirational despair by a fallen leaf from a chestnut tree . . . .'

Munnings, like Bell, was acutely conscious of his birthright and concerned about the detrimental effect of mechanization on farming. The two men often discussed the painter's dream of a revival of the old country values. Bell saw both Cobbett and Sir Roger de Coverley in this 'eloquent champion of Old England'.

Painter and author appreciated each other's work. Sometimes, Bell watched Munnings painting a big canvas in his studio:

> He would say [Bell wrote,] 'Do you realise the difficulty of getting all those hounds' legs arranged in a composition?'
>
> It looked to have been done with such ease .... But standing there watching him at work made me realise something of the niceties of judgement, the headwork as well as the handwork, the exact spacings, the angle of a hat, while keeping the zest of the thing, as though it were as spontaneous as one of his ballads.

Both men preferred Munnings's earlier pictures to his later, lucrative commissioned ones:

> His pony Augereau, pulling the dealer's cart, never moves out of the picture frame [Bell wrote], yet seems really to be going somewhere .... For Shrimp time stands still in the days of his youth; there he is, for ever riding wild horses against a background of storm, there he is driving Augereau in the dealer's cart.
>
> 'Couldn't do such good work today,' Munnings said.
>
> 'Why not?'
>
> 'I've got too bloody respectable,' he growled, gnawing a corner of his handkerchief – a habit of his.
>
> Bell understood: 'Nothing he painted was ever so satisfying to him as that horsey hurly-burly under the huge East Anglian weather of those gypsy themes.'

Coarseness in the painter marched side-by-side with an artist's sensitivity. He asked Stanley Wade to type out three limericks which he loved to recite and which he wanted to show the Prince of Wales at a dinner. They read:

> When Titian mixed his rose madder,
> His model he placed on a ladder,
> Her position to Titian suggested fruition
> So he mounted the ladder and had her.
>
> There was a young lady called Gail,
> On whose chest was the price of her tail,
> While on her behind, for the sake of the blind,
> Was the same information in Braille.
>
> There was a young lady named Ramson,
> Who was raped seven times in a hansom,
> As she clamoured for more, a voice from the floor
> Said, my name it is Simpson, not Samson.

During those prewar summers another young companion of Munnings's was twenty-year-old Eversley Belfield, later a military historian. Often, when Violet was at their Exmoor cottage Munnings invited Belfield, like Bell, to tour the local countryside in the back seat of the Yellow Peril. Riding high enough to see over the Suffolk hedgerows they pottered along quiet lanes, stopped at old churches and fine farmhouses and walked back for a closer look whenever 'A.J.', as Belfield called him, saw one that particularly appealed to him.

They went to Newmarket races, where 'A.J.' spent the whole day by the starting-post, making preliminary sketches. He was far more interested in the riders jockeying for position before 'The Off', than in a view of the finishing post.

He was not painting much at that time. He told Belfield he did not need the money and he was so heavily taxed that he saw no point in working on lucrative equestrian portraits, which meant staying in country houses where he had to be polite to the kind of people he did not like much.

Usually, on their outings, they ate their sandwiches at country pubs where 'A.J.' chatted with the locals as if he were one of them. 'He seemed to belong there, far more naturally than with his smarter friends,' his young companion noted. 'He seemed like a farmer.'

After lunch they often walked for five or six miles over the fields and Munnings usually 'got carried away by one of his obsessive hates'. Belfield listened to his tirades about the willows in the water-meadows which were no longer pollarded, and to his violent anti-semitism because he felt the Jews dominated the art world, and considered that his sort of painting was slick, commercial stuff, done solely for cash and snobbery:

> He asserted that all modern art of the type he loathed was done by Jews [Belfield said.] I always protested that Picasso, his *bête noire*, was in fact a Spaniard (like Velasquez and El Greco, I sometimes added). He would then switch his argument saying that Picasso owed everything to the Jewish art dealers and critics who were fooling the public to make money for themselves by selling his works for astronomically high prices.
>
> He was pro-German [Belfield added] and was angry at

> Churchill's anti-German speeches. He believed Soviet Russia was a greater menace than Nazi Germany. He also loathed the Post Impressionists and modern art. At first I tried to argue with him a little but found it hopeless against his torrent of words.

Sometimes Belfield went back with him to Castle House for a meal of bread and cheese, produced by his ex-groom, Cooper, whose wife was looking after Violet on Exmoor. After the meal, the painter talked about the books he was reading – history and biography as well as novels and poetry – and recited and reminisced. He had a fund of stories, ranging from his days at Lamorna, to the night when he deceived a group of so-called wine experts by giving them sparkling Mosel with champagne labels on the bottles.

The small dinner parties held when Violet was at home were memorable occasions for Belfield. Munnings read aloud or recited and Violet, tired after a day's hunting, fell asleep on the sofa and snored loudly to infuriate her husband.

> Once he threw a book at her [Belfield said] but missed and hit the person beside her.... They would quarrel loudly and at length so that it became very embarrassing and people would make excuses to leave. He would turn to her and say, 'Look Violet, what you have done with your bloody bad manners: our guests are leaving.'
>
> She would reply, 'It's all your fault. They've heard you reading your old ballads before and are bored with them.'

Violet once suggested that her husband might adopt Belfield. It seemed that their childless state was never far from either of their minds. Belfield never commented on his own reaction to the suggestion.

He noted that both Munnings and Violet offended quite a number of the local people by their rude aggressiveness. He quoted the time when 'A.J.' telephoned a couple and asked them to dinner. When they arrived, feeling rather pleased at the unexpected invitation, 'A.J.' opened the door, stared at them and said, 'I didn't mean you, but the other people with the same name,' and shut the door on them.

'I'm sure,' Belfield said, 'both Violet and A.J. realised that they could never find another partner better suited or more congenial.... He was very proud of her beauty and spirit.... Violet was equally proud of his achievements and she had no doubt that he was the greatest living British artist and she entirely supported his views on art.'

Her faith was justified at his financially successful exhibition at the Leicester Galleries in London, in 1938. Afterwards, feeling 'free as air', he joined Violet at Exmoor where he rode vigorously – often hacking forty miles a day – and spent the evenings quietly with Violet. His happiness was reflected in the diary he kept spasmodically, 'I sat in the shadow of an aged thorn in bloom, painting massed white blossoming trees below, casting their shadows on the hillside and their scent all around. Farther below, the gleam of a small stream rippling over stones in the sun, its sweet, silvery music ascending, mingling with the blackbird's song.'

Adrian Bell went to stay and he and Munnings were driven about the countryside, as they had been in East Anglia, and complained because men were no longer farming the land. But there tourism, not mechanization, had taken over.

Sometimes, they abandoned the car and walked with back packs. They walked up the Doone Valley in pouring rain and, soaked to the skin, lay down and drank from a stream and filled their water bottles. Hours later they returned to the car, took off their shoes and socks, wrapped their legs in newspaper, and, 'looking,' as Bell said, 'like a pair of ruined Morris dancers,' called in at a smart hotel and asked a surprised waiter for whisky.

They drank cider at fourpence a pint but, more often, they were content to drink from the springs. Munnings was, gastronomically, a reformed character. He was on the then popular Hay Diet, because of his gout and hardly touched alcohol.

They visited the homes of Coleridge and Wordsworth and walked where the poets had walked. They lay on the cliff edge for a long time, contemplating the meadows sweeping to the sea and imagined the country as it was in the poets' time, before it was invaded by trippers. 'If only one could keep this feeling,' Munnings said, drowsily. 'If only one could keep it....'

Later, Bell wrote of that moment when he had looked at the stunted oaks and beeches, with their blotched trunks, and had thought of the polished trunk of an East Anglian beech ... and of the bright broken skies, clean blue, dazzling silver, and shadowed blue-black. 'I knew,' he wrote, '... why it is that we East Anglians never forsake our country for long for any other. I knew that my friend, though he says there is nowhere to ride where he lives and that these wild moors are just what he wants, I know he'll never live here, only stay.'

Politics intruded. Towards the end of the year, Munnings was invited to stand as President of the Royal Academy in succession to Sir William Llewellyn. It was an honour beyond the wildest dreams of a miller's son, who was happiest painting horses and sharing the life of the gypsies. Violet had mixed feelings and expressed them in a letter her husband always treasured. It read:

> If you became President you could do so much to lift up the dying Academy and make it a live place.... From my own point of view, I hope you won't be President because of the social side. You *must* not let the R.A. down if you take it on. Your clean and pure outlook would greatly influence art schools and help crush the viper of 'modern art', the distorted outlook of unbalanced minds and unhealthy brains.
>
> You will admit that I have done nothing to influence you until now, when you tell me that at last you have allowed your name to be put down. You have enough money if you only paint 2 *good* pictures a year (and sell all I am dusting now in the studio). You are not rushed into the position, as you have rested (and a *well*-earned rest) since April, and have had time and opportunity (riding and walking alone on Exmoor) to consider it from every point of view.
>
> But consider well: are you prepared to alter your life, habits, enter into a great position which in 100 years will be *remembered* and spoken of as a great office conducted by a countryman who *saved British art*?
>
> If not, leave it alone. *What thy hand doeth, do it with all thy might.*

He allowed his name to go forward but came third out of the nine candidates, from which Sir Edwin Lutyens was elected. His time would come.

Meanwhile, Violet gave him a present of one of Constable's sketchbooks. It was fitting, she thought, that '... this little sketch-book should now be *your* personal property, and *your* fingers turning the leaves. It will go down to posterity with *your* sketchbooks. Often have I thought he may live again in you and your work.'

Munnings was in Dedham on the night of 26 July 1939 when the East Anglian School of Painting, run by Cedric Morris, was gutted by fire. Morris, an avant-garde artist, was known as 'the Cézanne of Newlyn'. His work was well-thought-of by some critics, but was too modern for Munnings. As the fire raged, Munnings was driven up and down the street in the Yellow Peril. He waved his stick, shouted 'hooray', poured invective against modern art and rejoiced that the School would have to paint out-of-doors, for a time at least.

A month later he was painting out-of-doors on the North Norfolk coast and staying at The Ship Hotel, Brancaster. On 3 September 1939, he was painting a picture of the square-towered Morston Church, silhouetted against the salt marshes and the distant sea. 'Nowhere could an artist have found a church in a more peaceful setting; a place of repose – a place to dream in . . . .' Suddenly, the peace was shattered: a boy on a harvest wagon drove slowly along beside the church wall and shouted: 'the war's started'. Munnings continued painting.

In the afternoon he had words with another boy, the son of his old friend, the writer Henry Williamson, who farmed at the Old Hall, Stiffkey. Munnings had used up all his canvases so he looked around Williamson's barns and granary for something to paint on. He noticed a square of mill-board in an old trouser press, extracted it and started work. Henry Williamson's thirteen-year-old son came up behind and stood watching him paint. Munnings precipitated the argument; he told the boy to 'clear off'. The boy retaliated: 'That's my father's trouser press! He wants it.' The painter shouted at him again, 'Go away, I tell you! Get out of it! I want to paint this before the light changes!' The boy stood resolute, 'When Dad comes he'll want to know why I let anyone in the granary, you know. You *took* that, didn't you?' Munnings continued to paint. 'Look at that light – wonderful!' he said. 'Can't you see how beautiful it is? What the hell's all this about *trousers*? Go away!'

Henry Williamson was a silent observer of the scene. He had just returned from London, unhappy and depressed, and the argument introduced a touch of normality to a world gone mad. He liked to study Munnings and featured him, thinly disguised, in the fifteenth and final novel of his saga, *A Chronicle of Ancient Sunlight*, which John Middleton Murry prophesied would prove one of the most remarkable English novels of the time.

The novel was called *The Gale of the World* and was set in Exmoor after World War II. Munnings was there to the life, riding in as the earthy-spoken horse-painter, Frederick Riversmill. 'He had a great store of country lore, like most people with the seeing eye and sense of fun,' Williamson wrote. Riversmill also had a painter's eye for a beautiful young girl, bickered with his wife and belittled spiritualism, Picasso, flying saucers and an East Anglia that was 'all derelict airfields and rusty wire barriers'.

'What a go!' Munnings would have said of the fictional portrait published ten years after his death.

CHAPTER XIV

In the Footsteps of Reynolds

On the day after the outbreak of World War II, the Yellow Peril arrived at Brancaster to take Munnings back to Dedham. After a night there, he hurried to London to arrange for the pictures and furniture from his Chelsea studio to be moved to the comparative safety of Castle House. Violet was in their Exmoor cottage at Withypool and was eager to return to Dedham. 'You and I are getting old,' she wrote, 'and I want to spend more of my life with you. Let us now decide to live at Castle House always.'

He was not ready for such a commitment. He told her to stay where she was, for the time being, and make the most of the hunting. Very soon there might be no more riding, he warned her. 'Don't wonder what *I'm* doing,' he wrote. 'When I'm here to myself I always get to work; the only time I'm really happy. Nothing to interrupt my GREAT MIND... I went up the river at one o'clock and came back at six. When you want peace, paint willows and lily-leaves.'

He added that he and their manservant, the soberly-dressed, black-jacketed Cooper, and Mrs Cooper were managing perfectly well. They had dug potatoes, picked apples and bottled fruit – the pears in a strong concentration of tawny port and cloves.

He bought candles, twelve biscuit tins, a bag of wheat and a mill to grind it in, while the Coopers made jam, melted pork fat into lard and salted and packed butter into jars. It was an echo of his boyhood home life and he even remembered to send his mother a cheque on her birthday.

In early October, he set off for London and met Eversley Belfield, waiting for the train at Ardleigh Station.

> I had just received my call-up papers [Belfield said]. When he learned this, he insisted on my travelling with him in a 1st class compartment and promised to take me to a place I would never forget. At Liverpool Street Station he got a taxi to the Cavendish Hotel in Jermyn Street. In World War I it had been a popular place for rich young men to spend their leaves. They used to keep crates of champagne there and Rosa Lewis had a good supply of attractive 'nieces'.
>
> Rosa was very surprised to see A.J. We were ushered into her private room which was lined with photographs of the famous and infamous. I was given a champagne cocktail, the first of several. It was the only drink Rosa provided. My health was drunk and soon others arrived and a lively party continued until long after I should have reported to the Army.
>
> Eventually, A.J. said we must go and called a taxi. Before we left he handed Rosa a fiver saying she was a good-hearted woman, too easily exploited by the unscrupulous now she was getting old. I was fairly tipsy by then and he took me to the Arts Club for something to eat.
>
> When his friends learned I was just going to the Army, more drinks were pressed on me. Finally I was detached and put in a taxi for Waterloo Station. Fortunately, Aldershot was a terminus so I had to get out. I managed to report to the Guard Room where a kindly bombardier saw that I was unfit for anything military, showed me my bed and ordered me to lie down until I felt better.
>
> I never saw A.J. again. For a short time I was a favourite companion but I don't think that I made a lasting impression on him and he had no compunction in dropping someone when he lost interest, for whatever reason. He was, I believe, completely self-centred, had a very powerful personality and used his gifts to fulfil whatever he felt he wanted to do. In this he was aided by his genuine spontaneity of behaviour, by his almost childlike enthusiasm for his 'craze' of the moment and by his real ability to enjoy entertaining others with his wit and conversation.
>
> When I knew him, I believe he was beginning to deteriorate and was becoming obsessed by his hatred of modern art, which, in the end, dominated his outlook on life.

When Munnings had seen Belfield off he dined at the Other Club. That night they clapped Churchill when he arrived, gave Lord Gort, Commander-in-Chief of the British Expeditionary

Force, a terrific send-off to France, and listened to an anti-government tirade by H. G. Wells.

Later, Munnings went to stay with Violet on Exmoor and, once again, he was captivated by the 'boundless moorland'. He painted West Country landscapes and hunting scenes and a portrait of a local girl, Miss Rosemary Hancock. She posed for him and he automatically shouted, 'Whoa, mare!' whenever she moved. He recited the whole of Gray's *Elegy* while he painted, indicating again, perhaps, that his aural memory was a great deal better than his visual one.

A welcome diversion from a life of complete freedom came in the summer of 1940 when J. V. Rank invited him to his home, Druids Lodge, Wiltshire, to paint some of his winners, including Southern Hero, Black Speck and Knight's Armour. He was happy there in the company of Rank and a guest, J. H. Thomas, former Lord Privy Seal and Dominions Secretary, who had been bombed out of his own home.

In September air battles over Britain reached their climax, the peace of Druids Lodge was shattered and Munnings received a telegram notifying him the army had requisitioned Castle House. His studio in Dedham village had already been taken over for refugees. He went to Dedham immediately and the military authorities allowed him to hire a removal firm to fill three downstairs rooms of Castle House, from floor to ceiling, with his furniture and bedding. He had new locks fitted to the doors, the windows boarded-up and he and Cooper buried the contents of his wine cellar under the floor of his studio, which was also boarded-up. He then took Cooper and a groom, Harry Bayfield, along with two of his horses, Anarchist and Rose, back to Exmoor. His other horses were sent to be slaughtered.

While painting on Exmoor he recaptured some of the old excitement of his days in the Ringland Hills. Instead of his own horses, there were herds of Dartmoor ponies to paint, which he tracked down each day with the help of Violet and Bayfield. The three would ride as near as they could to the grazing grounds and, without disturbing the ponies, he would dismount and send his companions back with his horse. Then, alone on foot, he carried his portable easel and stool, eight or ten canvases and a brown paper roll containing twenty or thirty paintbrushes until he had found the right spot to work, as near the herd as possible.

Sometimes he lay there, waiting patiently for the weather to give him the light and shadows he wanted. One day, at Bagworthy Water, twelve miles from home, he found he had forgotten his brushes. The countryman was undeterred. He experimented with scraps of rag tied to a stick, thin branches of tree chewed into fibres, and with tiny fir cones matted with grass. A teazel proved the best substitute. The next day, he returned to the spot to paint the same scene with brushes. The two pictures looked identical.

He did a portrait of his beloved Anarchist, tethered in position between the garage door and a horse box, and with a hay net suspended in front of him to keep him happy. His owner still found it difficult to capture a horse's stance in a picture. 'I go for the attitude,' he wrote. 'I paint him looking at me, a three-quarter side view, almost side, seeing into his chest. The road and hills behind me.... He continually turns his head, all alert and listening, towards where I stand, sheltered from any wind by the horse-rugs on the line.'

That day, after two four-hour spells of painting and fortified by a large swig of rum, Munnings rode Anarchist and led Cherry-bounce on to the Moor for exercise. '... as the rum worked I drew the led animal (Cherry) to me and encircled her neck with my right arm, and patted her, and talked to her, and she arched that lovely neck and stepped out and swished her tail. What a thing is over-proof rum!' It is doubtful if he was ever as demonstrative with Violet but his love of horses was as great as ever. A few days later, he was thrown by Anarchist.

He was riding one-handed, because of gout in his right wrist, 'Suddenly, as I came to the last white gate,' he recorded in his diary, 'he shook his head, put it down, jumped up in the air, twisted his body and came down and up and down, and I, with only one hand, just got chucked off on my back, and then he gently stood on my ankle to show his love and thankfulness.'

It was the only mention he ever made of being thrown. He was winded and hurt and rode home 'in deep resentment', with two broken ribs and 'a hell of an ankle'. The next day he was outside, painting again, despite the gout in his right wrist.

Nothing deterred him. He was painting entirely to please himself and his output was prodigious. Sometimes he worked on several canvases together. He was spurred on, perhaps, by the knowledge that there was a ready market for everything he did and he was likely to earn as much, if not more, than he earned through his onerous equestrian commissions which, so often, involved him in a complete change of life-style.

There was time for writing poetry at Withypool, not the boisterous ballads, but gentler verses reflecting his thoughts on life and the countryside when he saw *Shadows on the Grass*, *Sherdon Water*, *Cloud Shadows*, *An Exmoor Lane* or *Tracks on Exmoor*. In *Vain Desires* he reiterated a lifelong prayer:

O let me lie by a running stream,
Playing over its stones all day,
Whose music soon becomes a dream,
And carries the mind so far away,
Into a distant, lazier land,
Further and further away . . .

They were very different from quite recent efforts such as a nauseating six-verse ode, with a rousing chorus called *The Tortured Coast of Norfolk*, written as a plea for conservation and presumably intended, in its unexpurgated version, for private consumption. The last three verses led up to his prophecy of the 1950 East Coast floods, more than a decade before they occurred.

Jews and fair-haired ladies
Are bouncing in the sea.
Mothers with their babies,
Hold them out to pee.
Motor cars are parking,
With hooting and with noise,
And little dogs are barking
At half-bred girls and boys.

French letters and banana skins
Are floating in the surf,
Tins and broken jam pots
Are scattered on the turf.
And if you go by moonlight
To see the sea at night

Don't sit upon the shingle
Or you'll sit upon the shight.

But nature she is waiting
And storing up the day
When she will send a tidal wave
And wash the sods away.
And when all the bloody sheds and huts
Are gone for evermore,
Troops of lovely seagulls
Will shight upon the shore.

In contrast to that vitriolic ode, Munnings, in the war years with Violet on Exmoor, seemed more at peace with himself than at any time since his early years at Lamorna.

His peace and painting time were shattered, however, by a letter he received on 31 December 1943, inviting him to allow his name to go forward for the presidency of the Royal Academy. The President, Sir Edwin Lutyens, was seriously ill and the invitation, from another member of the Royal Academy, read:

> Dear Munnings,
>
> We should, next December, be faced with the election of a new P.R.A., but alas! our dear Ned is sinking rapidly, and I am told by his secretary, it is only a matter of days.
>
> He has endeared himself to all members by his single-hearted devotion to their interests and to those of the R.A. . . . .
>
> The immediate object of my writing to you is to express the profound hope that you may find it in your heart to allow yourself to be nominated for the Presidency . . . .
>
> It is an annual election: you need not feel you will be saddled for a long term with duties that have become distasteful to you. Give us a chance to make them otherwise. Those to whom I have mentioned the question are your whole-hearted supporters.

'Of course you'll stand,' Violet said, 'but I won't influence you. Think it well over. Remember the tie it will be.' He remembered and shied away 'like a horse at a milestone'. He went for a ride to 'think it well over'. Later that day, he wrote agreeing to stand for election, when the time came, but asked for consideration and fewer Council meetings if elected. They assured him all would be well, meetings would be fewer and a deputy would be appointed to help him. If elected his name would be in the Birthday Honours List.

Lutyens died on New Year's Day and the ballot for President took place on March 14th. The contenders were Munnings, Augustus John, Gerald Kelly, Philip Connard, Harold and Dame Laura Knight, Sir William Reid Dick, Meredith Frampton and Sir Giles Gilbert Scott. Munnings beat Augustus John into second place by twenty-four votes to seventeen.

John had been a reluctant candidate: 'P.R.A. is only an extension of R.A. I would have no logical reason to refuse,' he had told Philip Connard, explaining why he had allowed his name to go forward, despite his doubts about his ability to cope with the official and social duties.

On his way to the election, Munnings, wearing black and white check trousers, spotted bow tie, black coat and vivid scarf, had passed 'the finest statue in London', that of Sir Joshua Reynolds, the first President of the Academy, in the courtyard of Burlington House. He hoped and feared to follow in his footsteps. When he heard he had been elected, he shouted, 'I feel like riding along Piccadilly on a horse. What a go!' Later, he wrote to an old friend, James Woodford, 'It was a great afternoon at the R.A., and the whole lot treated me like a swell.'

He was staying with his sculptor friend, Whitney-Smith, in Priory Road, St John's Wood because his Chelsea studio had been damaged by bombs. That night he dined with friends in what was left of the Arts Club. It, too, had been badly bombed and the painting he had lent to the club, Tissot's *La Danseuse le Cord*, had been destroyed.

When the air raid sirens sounded and the noise of falling bombs could be heard, celebrations were adjourned to the reinforced basement. In the small hours of the morning the new PRA and Whitney-Smith, both full of wine, walked home under a fire-lit sky, past burning buildings in Edgware Road, flooded streets, fire brigades and ambulances. There were no taxis and the Underground stations were packed with sleeping people. 'Pictures of hell,' Munnings wrote.

Nothing, however, daunted his hopes for the future of English art. Remembering that night, he wrote in his intermittent memoirs:

> I believed in tradition, with the sure knowledge that the great men of the past, like Michelangelo, Rembrandt and all the company of Masters belonging to a great age, could never be surpassed in drawing and design, that in our age we could yet see things as they were and carry on to a future of sound painting and interesting outlook.
>
> That abnormal fooleries, distortion – the outcome of disgruntled, cunning, incompetent minds – would be denounced by a Press worthy of England; that young art boys, glad of good, easy jobs on the Press, Art Councils and such like, would wag their beards for the last time on the wireless.

He returned to a snowbound Exmoor to collect his morning suit in preparation for going to Buckingham Palace in June, to receive his knighthood, and to answer the hundreds of congratulatory messages and telegrams that poured in. He evolved a formula for his replies. To acquaintances he wrote, 'Stacks of letters, but thank you for yours.' To friends he wrote, 'Thank you very much. What a go!' To those who had used his own catchphrase in congratulating him, he replied, 'Bless your good soul – thanks!'

There were exceptions in his replies when letters really moved or amused him; Brendan Bracken, Minister of Information, in his letter of congratulations, suggested that if anything happened to the Poet Laureate that job should also be conferred on him. 'Jack M.' (Lord Mottistone) wrote as 'one of your oldest and greatest admirers': 'I see you now in your quaint civilian costume, painting Warrior and me at Smallfoot Wood, and, again, on a bright sunny morning right in the middle of the March retreat, painting Antoine of Orleans on his black horse.... What fun we had together.' Munnings replied, 'My dear Lord of the Isle, Only you could have written that letter and I thank you from the bottom of my heart....'

His 'very dear, dear Rosa' (Lewis) wrote from the Cavendish Hotel; a former nurse and the son of his old bank manager congratulated him from Harleston; while an old lady who had worked at Caley's said how delighted Shaw Tomkins would have been to know of his great success; his mother said it was just what she had been expecting.

Messages of goodwill flowed from a half-forgotten past. The present promised to be more controversial. Gerald Kelly wrote from Windsor Castle where he was painting two, full-length, state portraits of the King and Queen:

> I voted for John [he admitted], I did so because I wish, above all things, to see the rising generation of artists reconciled to the Academy; and I felt that John was the candidate most likely to bring about this consummation.
>
> You beat him handsomely, and I accept the situation. It is the easier for me to do since for many years I have greatly admired your paintings, and still do so.
>
> I feel certain that we both love this institution, the Royal Academy, and wish to see its traditions honourably maintained. For my part, that is my sole objective, as it is surely yours.
>
> The more successful the President, the better for the Royal Academy.
>
> In every point that I can, my support, for what little it may be worth, shall be at your service.
>
> If we should differ I may feel obliged to contest the point at issue, but always, let me assure you once more, in what I conceive to be the true interest of the Royal Academy.

For the moment, Munnings was unusually conciliatory:

> I had hoped John would have to bear the burden and set me free [he replied]. Since it has fallen on me, I want you all to be good friends of mine.
>
> You and I will never disagree about the things that matter. Art is long, etc.

He could not have become President of the Royal Academy at a more stressful time. The sound of flying bombs and rockets dominated tedious Council meetings at which he ignored protocol. Total disaster was frequently only averted by the tactful intervention of the loyal secretary, Sir Walter Lamb. Munnings was doing his best and he accepted rebukes with surprisingly good humour.

He stayed at the Devonshire Club but sleep was usually impossible during the heavy air raids, punctuated by the roar of doodlebugs. 'Drink was the thing that was needed in those desperate days,' he wrote. Drink, however, brought on a crippling gout attack – the worst he had ever had, which was only relieved by a lumbar injection.

The day-to-day business of the Royal Academy kept him from his paints and brushes and he turned to pen and ink for an outlet for his creativity. He gave vent to his boredom at serving on the

Selection Committee for the Academy's Summer Exhibition by writing a ballad of more than a hundred lines beginning:

> Oh, who can say what toiling hours are spent
> Upon the many pictures yearly sent
> By youth and age to hang upon the walls
> Of this Academy, which each year palls
> Upon the sight of those who hope for better?
> Alas! When shall we break our rusted fetter
> Which chains us to our ancients in their age?
> When shall we start afresh, with cleaner page?

He considered publishing a book of his poems and sent a selection to his former literary admirer, John Masefield, for his opinion. The Poet Laureate's reply was cautious and not very encouraging:

> My Dear President,
>
> With some misgivings, I send you some of the notes suggested by your poems. I'm afraid they may seem rather on one note; and inappreciative. Please do not think that. I have much enjoyed the 3 big tales, the Cottesmore Ball, the Larkbarrow and Cherry Bounce*. You ought to have another go at these, and when you have done them AND ILLUSTRATED THEM, it will be peace, perhaps, and a grateful Nation will surely raise you to the Peerage.
>
> Please forgive me, if the judgements seem now and then harsh or unhelpful; the main effect made on me has been one of enjoyment.
>
> With our greetings and regards to you both,
>
> John Masefield.

Another letter was more reassuring. Masefield wrote:

> You have a lot of natural talent for writing, an easy, gay power, and a gift for narrative. DO, I beg you, finish your narratives. Cherry Bounce has unusual qualities.
>
> Do believe me. You believed me about Anthony Bell; and I have grown lots wiser since then....
>
> You ought to do a Haunted Mill story, and use your River sense in the setting.
>
> If any comment by me can seem of any use to you at any

* The last two long narrative ballads were written while he was riding on Exmoor, as was probably the first. It was 490 lines of rhyming couplets with an alternative ending.

stage of your writing, please send along the script, and your chief admirer will gladly give what comment he can.

The frustrated painter shelved the matter and turned his pen to other uses. He wrote letters to *The Times* and newspaper articles including one to *The Studio* magazine, in which he reflected on the Academy's Summer Exhibition of 1944. He described how he had toured the galleries after closing hours, stopping before the pictures he liked the best, which invariably made him exclaim, 'How does the fellow do it?'

There was a scarcity of good landscapes that year, he noted, probably because in wartime the landscape painter had nowhere to go. He advised him to go into the country, when he could, and make endless studies of weather effects, *always working*. 'One day, it might be late in life,' he said, 'he will at last grasp something of the truth, creating entirely fresh and living landscapes, and so prove what can be done with nature as a supreme guide, and perhaps with the use of some perfectly primed canvas which has yet to be discovered. Alas! How many of us long for the perfect surface, for one of the secrets of good painting lies in the priming we are painting on.'

From writing he turned to music for relaxation. He went to several afternoon concerts with a friend, another Dedham painter, Maurice Codner, and particularly enjoyed listening to Chopin.

He also found unexpected solace in the atmosphere of Burlington House where he could surround himself with glorious antiques such as he had always dreamt of doing. The Assembly Room, with its painted ceiling, contained a choice Sheraton sideboard, a set of mahogany 'Nelson' chairs and a large Constable landscape insured for £40,000. The Georgian silver delighted him most. Every piece was a traditional gift from a new member. Munnings, in his turn, had donated a pair of silver, crested candlesticks.

There were other candlesticks, salt-cellars, rose bowls and tea services, always in use at appropriate occasions. Munnings was particularly fascinated by the large set of silver dessert plates, all the same pattern, each engraved with the name of a donor. As the port went round he never failed to examine his plate and thrill if he found it had been given by Sargent or Landseer or, perhaps, by Etty or the great Sir Joshua. The plates provided unfailing topics of conversation. To use and handle such treasures bridged the years and were ample compensation for the tin hip bath, available to him in the sparse Presidential accommodation in the magnificent building.

He took hot baths at the Athenaeum Club, for his Presidency of the Academy entitled him to honorary membership. He soon made his presence felt there and some older members found it very disturbing. 'He acted on their cloistered calm like a sudden purge on a well-ordered stomach,' wrote his writer friend, James Wentworth Day, after he had lunched with him there.

At one lunch, Wentworth Day was hoping to enlist Munnings's support for local opposition to a proposed new Essex power station. The painter was completely uninterested until he was told it would draw off water from his beloved River Stour and it would no longer flow under Flatford Mill, where he loved to paint. 'That went home,' Wentworth Day recalled. '"Water!" Munnings roared. "There's not enough water anywhere. Y'know why? Every time an old woman piddles half a pint, she pulls the chain and away goes a gallon .... When I was a boy, we used to piddle in a bucket and chuck it on the garden. Grew better lettuces." There was a stunned silence .... In the distance an elderly protesting voice was raised: "There's that damned ostler fellow at it again!"'

As they left the dining room they passed a table of bishops including the writer's cousin, who waved an acknowledgement. 'I see you're in lively company,' he said. 'Munnings glared,' Wentworth Day recalled. '"Y'know that lot of black crows do you? Look at them. They rob the Offertory plates on Sundays and come up here on Mondays to booze it all away. Crows! Black crows!"' Wentworth Day said he was not surprised when Munnings was suspended from the Club's membership for six months for tickling a pretty waitress under the chin and saying: 'You're a damned paintable gal!'

He still loved to shock. 'I made those old boys jump a few times,' he confided to the Head Porter at the Academy, after he had lunched at the Athenaeum and had read aloud a particularly coarse Norfolk rhyme. Nevertheless, he had staunch admirers at the Athenaeum, particularly among the intellectuals. They included Professor John Mavrogordato, Fellow of Exeter and sometime Professor of Byzantine and Modern Greek Languages and Literature at Oxford, who appreciated Munnings's 'infectious pleasure in life, somewhat rare!'

The painter's great friend was C.K. Ogden of *Basic English* fame. He liked Munnings, he said, because he was 'pleasantly eccentric.... Well perhaps eccentric is not the right word. Weird, shall we say? I find him weirdly amusing.' With Munnings the friendship went deeper. The two men invariably dined together and finished the meal with a glass of Benedictine laced with brandy and one of the painter's rhyming ballads. After Ogden died in 1957, Munnings never entered the Club again.

Munnings's Presidency, after its wartime start, coincided with a propitious time at the Academy. In 1945, the year of Germany's surrender, more than 200,000 people visited the Summer Exhibition; arrangements were made for the Painting and Sculpture Schools to reopen; there was talk of resuming the large loan exhibitions and the post of Professor of Architecture was revived.

The first post-war loan exhibition was 'The King's Pictures' and proved extremely popular. It consisted of five hundred masterpieces, from royal palaces, which had been hidden in safe places during the War. More than 366,000 visitors queued to see the Dutch and Venetian paintings, the early Italian works collected in the nineteenth century by the Prince Consort and the unrivalled series of portraits by Holbein, Van Dyck, Reynolds, Gainsborough, Lawrence and others, before they were rehung in their rightful homes.

Munnings was proud to be President on such an occasion. King George VI gave several private parties at the Academy and told Munnings he did not know he owned so many fine pictures. Munnings met the King again that year when he went to Buckingham Palace to receive the insignia of a Knight Commander of the Victorian Order. They talked about the King's racehorse, Sun Chariot, and her foal. Munnings had painted the mare in 1943, before she went to stud. It was his latest commissioned portrait of a racehorse. The King asked why he had his arm in a sling and the painter replied, 'Sprained my wrist, Sir.' He did not want to admit it was swollen with gout.

Later that year, a large exhibition of Munnings's work was held at the Leicester Galleries and yielded nearly £21,000, the highest return of his life. £12,000 was taken on the first day. He had painted for years, preparing it, and it included many of his Exmoor pictures. Nevertheless, many of the art critics were unimpressed.

Not so Sir Desmond MacCarthy, literary critic of the *Sunday Times*. He wrote to Munnings:

> ... at last lovers of pictures are asserting their faith that painting is a *representative* art, a principle which no one doubted till lately ....
>
> If your name had been Degas, how 'the critics' would have raved about your skill in recording movement and the gait and gestures of horses.

Munnings was also bitter because the proceeds of the exhibition were treated by the Inland Revenue as one year's earnings and he was taxed at 19s.6d. in the pound, despite an appeal to the Treasury on his behalf and on behalf of all one-man shows. To add to his aggravation, his best pictures were bought by dealers and resold at good profits.

He maintained an in-built disrespect for all dealers, although he accepted that many had done much to help his reputation. He reserved his distance by addressing them by childish, fancy names in his brief communiqués. Stanley Wade was 'Dear Sir Wade', Oliver Brown of the Leicester Galleries was 'All-over Brown' and James Green of the Bond Street Galleries was 'Dear Viscount Worcester Sauce'.

That year his mother died in Norwich, at the age of ninety-five, and he received the freedom of the city, an honour rarely bestowed even on its own citizens. The ceremony took place in St Andrew's Hall where, long years ago, he had watched Henry Wood conduct and listened to the music of Sir Edward Elgar. He spoke movingly about his youthful days in Norwich and the Lord Mayor's brother, Tom Copeman, editor of the *Eastern Daily Press*, wrote in his diary, 'Munnings, who for one dreadful moment lost his notes, gave a wonderful impression of his love for Norwich and of the happy freedom of his early painting days – gorse – commons – village inns ....

Unfortunately, the impression he left at a subsidiary function, a reception given that afternoon in his honour by the Norwich Art Circle, was far from wonderful. The Chairman, James Starling, remembered it as the most embarrassing occasion of his life.

It was held in the Art Gallery in the Castle Museum and, at

the outset, Munnings caused confusion by avoiding the official welcoming party, headed by the Museum's Curator, Miss Grace Barnard. Eventually, Starling ran him to ground in a side gallery, talking to a terrified, young girl steward who was admitting she did not know that the painting they were standing before was by John Crome. Starling said, 'Munnings was telling the girl that if she didn't know the work of such a famous local painter, she certainly wasn't entitled to take the rate-payers' money and she ought to be given the sack, there and then. He then told me he didn't want to waste time meeting Miss Barnard.'

Munnings met Miss Barnard in the Main Gallery at the official opening of the reception when Starling embarked on a congratulatory speech. He was just describing how Munnings had his first picture accepted by the Royal Academy when the painter jumped up and said, 'If you don't stop this I shall walk out.'

Starling cut short his speech and invited Munnings to say a few words. 'Munnings immediately attacked Miss Barnard about the lay-out of the Gallery,' Starling said. 'It had a long seat down the middle with a palm tree at either end. Munnings said "You've got a gallery full of Norwich School paintings and you have to have bloody palm trees. . . ." The reception ended in confusion.' It seemed as if the painter who loved the freedom of the road, the sound of the river and painting in the open air, had had his fill of civic duties.

That night he was the guest of honour at a dinner given by the English Speaking Union. In his speech he said how depressed he had been by his own pictures in the Norwich Art Gallery. He then launched into a long prose passage which mystified most of his audience, and sat down. Few realized it had been a passage from Borrow's description of Norwich in *Lavengro*; 'a terrific feat of memory', according to the Chairman, R. H. Mottram, the novelist.

Soon afterwards, it was a less flamboyant and an essentially modest speaker who addressed an audience at the Centenary Celebrations of Ipswich Museum. 'You have to know everything about your characters,' he wrote, 'like Thackeray when he wrote *Vanity Fair* or like Tolstoy when he sat down to the first chapter of *War and Peace*. I have tried to paint horses. Why do I fail? Because I don't know enough about them . . . .

Never-ending responsibilities conspired to prevent him from

painting. He moved into his Chelsea studio as soon as it was repaired and into Castle House the moment it was derequisitioned. A gregarious PRA, he hosted dinner parties in the Assembly Room at Burlington House on the slightest pretext. The antique-lover delighted in playing host in such a magnificent setting and went into the lovely room before his guests arrived to enjoy the sight of gleaming silver, the glow from the red shades over the candlesticks and the fire burning in the grate. The setting more than compensated for post-war rationing and indifferent wine.

He contrived reasons to entertain. He waxed vitriolic at a dinner he gave for a sprinkling of Academy members and men who had written to *The Times* about the Picasso Exhibition at the Victoria and Albert Museum. He gave a dinner to the Hanging Committee and a lunch to the newspaper editors on the press day of the Summer Exhibition.

Guy Schofield, the elegant editor of the *Evening News* and later of the *Daily Mail*, was a guest at the most interesting dinner Munnings ever gave. His invitation was the outcome of the support his paper gave to the highly controversial Chantrey Bequest Exhibition at Burlington House, in February 1949. Munnings rated that exhibition as the greatest achievement of his Presidency.

It consisted of four hundred pictures which the Royal Academy had bought, over a hundred years, from a large trust fund left by a wealthy artist, Sir Francis Chantrey, to form a permanent British art collection. Most of the pictures had found their way into the vaults of the Tate Gallery without ever being seen by the public which, in many cases, was just as well.

They included many famous Victorian paintings, some by Millais and Holman Hunt, as well as works by Sargent and three by Munnings himself; *Epsom Downs: City and Suburban Day* (1920)*; *From My Bedroom Window* (1930) and *Their Majesties' Return from Ascot, 1925* (1926 and 1938). Munnings hoped an exhibition of traditional paintings would counteract some of the growing interest in abstracts, which he so abhorred.

Most art critics rallied against him. They slated the exhibition as: 'a freak show'; 'the funniest and saddest show ... which fully justifies its sojourn in the vaults;' and 'Britain's first exhibition of

* Numbers in brackets show the dates when the paintings were exhibited in the Royal Academy.

Decadent Art'. The *Evening News* stood alone. Moreover, its own editor turned reporter and wrote a long article endorsing the Exhibition not because of its artistic merit but because he saw it as a moral challenge.

> Pictures are not painted for artists and critics alone [Schofield wrote] – at least we might be allowed to contend so.... Gradually these old pictures overwhelm you with a sense of two worlds – or, more accurately, two minds. The instinct, the conception of life and purpose, in them is unpleasantly far from ours.... You realise that the distance between Frank Bramley and the abstract art of today is the distance between Charles Kingsley and Stalin. It is the divide which parts God – however gropingly sensed – from arrogant agnosticism.
>
> The challenge of the Chantrey Exhibition is not one of artistic technique or taste, but of moral significance.
>
> Those Victorian artists looked *outward*, with aspiring eyes, upon a world of stable values, acknowledged principles and accepted duties. Good was good and bad was bad and that which was good was known to be good and that which was bad was known to be horrid. They did not look *inward* upon their own fretful minds out of a faithless and codeless world adrift.

The article attracted a great deal of controversy in the press and gigantic audiences to the Academy. The delighted President ordered four thousand reprints to distribute free to visitors.

Gerald Kelly was up in arms at the press Munnings received.

> My dear A.J.,
> Oh, how I wish you hadn't this appetite for publicity. I'm shocked at your 'bustling catchpenny tactics'. Alas, alas! ... The same sincerity which is so lovable – yes but you mention living artists and members of our body.* It's not fair. You shouldn't do it. It makes so many of us ashamed. How difficult it is to write, to paint, to criticise and to collect well and wisely!
>
> Yours ever,
>
> Gerald Kelly.

* Schofield had named several painters in his article.

Munnings was unrepentant. He arranged a small dinner party at Burlington House to which he invited Schofield. 'Nine o'clock sharp and wear your black tie,' he said with a chuckle. 'The richest chuckle I've ever heard,' said the tall, spare, Yankee-looking man, as Munnings described him. His fellow guests were Arthur Watson, editor of the *Telegraph*, and several elderly R As and A R As.

> We stood about in one of the large galleries, making conversation [Schofield said]. Suddenly, without warning, Winston Churchill walked in. We all adjourned to a smaller room for dinner. All the Academy silver was out and there was a flunky standing behind every chair.
>
> When coffee came, Munnings said, 'I'm sure you're all wondering what this is about.' Then, from under his chair, he drew out a roll of parchment and, turning to Churchill said, 'Now Winston, this is your Diploma as a Royal Academician Extraordinary.' Winston was completely surprised and delighted.

It was the only time in the Academy's history that the title was bestowed.

Churchill had been an enthusiastic painter for more than thirty years and his works were first shown in the Royal Academy's Summer Exhibition in 1947, thanks to Alfred Munnings. The painter's acquaintanceship with Churchill at The Other Club had resulted in an invitation to lunch at Chartwell to see his pictures.

Munnings had never seen such stacks of paintings on open-air themes. They hung, one above the other, in a galleried studio and were piled against the wall of a kind of summer-house; all thirty-by twenty-five-inch canvases. Munnings immediately realized Churchill needed that amount of space to express himself. His immediate reaction was: 'Attack, attack was written all over them. Have a shot, paint what you see. Maybe it was a glorious escape for a great mind.' 'They're nothing,' Churchill demurred, ' – just sketches.' Munnings thought otherwise. Many of those works had the vital touch. 'My dear Sir,' he said, 'Nature has been your inspiration. The poorest efforts before Nature have something in them that others have not. Many of these paintings are better than you think.'

Eventually, Munnings persuaded Churchill, who was then seventy-four, to submit six of 'my poor daubs', as Churchill called them, to the 1947 Summer Exhibition of the Academy, under the pseudonym of 'David Winter'. Munnings could hardly contain himself when the Selection Committee approved them all*. He waved his arms and exploded: 'Good job you passed them! They're Churchill's.' From that time Churchill's paintings were exhibited in the Royal Academy every year until his death.

Meanwhile, after the dinner at which Churchill was made an Academician Extraordinary, the guests were taken on a tour of the Chantrey Bequest Exhibition. One by one the elderly gentlemen slipped away. Munnings was hit by an appalling attack of gout but Churchill showed no signs of leaving and, around midnight, sent for his overcoat because the galleries were getting chilly.

> By this time [Schofield said], there were only four of us left; Sir John Rothenstein, Winston, Munnings and I. I tried to get away but Munnings, who was sitting on a settee groaning, said 'For God's sake, stay.'
>
> Winston beckoned me over to a picture by Holman Hunt he was looking at. It showed a fellow in a scarlet coat and Winston said, 'Only a great artist can use scarlet.'
>
> Below the painting was a quotation from *Measure for Measure*. It read: 'Death is a fearful thing – Claudio'.
>
> Winston said: 'That isn't true.' That's something I've always remembered.

Eventually, Munnings, tired out and in agony, could contain himself no longer and called out, 'Winston, when the hell are you going home?' 'I shall go home when I feel like it,' was the reply but the Academician Extraordinary left soon afterwards.

Munnings nurtured his friendship with Schofield and the sensitive, shrewd journalist saw beneath the rumbustious character, who often offended by his brusqueness and rudeness. Schofield thought he was an outspoken, endearing throwback to the eighteenth century, who would have fitted in perfectly with Dr Johnson.

He saw the sensitive side: Munnings telephoned him one day and asked him to come to the Athenaeum as soon as he had got 'that bloody paper of yours to press'. He had something to show him. 'He had been racing,' Schofield said, 'and the "something"

* *Fontaine de Vaucluse*, 1948; *Sunset. Templeton, Roehampton*, circa 1920; *The Palladian Bridge, Wilton*, circa 1925; *Sunset, Cannes Harbour*, circa 1923; *Winter Woodland*, circa 1925; *Lake near Beccles*, circa 1929.

was a beech leaf. He waxed enthusiastic over its beauty. "Look at that," he said. "The delicate symmetry, the beautiful pattern. And they say everything has been painted, but not many artists could paint that."'

The two men frequently dined together at the Athenaeum and, when Munnings and his party were left alone in the dining room, he sometimes ordered the steward to put out the lights and gave highly dramatic renderings, by candlelight, of Edgar Allan Poe's *The Raven* or his own poems and ballads – some lyrical and sentimental, some full of a bawdy schoolboy's sense of humour.

> He loved the sound of his own voice [Schofield said]. One night he used it to good effect when we were trying to find a taxi in Grosvenor Square, after a party. No taxis would stop for us, however hard we shouted. Presumably, they were on their way home.
>
> 'It's no use shouting for a taxi,' A.J. said. 'You've got to sing for them,' and he burst into 'Shall we gather at the River?' We'd no sooner got through the first chorus when a taxi drew up, the driver shoved his head through the window and shouted, 'Which river Guv?'
>
> He was enormous fun. Some prissy people disliked him, but it was all good-humoured.

Soon, there was to be a very tangible outcome of their friendship.

9. "Does the Subject Matter?"

Sir John Rothenstein (then Director of the Tate Gallery), Humphrey Brooke and Professor Mavrogordato examining a piece of 'contemporary' sculpture with Munning's dog Toby. Above are the 'three daubers' whom Munnings criticised so famously in his inaugural lecture as President of the Royal Academy.

10. Studies of Hyperion

Lord Derby's Hyperion, winner of the Derby and St Leger in 1933. Munnings wrote that the finished painting in 1937 was 'my one and only good painting of a horse'.

CHAPTER XV

Final Challenges

One day, in 1946, a twenty-two-year-old corporal in the Royal Army Veterinary Corps at Colchester was glancing through a local newspaper in the barracks when an item about the President of the Royal Academy caught his eye. The soldier was not much of a reader, but the name that leapt out at him from the newspaper had been impregnated on his mind since childhood. The man's name was a family legend. It belonged to a painter his father had spun tales about whenever he spoke of his young days before he and the man lost touch. Now, according to the newspaper, the painter lived only a few miles away.

The corporal was George Fountain Page, son of another George Fountain Page, or 'Shrimp'. He found his way to Castle House, Dedham as soon as possible and asked for Sir Alfred Munnings. 'You're Shrimp all over,' Munnings repeated in bewilderment, for he had always believed that Shrimp had been killed in World War I. Now, he learnt that he was alive and married with three children and lived in Leicester.

A few weeks later the corporal borrowed a Morris 8 and drove his father from Leicester to see Munnings. It was the old Shrimp, stocky and perky, who had hardly changed, Munnings thought, as they talked over endless tankards of beer. 'They talked all day,' Shrimp's son said.

Shrimp told his former master that, since they parted, he had always lived in caravans. His present one was parked in an old stable yard in Leicester where he had three horses out to grass and made a living wheeling and dealing. During World War I, he might have been close to Munnings. He had served as a lance-corporal in a horse regiment in France and had twice been mentioned in dispatches. He was injured just before the Armistice and lost the tip of his index finger. After the war, he married a beautiful dark-haired Romany, had two sons and a daughter and travelled the road.

His son took up the story: 'A better mother and father you couldn't want,' he said. 'We were always warm and well fed and we'd plenty of coal because we always parked near a railway. Although Pa drank a lot we were a close-knit family. We had no schooling but Mother taught us to read and write.'

Shrimp told Munnings that when World War II broke out, he parked his van permanently in Leicester and became an air raid warden. During a raid in 1942, he was blasted across a factory yard and lay in hospital for a week suffering from amnesia.

Munnings and Shrimp never lost touch again. Munnings visited Leicester several times over the years. On his first visit, he took a large birthday cake with him because, although Shrimp had no idea when he was born, the cake probably symbolized the rebirth of their friendship. Shrimp paid at least two more visits to Dedham.*

* * *

In 1947 Munnings still had an urge to appear in print, despite John Masefield's lack of enthusiasm about his book of poems and ballads. The painter had drawers full of verses, incomplete diaries, jottings and letters and, once or twice, encouraged by friends, he had tried to arrange them into an autobiography. He just did not know how to start the book, he told his new friend, Guy Schofield. The journalist offered to have a look at the material.

He received a huge parcel of scribbled notes, typescripts and press cuttings from the would-be author, made a brief assessment and typed out his own idea for the first two or three pages of Munnings's book. He began it reflectively and dated the opening retrospectively, at an important time in the painter's life:

> This is written on Tuesday, 13th June, 1944 [read the opening paragraph]. I was elected President of the Royal Academy in March. The Birthday Honours List appeared last Thursday, and I am still receiving letters from friends of today, friends of the past and even from people I do not know. This being

* In 1968 Shrimp left a public house after drinking half a pint of beer. He said he felt ill, went to bed, refused to see a doctor and died during the night. He had fourteen grandchildren and twelve great-grandchildren.

> a real Exmoor day – a day of driving wind and rain – I lay in bed reading more letters. Then I fell into a reverie.... Who would have thought I should ever be President of the Royal Academy or be knighted by the King? What a go!

The reverie turned to Munnings's horses; those at Exmoor and down the years to the greys at his Aunt Rosa's wedding and to Merrylegs, the name of his first pony and, earlier still, of his first toy. Munnings found it easy to continue in the same vein; in fact, he just could not stop writing.

'It was just as if I'd triggered something off,' Schofield recalled. 'He saw when to start and how to start. We met frequently after that and often he would slap his thigh and say, "Guy, I've just done a damn good chapter. Let's have a bottle of claret."'

The meticulous journalist thought the result was 'slap dash' and deplored the way Munnings 'just plonked everything down'. However, during their frequent meetings he enjoyed hearing Munnings's opinions on art. 'If you like a picture,' Munnings told him, 'and you're an intelligent human being, well, that's a good picture and there's no reason why your judgement should be regarded less than that of the art critics.'

He knew his own work was good but not great, Schofield said. He added: 'He had no vanity and always conceded the great artists were better than he was. "How did he do it!" he often said, looking in admiration at the work of other painters.'

Munnings wrote prolifically. Expressing himself in words probably afforded him release from the tedium of the Presidency, which allowed him little time to paint. The task of shaping and sorting several thousand pages of typescript and choosing from as many photographs fell to a young editor, William Luscombe, who was running a new publishing business, virtually single-handed.

Luscombe had approached Munnings at least a dozen times before the painter reluctantly agreed to meet him, 'to silence him' about publishing his memoirs. Ultimately, to the surprise of the trade, he chose him, from strong competition. The painter was, perhaps, irrationally impressed by the fourteen-stone Luscombe's ability to paddle a canoe from Dover to Calais in six hours and two minutes.

Luscombe needed all his strength and endurance during the five years in which he had to cope with Munnings's unpredictable moods, his perpetual drive for perfection and his bursts of wild enthusiasm, when he expected his publisher to work round the clock, seven days a week. The two became firm friends, although while Luscombe was working on the manuscript he was eventually forced to find refuge in the Reading Room of the British Museum to escape from Munnings's long and persistent telephone calls.

Violet Munnings drove him to the station after his first hard-working weekend at Dedham. 'Mr Luscombe,' she said, 'you look as though you've been crucified.' The man, more than forty years younger than her husband, replied, 'I have.'

He was there on Munnings's birthday when the painter insisted on buying a brace of pheasants for dinner, although Violet warned him they should hang for a few days before he ate them. When he tasted them at dinner that night he flew into a towering rage and left the table, swearing at the top of his voice. 'What impressed me most,' Luscombe said, 'was to hear the voice slowly fading into the distance as he passed from room to room.'

There were happier interludes. They went racing at Newmarket and Luscombe learnt how Munnings made a rare study of the finish of a race, as opposed to his usual paintings of the start. Before the days of starting stalls, horses and riders jockeying for position behind the tape gave the painter more time to record his impressions. However, the finish was over in a flash. Munnings tried to overcome this by sketching the finishes of six races in one afternoon and created a composite picture from six sets of racehorses, brought to a standstill, their nostrils extended, their tails quivering, when the jockeys dropped the reins, dismounted and unsaddled. But the technique did not work. The impression never came alive.

Such painting respites were rare during Munnings's term of office and, by 1948, the President of the Royal Academy was a tired man. Gout attacks disabled him for weeks at a time; his obsessive hatred of modern art dissipated his energy, as Eversley Belfield had noted, and he had to stay in London when he longed to be in the country and paint. He tended to delegate irksome responsibilities and, in 1947, had handed over the organization of the exhibition of the King's Pictures to Gerald Kelly, saying he was 'not quite up to the mark'. His frustration mounted and he decided to resign the Presidency.

Meanwhile, he caused an unfortunate scene at the Garrick when he loudly called John Rothenstein a bloody Jew and said that was why he staged an exhibition of the work of Chagall, another Jew. His audience, including Robert Lutyens, descendant of his former mentor, protested vehemently whereupon Munnings attacked Lutyens, saying his grandfather had been 'a real painter and a great architect,' but he had built neither cathedrals nor bridges. Lutyens's letter of complaint to the Club officials resulted in Munnings receiving a stern rebuke from the secretary. Perhaps the Club feared a demand for an apology might result in a scandal that might reach the newspapers.

Suddenly, his frustration abated when, unexpectedly, an irresistible idea from the new Academician Extraordinary made him change his mind about resigning the Presidency. Churchill suggested that Munnings should revive the Royal Academy's annual banquet, after a lapse of ten years. This men-only function had been started in the days of Sir Joshua Reynolds and was held on the Wednesday evening preceding the Private View of the Summer Exhibition. It had been an art event of the year, reported in most newspapers and, since the 1920s, had been broadcast live on BBC radio.

The idea stirred all Munnings's initial excitement at following in the official footsteps of Reynolds. He agreed to the dinner providing that Churchill promised to make a speech. The inveterate party-giver also decided on innovations to lighten a traditional, heavy, solemn affair, held in the largest gallery at Burlington House and attended by two hundred and forty men but no women, for even the four or five lady R As were excluded. He would have a toastmaster 'in full splendour' and arrange for the Royal Artillery Band to play 'The Boys of the Old Brigade' to which the company could sing, before speeches by the Archbishop of Canterbury, the Duke of Gloucester, the Lord Chief Justice, Lord Montgomery, Churchill and, of course, by Munnings himself.

Munnings had never spoken in such distinguished company and, a few days before the banquet, he discussed his speech with Stanley Wade and a friend, over dinner at Claridge's. He was a conspicuous figure, Wade recalled, in check trousers, a yellow waistcoat and a carnation in his black jacket.

He became more conspicuous. Their table was soon the focus

of attention as Munnings, in a loud voice, lambasted modern art, particularly the work of Francis Bacon. He told Wade and dozens of people within earshot, that he wished he could say as much at the Royal Academy banquet but felt it would be fouling the artistic nest to decry other painters, even though he detested their work. Wade disagreed. He insisted that, on such an occasion, the President should be allowed to express his true feelings.

It was the encouragement Munnings needed. Neighbours were fascinated as, in an even louder voice, he amplified his points and only drew breath to order a fish dish that was not on the menu. The Head Waiter was summoned and Munnings remained adamant that a restaurant of that quality must always be able to produce just what the client needed. After a long delay, the requested fish dish arrived.

That was not the end of the unscheduled cabaret. In stentorian tones he requested the waiter to 'Bring me some applie pie like my mother used to make.' Apple pie was not on the menu either and the restaurant waited again while the Head Waiter disappeared and returned bearing, in impeccable style, a pie that seemed to fill the bill.

Munnings ate it with great gusto, Wade recalled, and then lapsed into a loud attack of hiccups. It seemed, however, the meal had been a significant triumph, for the confident diner, with two victories under his belt, told Wade that he had decided to take his advice and express his views on modern art at the Academy dinner.

Later, he hinted to one or two of his R A colleagues that Churchill privately supported his intentions to 'have a go' at the way the Academy and other powerful bodies condoned modern art. Churchill had, in fact, made no secret of his attitude and Reginald Pound had already quoted him in his book *A Maypole in the Strand* as saying: 'Modern art is deluding the people.'

Munnings was, fundamentally, a simple soul and his extravagant vitriolic outpourings against modern art probably covered up his fear that it might spoil his own vision of nature. He considered most modern art affected, and designed merely to be sensational. His East Anglian suspicion may also have been aroused and he could not believe such paintings meant anything to their creators. In addition, he was infuriated by so-called artists who had not served such a long apprenticeship as he had and were not prepared to spend a life-time in study.

At the 1949 Academy banquet, A. J. Munnings, the first landscape painter to be President of that august institution, made a blunt sixteen-minute speech, largely off the cuff, with the aid of only a few notes. It created Academy history. The BBC's switchboards were jammed with telephone calls even while the next speaker, Winston Churchill, was still speaking. Several dissenting diners were heard over the air and at least two objectors had to be ejected forcibly from the gallery. Afterwards, Sir Walter Lamb warned Munnings that he could expect at least six libel suits against him.

He delivered his speech with an ease of manner and a sense of oratory, brought to a peak by a few pre-dinner sherries, champagne with the meal and a final sip of wine. With perfect emphasis and timing and a masterly display of rhetoric, he lashed out at the Academy, the Arts Council, the Tate Gallery and at Anthony Blunt, Surveyor of the King's Pictures who, he complained, had said Reynolds was inferior to Matisse. He blamed them all for accepting those 'foolish daubers' Cézanne, Matisse and Picasso, whose influence, he maintained, had defiled the British tradition:

> On my left, I have the famous newly-elected extraordinary member of the Academy – Winston Churchill. He is beside me because once he said to me, 'Alfred, if you met Picasso coming down the street would you join with me in kicking his something something . . . ?' I said, 'Yes Sir, I would.'
>
> Perhaps I should not mention names, but I do not care, since I am resigning at the end of this year . . . I do not wish to go on with an Academy that says – their profound minds working and thinking – 'Well, there *must* be something in this modern art; these writers are getting busy, we must give the jugglers a show . . . .'

As President of a body of men who were shilly-shallying, feeling there was something in this co-called modern art, he queried whether the members of the Royal Academy were worthy of the building in which they were housed.

> I myself [he said] would rather have – excuse me, my Lord Archbishop – a damned bad failure, a bad, dusty old picture where somebody had tried to do something, to set down what

> they have felt, than all this affected juggling, this following of what – shall we call it the School of Paris? (I trust the French Ambassador is not here tonight.)

Sacks full of letters from all over the world showed that, generally, the public agreed with him and heartily approved of the way in which he had made his case. The disapprovals included forty objections sent to the BBC on his use of the word 'damned'. The only complaint that upset him was Churchill's private protest, telegraphed to him on the day after the banquet, rebuking him, strongly, for the way he had publicized a private joke between them. Munnings admitted he might have gone too far.

He had certainly gone a long way towards fulfilling Violet's original conviction that, as President, he 'could do much to lift up the dying Academy and make it a live place'. No President, before or since, had done so much to introduce art controversy into the homes of people who had never heard of Picasso or Cézanne. Meanwhile the directors of several British art galleries sent an open letter of regret to Matisse and Picasso.

No President had elicited such support from an army which included doctors and vicars, the Transport and General Workers' Union, his peers, like Lionel Edwards, who commented, 'Well done, A.J.! I was delighted to see you had a crack at them,' and from Lord Dunsany who wrote, 'Thank you very much for all that you said, sanity's tottering throne will be steadied by it.'

Later, he could hardly believe he had said it. When he heard a private play-back of the speech at the BBC he chuckled with glee and asked repeatedly, 'Did I say *that*? What a go!'

His resignation as President took effect from the end of the year, as he had promised, and 'joyously, he returned to painting' – often at Newmarket, 'the most beautiful course in the world'. His race cards were scribbled with sketches and phrases expressing his pleasure. 'Happier by far than I have been these twenty years,' he wrote on a card as he walked by the river. '... I had sought and found the spot I must find at the moment or die. So satisfying were my surroundings that it is impossible to express my feelings ...' Yet, even in Arcadia, he was dogged by the abhorrence of modern art.

One of the first acts of the succeeding President, Sir Gerald Kelly, had been to reinstate Stanley Spencer, ARA, one of Munnings's *bêtes noires*. Spencer had resigned from the Academy in 1935 because the Hanging Committee rejected two of his six pictures submitted for the Summer Exhibition. Munnings's annoyance at the reinstatement festered when, in the 1950 Summer Exhibition, Sir Gerald commemorated Spencer's return by hanging several of his largest and most important canvases together, including four *Port Glasgow Resurrection* pictures. Spencer's return was the talk of the 1950 Academy, where Munnings's three Newmarket scenes and three landscapes went comparatively unnoticed. A touch of cynicism could be detected in the title of one of them: *Not yet a dumping ground for tins and rubbish*.

In the autumn, Munnings's dislike of Spencer reached bursting point when he found a small Spencer painting, which he considered obscene, in an obscure dealer's London gallery. He was particularly disgusted because he usually associated Spencer with religious themes. He borrowed the painting and also some of Spencer's genitalia drawings which he considered improper, had them photographed and showed the photographs to the police, urging prosecution under the obscenity laws. The resultant enquiries led to sensational accounts in several newspapers.

Sir Gerald Kelly returned from a trip to America in time to convince the Director of Public Prosecutions that the case should be dropped. It was unlikely to have succeeded, however, for even if the pictures were obscene, which was doubtful, there was no evidence that they had been exhibited, which was a requirement for conviction.

Once again, the past President had shocked the Academy and the next Council meeting recorded the following minute:

> The President read extracts from newspapers dated between 1st and 21st October 1950 showing that Sir Alfred Munnings had sought to defame the character and art of Mr Stanley Spencer by showing certain unexhibited paintings to members of a London club and the police. It was agreed that it was highly reprehensible that a Member of the Academy should attack another in this way, and that the President would personally assure Mr Spencer of the Council's regret for the occurrence and their readiness to assist him if further attacks of the kind were made on him.

Munnings never spoke of Spencer again.

Meanwhile, the tension between him and Churchill was short-lived. Churchill, at the age of seventy-four, had taken up racing as a hobby and had acquired a French colt, Colonist II, who won thirteen races for him in his first three seasons. He was a grey and, after Munnings had watched his third win at Ascot, he longed to paint him. Coincidentally, a letter came from Churchill inviting him to do so.

> ... the most wonderful letter I ever received in my life [Munnings replied with boyish enthusiasm]. What a horse! What a hind leg, what hocks! I could paint him with my eyes shut.
>
> I do not paint horses with races ahead, or when the late autumn gives them a coat like a bear. He will be a picture in the Spring.

He was. Munnings was back in his own environment, writing about it as well as painting it. *An Artist's Life*, with one hundred and forty photographs, including many illustrations by him, was published in November 1950. The bulky volume, which had needed much costly resetting because of his afterthoughts, dealt only with the first forty years of his life and was a series of jottings rather than a structured autobiography, despite William Luscombe's valiant efforts. Nevertheless, it was a fascinating and full-blooded *tour de force* and created great interest, including an invitation to speak at a Foyle's Literary Lunch. Obviously, there should be a sequel. It turned out there were two: *The Second Burst* and *The Finish*, both also large books, copiously illustrated and published, consecutively, in the next two years. All were dedicated 'To My Wife'.

The critics were enthusiastic for a variety of reasons. The books, although chronologically inconsequential, had an endearing spontaneity, passages of lyrical writing and a wealth of appeal: 'Munnings gives us a precise analysis of his methods of attack on a painting.... In short, unceasing study eternally nagged at by the thought, "It can't be done,"' wrote Norman Lindsay, sympathizing with 'the hell of a job' which those commissioned portraits of horses had been. 'No one,' he added, 'who is concerned for the dignity of art can afford to miss this.'

The author's friend and admirer, James Wentworth Day, wrote of the books as 'cameos of perfection', while in a more considered and unbiased vein, the prolific author, R. H. Mottram, applauded their remarkable exuberance and enthusiasm, 'often shown', he wrote, 'in "shorthand" notes of momentary moods, snatched and fixed and put away safely until the time comes to elaborate them,' and by the 'sheer zest of living' they expressed.

Inevitably, Munnings was inundated with invitations to lecture. The Council of the Royal Academy invited him to speak on Stubbs and Constable at the Royal Institute in Albemarle Street. The hall was packed for both lectures and, although Munnings confessed he had never attended a lecture and knew nothing about giving one, he rose to the challenge enthusiastically.

Humphrey Brooke, the new Secretary of the Royal Academy, said, 'He instructed me to fill the water-bottle on the desk with neat gin. So fortified, he held the attention of enthusiastic audiences of over six hundred, the largest since Marconi had lectured there, for over two hours using no notes and with disregard of the Institution's regulations*.'

His style of lecturing proved as unpredictable as his writing. In his first one, he did not mention Stubbs's name until he had been speaking for one hour. Then, peering into the hall he called out 'Are you awake, Violet?' to a roar of amusement from the audience, whom he enthralled for another hour with a penetrating and knowledgeable discourse on Stubbs.

He found he could use his lectures as umbrellas for airing any topic he felt strongly about; from the shortage of studio space in Chelsea and the subversive activities of the Arts Council, to ecology and modern farming methods and, of course, his disgust at modern art.

Surprisingly, the champion of so many causes seemed unconcerned about an infringement close at hand; the increasing number of forgeries of his pictures. In 1952, he returned to Norwich for a luncheon to celebrate the publication of his book and afterwards, walking up the picturesque cobbled Elm Hill, the oldest street in Norwich, with the writer Eric Fowler, he said, with a wry grin; 'D'you know, there's been a sight more Munnings sold in this street than Munnings ever painted.'

That day he went on to the Castle Museum where a friend found him standing in front of his picture, *Sunny Jim*, painted in 1901,

* Lectures invariably lasted one hour.

which showed Old Norman leading a Suffolk mare and foal along a poppy-sprinkled path beside a hedgerow of flowering elder. James Reeve had bought it for the Museum for £85 – 'a vast fortune' to Munnings in those days. 'My God! I wish I could paint like that now,' he said.

Predictably, gout and an attendant awareness of increasing disability, added to the rarely-spoken fear of diminishing sight in his one eye, aggravated his irritability. Earlier in the day, at a signing session for his books at a Norwich store, ignoring the long queue waiting for his signature he became involved in an argument about one of his pictures with a lady at the head of the queue. The crowd grew restless until the book buyer, Bertie Stone, persuaded the first customer to move on. The next customer was an elderly gentleman, clasping his three volumes of Munnings's autobiography. Munnings signed the first, picked up the second and said, 'That's not bloody-well mine,' and hurled it across the store. Apparently, the old man had accidentally included a similar-looking book by another author.

The novelty of authorship soon wore off, as Munnings's patience was strained by the increasing correspondence and public demands it entailed. 'I have more to do than sign books for people,' he wrote in reply to the widow of an old Norwich friend who asked him to autograph her copy. 'Damn the book. I refuse to sign another.'

However, his enthusiasm about publishing was renewed when Violet wrote the memoirs of her beloved black pekinese, Black Knight, whom she had taken everywhere with her, since 1945. *The Diary of a Freeman*, purported to have been written by Black Knight himself, told how he was carried in Violet's little black velvet evening bag to Buckingham Palace for Munnings's investiture, to a royal Garden Party and to a party before the wedding of Princess Elizabeth. One guest thought his head, sticking out of the bag, was 'a very unusual trimming'. He went in the bag to the Lord Mayor's Banquet at the Guildhall where he was made an Honorary Freeman of the City of London.

When the press grew wise to the contents of Violet's evening bag, Black Knight was transferred to an orchid-covered muff from which he viewed the wedding of Princess Elizabeth at Westminster Abbey. He became something of a national curiosity and sent a telegram to Princess Margaret 'in humble duty and obedience' on her twenty-first birthday, to which she replied in a message signed 'Margaret' that same afternoon.

Munnings, thrilled with the success of his own autobiography, tried to mastermind the whole production, which was the last thing Violet wanted. This was to be her book. However, she was happy for her husband to provide sketches to be inserted in the text. He also did a delightful oil painting of the four-legged 'author' sitting on a desk between a silver inkwell and a pile of books for the frontispiece. When the material was due at the publishers the arguments between Alfred and Violet were so intense that, in a fit of pique, Munnings painted out his signature on the painting. However, peace was restored before the book was printed and his name appeared on the fly-leaf as illustrator, beneath the name of Black Knight as author. Violet's name did not appear.

The book was very successful and the proceeds were donated to buy an ambulance for the People's Dispensary for Sick Animals. Sadly, Black Knight could not attend the launching party of his book because he had a cold, but Violet could be seen scooping titbits into a paper bag to take home to him. Violet maintained that Black Knight even picked out winners at race meetings, by barking at his chosen horse in the paddock. Even after his death in 1955 at the age of ten, Black Knight continued to accompany his mistress for she had him stuffed.

Munnings was painting enthusiastically again, at all the major meetings, but most frequently at Newmarket where, invariably, he was at the starting post. 'A hundred times have I seen this sight and yet it was more beautiful than ever,' he wrote on the day of a Cesarewitch .... 'Each start was a fresh picture for me, as they have been, meeting after meeting, year after year ....'

They cared about him at Newmarket. Lads riding on The Heath tipped their caps to him and called out 'Mornin' Sir Halfred', and the Jockey Club loaned him an old horse-rubbing box on the course as a studio. It was some two hundred yards from the start of the 2,000 Guineas, near the Rowley Mile, and the Jockey Club had lights inserted in the roof. He was also given permission by the Clerk of the Course to drive a car to the starting-gate.

One day, there was a knock at the window of the hut and a man announced he had travelled nearly 3,500 miles to see him and buy a painting. Munnings was indifferent, at that time, about selling paintings, but he loved the originality of approach and was eventually persuaded to sell one or two pictures – even though the enterprising purchaser turned out to be a director of the New York picture dealers, Wildenstein.

Munnings often predicted to Stanley Wade that, after his death, his paintings would realize very high prices. Wade thought there might be a steady price rise but never visualized the phenomenal increase by which, within twenty-five years of the painter's death, *The Start at Newmarket* sold at auction for £220,000, then a world record for a work by a twentieth-century British painter.

Munnings, meanwhile, was perplexed by the lack of interest in his landscapes and, one day, showed Wade a pile of some fifty landscape sketches without horses, in his studio. 'Is it not amazing, Wade,' he asked, 'that these, to my mind, are my best work and yet there's not a sod in the world who wants to buy them? For instance, you could have them for £50 a piece.'

Wade missed that opportunity, although, over the years, his firm bought hundreds of Munnings's paintings, most of which they reproduced as prints.

> Whenever he came to sign reproductions (usually five hundred at a time) [Wade said], he always insisted on having a particular grade of pencil. Should a point break, he would fling the offending weapon over his shoulder. He felt that, out of respect to him, only a Director should turn over the sheets.
>
> He was the quickest artist ever to sign copies and, while signing, would keep up a running commentary about the subject before him and would criticise my own failings in a colourful fashion. He invariably walked off with all the pencils.

Tony Nevill, a director of the firm, was a youngster and had never met Munnings when he was sent to Dedham with a two hundred and fifty edition of a large print for the painter to sign. He was warned not to drive up to the house, that the painter would demand cash for each print he signed, and he should take twenty-four sharpened pencils.

> I loved his pictures [Nevill said], and this was one of the highlights of my career.
>
> It was a very hot summer's day and I staggered up the drive

> carrying the prints in four parcels and just made it to the front door. I rang the bell but nothing happened. Then a voice from above shouted, 'You bloody tradesman. Use the trademen's entrance.'
>
> I went round to the back door. He shuffled down and let me in and I told him why I'd come. He said, 'I can't sign those. I haven't a pencil.' I produced a pencil and he still refused to sign them. He said he didn't feel well and dropped the pencil on the floor. After half-an-hour he hadn't signed a single print and told me to go and leave the prints and the money with him.
>
> I said I would leave them with Lady Munnings and his reply was unprintable. I then told him that this was to have been the greatest day of my life and it had turned into the most disappointing and I was going and taking the cash and the prints with me.
>
> 'You're a cheeky young sod,' he said. 'Wait here.'
>
> He went off and came back about ten minutes later with two huge tulip glasses full of brown liquid. They were full to the brim and he didn't spill a drop. He said it was cask sherry and should be left to settle. It took about twenty minutes and tasted like pure fire-water.
>
> He then sat down at a table and signed one print. He then asked me which of his books I liked best. I said the second and he asked me why I didn't prefer the first. I said I thought the second had more meat in it and, anyway, no one was very interested in his early works.
>
> He was terribly interested to know someone who had read his books. He then signed every print. It took him about two hours.

It was probably no idle excuse when Munnings told Tony Nevill that he did not feel well. The tear duct of his good eye was blocked, his left thumb 'felt dead' when he held his palette for any length of time and he was obliged to sit at his easel. Moreover, there were medical signs of cardiac disturbance. Nevertheless, he battled on, finishing a picture he had started six years previously called *Moving Up Under Starter's Orders, Newmarket.*

It measured forty-eight by ninety inches, one of the largest canvases he had ever tackled, and was shown in the 1954 Royal Academy where it was bought by E.P. Taylor, the Canadian industrialist. Among his other five pictures that year was one of his last equine studies, *Newmarket Incident: Runaway*, a forty by fifty inch picture of a jockey struggling to control a racehorse that had broken away.

He and Taylor met each other for the first time at a private dinner party at the Athenaeum. A fellow-guest was James Gunn, who was painting Taylor's portrait. Gunn asked Munnings's permission to use the large racing picture as a background for the portrait and Munnings was delighted until Gunn remarked, 'I find painting a horse much easier than painting a man.'

Taylor had the portrait reproduced for his Christmas card, whereupon Munnings, still furious at Gunn's remark, threatened legal redress, if not for breach of copyright – which he had sold with the picture – then for the poor quality of reproduction. He insisted it had damaged his reputation but again, as with the Spencer case, he was forced to climb down. Such incidents helped to undermine his health and sapped his energy. He was not interested when he was asked to paint Queen Elizabeth II and Foxhunter, the great show-jumper.

Horses were still his main interest and, in one of his last lectures, he reaffirmed his life-long love for them. He was besotted by horses, he told students of London University's Royal Veterinary College's Medical Association – the oldest Veterinary Society in the United Kingdom, when he spoke to them about his life and work.

A student in the audience, now Dr John Bleby, Director of the College's Postgraduate Unit, recalled how he held the packed meeting enthralled, without using a single note, for more than an hour.

> You could have heard a pin drop. He told us if there were no horses in the world, life would not be worth living. He said he expressed his love for them through painting and by studying them and he never tired of looking at them.
>
> He spoke with his eyes closed and swayed backwards and forwards, as if we weren't there. He spoke of the smell of the dew at early morning gallops and the clatter of horses' hoofs and the start of a race with the horses milling around, waiting to get under starter's orders; a moment of tension with their nostrils flaring and their adrenaline flowing. 'Always the start – never the finish,' he said.
>
> He then made a plea for stallions which I've never forgotten. He said that, after a stallion had raced for three or four seasons and won two or three classics, he became a valuable stud animal. When that happened, his whole life, everything

> he'd been trained for, stopped overnight. The poor animal would hardly be ridden and would get fat and go to seed.
>
> He felt very upset about that and suggested that if any of us, as potential vets, went into horse practice, we should make sure that old racehorses were ridden every day, if only by stable lads.

He had, in a small way, repaid a little of the debt he owed to the creatures he loved best in the world.

By that time Munnings's hands and feet were distorted by gout and painting required a great effort. At the start of 1956, he entered Ipswich and East Suffolk Hospital to be treated for cardiac asthma. He was a memorable patient because of his bad language, his tempers, his refusal to follow a prescribed diet and his determination to go home. Yet, he endeared himself to the nurses.

He was released after three weeks and, from a wheelchair, corresponded feverishly with Humphrey Brooke about a Retrospective Exhibition of more than three hundred of his works to be held in the Diploma Gallery's four salons at Burlington House from March to June. He was only the third painter to be honoured with a one-man show at the Royal Academy in his lifetime.

He implored Brooke to get the skylights done over with muslin at once because the heat would be unbearable in May and June. 'Remember my poor old artist's temperament and that I painted them all,' he wrote. 'No painting can stand the sun. It becomes a joke, a skinned piece of paint on canvas.'

He made suggestions for hanging the pictures. They ranged from his first Royal Academy acceptance, *Stranded*, to a recent horse study painted for Violet the previous year. One hundred and ten of the works had been lent by the artist and, of those, sixty were pure landscapes. 'Not too many of those bloody commissioned pictures,' he implored Brooke, explaining they showed up his 'tricks' of which he was ashamed.

He sent instructions, through Brooke, to James Gunn who was to do a television introduction to the Exhibition. 'Tell Gunn from me, all the change and variety is ready if an artist paints from Nature. Nature can give lovelier surprises than all abstractions .... Nature has always beaten me, but all I've done that's any good is from Nature.'

In an introduction to the Exhibition Catalogue, Anthony Devas,

A R A, recommended that all art students should see the works of 'so uninhibited, rumbustious and English a painter'. He wrote:

> He paints all day despite the rain and the wind, despite the restless champing of his chosen models, and despite, too, the discouragement of the modern critic, and he'll not be content with his first attempt to capture his dream – he'll do it again and again. The work involved is prodigious – it makes one think of the studios of the old masters, but unlike them, he has no students to help him.
>
> ... This is the real world – this delightful response to life, this love of simple and ordinary things, and the enormous skill and technical accomplishment displayed in the more elaborate commissioned works – that too is the real world for painters, for that craftsmanship is the backbone of the masterpieces of artists as diverse as Stubbs and Botticelli, Rembrandt and Degas.

Munnings was not well enough to attend the Exhibition and had to be content to watch the television broadcast and read the press criticisms. The critics were divided in their opinions, and two or three of the pro-moderns seized their opportunity to hit back at him, to retaliate for his forcibly-expressed views in speeches and letters to the newspapers.

He sent a copy of a 'letter' which, to his annoyance, *The Times* had refused to publish, to Lady Wentworth, with whom he was in correspondence about buying a grey Arab. It began:

> If you want to be reviewed
> By *The Times* with promptitude,
> You do a monster nude
> To weigh a Ton,
> With a belly to protrude,
> Of genetic magnitude,
> To shock the multitude
> Excepting one –
> Who thro' the night with vigour,
> Writes up the abstract figure,
> In a column growing bigger,
> For *The Times*
> Which he does for precious readers,
> A cultural lot of bleeders,
> Who never read the leaders
> Or the crimes.

Later in the year he stayed away from the Royal Academy banquet and told the newspapermen that he did not want to see his work hung next to some of the bits of nonsense that were allowed in. He may also have been concealing the fact, even from himself, that he did not feel well enough to go.

Nevertheless, his perverse opposition to modern art was there for all to see. One of his six pictures was the season's most controversial painting, a lampoon on modern art, which the President, Sir Albert Richardson, had tried his best to prevent him from showing. His misgivings were as much for Munnings's painting reputation, as for the reputation of the Academy.

Does the Subject Matter? illustrated Munnings's attitude to the way he thought modern art was threatening the traditions and authority of the Royal Academy. It showed a piece of contemporary sculpture being examined by a rapt Sir John Rothenstein, Director of the Tate Gallery, a noncommittal Humphrey Brooke, a thoughtful John Mavrogordato and a slightly bewildered young lady in pink from Selfridge's fur department. In the background, Professor Thomas Bodkin, Director of the Barber Institute of Fine Arts in Birmingham, and an elderly gentleman were examining another work while, hanging on the wall above, were copies of three Picassos. Munnings had written under the title in the catalogue:

> And why not purchased for the State?
> The State, alas, has come too late.
> Because the subject's so profound
> 'Twas sold for twenty thousand pounds.

The picture had been hung only after long and voluminous correspondence between Munnings and the Academy officials. To Richardson, Munnings wrote, 'You have attacked, in biting phrases, work of modern architects. This gave many of us hope: now you tremble at a humorous picture aimed at modern art ... and now that I am trying to hit back for tradition in paint, as you do in words, you object. For me it is a setback I least expected. After all, Sir, what in God's name is there to fear?'

There was no artistic merit in his 'little joke', as he unrealistically called it. Whether it was a good or a bad joke was left to the public to decide when they tracked it to its inconspicuous position in

Gallery IV. However, the controversy it had provoked probably gave Munnings the impetus he needed to travel to London and see it *in situ* for himself.

As for his devotees who feared the crude illustration might jeopardize his reputation, they need only look at the crowds flocking into his Exhibition in the Diploma Gallery to feel reassured. He donated £300 to the Artists' Benevolent Fund in gratitude to the Academy for the Retrospective Exhibition.

Perhaps the arguments provided the tonic he needed. There was a remission from gout and he was at every Newmarket Meeting again, sketching horses and riders and working on the sketches in his Dedham studio until the small hours. He also fulfilled a promise to the Queen and painted several studies of her racehorse Aureole.

On good days his energy was tremendous: one night, after a day at Newmarket, he was driven to London for an evening at the Athenaeum with friends, and soon after midnight excused himself to get back to Dedham because he intended to be at the first race at Newmarket the following day.

Two pictures of the Queen's horse Aureole fetched high prices in his very successful one-man exhibition run by James Green at the Bond Street Galleries. He gave £1,500 raised by one painting of Aureole to a fund to buy Gainsborough's birthplace at Sudbury and donated £1,000 from the other to Hungarian Relief. Nearly all the one hundred and eighty pictures and drawings – many of them boyhood works – were sold. One admirer came from Canada especially to see the exhibition.

Yet he could sympathize with less-successful young painters. Early in 1958, James Noble from Norwich had his first one-man exhibition in the Bond Street Galleries, which unfortunately coincided with the worst financial crisis since the war. Munnings visited the Galleries and saw that hardly a picture had been sold. He told Green to invite the editor of the *London Evening News* to the exhibition, mention his name, and ask him to give the young painter a write-up. 'We got a wonderful piece in the paper, a few days later,' Noble recalled. 'Within a week we had almost sold out.'

Munnings was at the opening of the 1958 Academy where all but one of his six pictures were racing scenes. Afterwards, he wrote to Guy Schofield, 'Do not let this opportunity slip, but slip to town one day yourself and write a *stinger*.... Let them know that one paper at least speaks its mind on this frightful letting down of Tradition on the walls of the Academy. ... My fervour is fast abating – it is for you to carry the lance and tilt now.'

There was little sign of his fervour abating when he appeared on a BBC television programme, declaiming one of his ballads. He had finally succeeded in persuading his publishers to issue a slim book of forty-three of his ballads and poems, illustrated by his own sketches. The television appearance was a result. The book was not a big success but his honour, in yet another medium, was at last satisfied, particularly when he was invited to read a few of the poems at a meeting of the Poetry Society.

He followed up the new publicity with more letters to *The Times* and the *Daily Telegraph*, complaining at the way scientific progress, particularly jet aircraft which roared over his home, was menacing the beauty of England.

By 1959 however, even writing was denied him. Humphrey Brooke visited him at home at the end of April and found him with both his hands bandaged in flannel, hardly able to move. He told Brooke that, as he would never paint again, he wished he were dead. The next day he telephoned Brooke at the Royal Academy and apologized for having been such poor company.

Early in June, James Wentworth Day telephoned him and said he would like to see him. 'I'm not fit to see a dog. I've done with this world,' he told Wentworth Day, in a sad, deep voice. 'Nonsense,' Wentworth Day replied, 'you've got another book in you yet. Your three-decker memoirs are absolutely classic. Time you wrote another one. Search your memory. It will come to you.'

'Only one thing will come to me – the graa-ave. You can write my epitaph,' he said and put down the telephone.

Next month he entered the Essex County Hospital at Colchester for treatment and, a week after he returned home, on 17 July 1959, he died in his sleep. There was a private cremation at Colchester and, a week later, a Memorial Service at St James's Church, Piccadilly.

The congregation overflowed from the little church out into the warm sunshine. They heard Sir Charles Wheeler, President of the Royal Academy, say that Munnings

> ... drank so deeply of the visible world that he became, at times, quite intoxicated with it and was led into extravagances which delighted some and exasperated others.
>
> So overwhelmed was he by the loveliness of nature that distortion was an anathema to him – a sort of violation of a holy thing. Quite incapable of understanding why it should ever be helpful or necessary to distort, he found himself quite cut off from many of the manifestations of present day art.
>
> The passage of time will, of course, determine the validity or otherwise of his so strongly held views but *no* passage of the years will ever prove his insincerity – for he had none. I myself have never known anyone less prone to it than he.

A conspicuous mourner at the service was Augustus John, wearing a wide-brimmed straw hat, daubed with black paint, for the occasion. Afterwards, he said, 'I think Munnings was greater than Stubbs. He made it move, had greater narrative quality and his groupings are better.' No epitaph could have pleased Munnings better.

Munnings's ashes were laid in the crypt of St Paul's Cathedral, where a memorial tablet was dedicated to him next to that of another Suffolk miller's son, the artist John Constable. Lines written on his death by his friend John Masefield, the Poet Laureate, were engraved below Munnings's carved profile:

> O friend, how lovely are the things,
> The English things, you helped us to perceive.

Over the years, this sentiment was endorsed, worldwide, in growing appreciation of his paintings, and, one by one, close friends tended to identify the inimitable elements of Munnings in their own ways. 'Time may well prove that, next to Winston Churchill, the most enduring fame for an Englishman of our generation will go to Alfred Munnings,' wrote that most discerning editor, Guy Schofield.

Ten years after his death, Stanley Wade, his print publisher for more than thirty years, described him with penetrating understanding in a catalogue for an exhibition of his paintings in New York:

> He had all the qualities of genius. The whimsical attitude of the eccentric, the charm of the schoolboy, the gripping power of a great man and the sheer never-to-be forgotten charm of

> the outstanding artist mixed on a palette with a little selfishness, a fine measure of wilfulness and a dogmatic attitude. But he fused these shortcomings in such charming combinations of colour that he almost concealed them, and I loved him for all the good points which never ceased to warm one's heart.

Munnings might have found it easier to accept the comment of his East Anglian writer friend, Adrian Bell. Bell read of his death in a newspaper in the White Horse Inn where they often drank together. Afterwards, he wrote:

> I tried to believe he was dead. Here today was an old man in the bar ... telling me how he had mowed his two acres of barley, and his one of wheat and tied it up ... a man after Munnings's own heart .... He went on talking of his mowing with the scythe, and his driving of the tall loads as a boy; trace horse, shaft-horse and the long harvest waggon ... I kept telling myself, yes, this is what we used to listen to, and here is the oak-ribbed bar of the 'White Horse', and the sunlight filtering in through summer leaves as it used to, but Munnings is dead ....
>
> On the day after Munnings's death I retraced some of the old routes. Green byways were his hobby. I stopped at Dennington Church where he had given a woman half-a-crown to wash the face of the effigy of Lord Bardoff .... In Stradbroke Church he got up in the pulpit and preached me a sermon on Life and Art ....
>
> I go into the inns we halted at, sit on the settles we sat on; go into the churches, see him in my mind's eye in the pulpit, preaching to me on life and art. Although he is no longer there, I can never think of him as out of all this.

Epilogue

The first and last time I met Alfred Munnings was on a Spring day in 1956. I was a young BBC radio reporter and had gone to Castle House with some misgivings to interview him on the occasion of his forthcoming Retrospective Exhibition at the Royal Academy.

The misgivings were the result of my Editor's parting advice when he sent me off on the assignment:

'Don't stand any nonsense from him,' he warned me. 'He can be a cussed devil and if he starts being difficult just forget about the interview and leave him to it.'

As I approached his house through the beautiful main street of Dedham village in the Stour Valley, past the flower-bedecked pubs and the great church that Constable immortalised in so many paintings, the misgivings mounted. I recalled the story of his vitriolic speech at the Royal Academy banquet and how the BBC telephone switchboards were jammed by listeners protesting at his foul language.

Near the edge of the village I came to the white ornamental gates of 'The House of My Dreams' as he called it and drove up to the part Tudor part Georgian cream-coloured house set among paddocks and meadows and great trees. Playing for time I sat in the car and noticed a fine chestnut, a wellingtonia, a great copper beech and a large plane tree.

He had his own misgivings when he bought the property:

'Still full of fears I began to wish that I had never thought of buying such a thing as a gentleman's residence,' he confessed in his autobiography. 'I should never be able to keep up such a place! Who was I? A mere painter. I was no retired general or colonel. Such men could play with a house like this, whilst I... What could I do with it?'

He could never have guessed that some eighty years later a painting of his would be sold for more than two and a half million pounds at Christies in New York.

I rang the bell and he opened the door – a welcoming genial host flaunting a yellow riding stock and still handsome in a rakish sort of way despite his seventy-eight years. Maybe my editor had been unduly pessimistic or had discounted this old showman's intention to get the maximum publicity for his three hundred or so paintings about to go on exhibition. Or perhaps this English eccentric had mellowed in his old age or the rumours about his devil-may-care brash character had been grossly exaggerated?

One day it would be my task to attempt to answer these questions – and more. But that was for the future, in thirty years time when I had undertaken to write his biography. Meanwhile, as a rather apprehensive visitor I crossed the threshold into the home of one of the greatest British painters of all time.

He was a perfect host and, as he took me on a tour of his home, he patiently and courteously answered all my questions. He was justifiably house-proud. The miller's son had become an English country gentleman with fine furniture arranged in an elegant setting whose walls were hung with an enviable selection of his own paintings.

There was one concession to his age. This was a glass dome built into the large Georgian hall so that he could use that part as a studio and did not always have to walk across the paddock to the main one.

But it was in his main studio, a hundred yards or so away from the house that I saw Munnings in his true environment, surrounded by a lifetime of painting memories. He told me how the thatched building that, from the outside looked like stables, incorporated his first studio, a sectional wooden building forty-five feet long, which was originally erected at Swainsthorpe in 1906. Thirteen years later, when he bought Castle House, it was dismantled and brought by rail to Dedham where it was erected on new brick underpinnings and extended to nearly double its size.

Inside, arranged surprisingly neatly, were easels holding partly-finished canvases, palettes daubed with paints, jars of brushes, painting stools and some of his hunting paraphenalia. A rainbow of jockeys' silks hung from the ceiling and gave a festive touch echoed in a large design for a backcloth for one of the Chelsea Arts Balls.

'It was for Sun-worship or some such theme,' he recalled with a smile prompted by some very happy memories.

I remembered reading his account of his first Chelsea Arts Ball:

'I took a box on the ground floor,' he wrote in his memoirs. 'Not only did I take a box, I took a jovial crew to fill it.... Revellers stripped off cloaks, furs and overcoats, revealing surprises, a lovely figure or two – visions of beauty.... Appearing from wrappings, the female form divine, gracefully curved and moulded – not in cold marble – was there, alive, warm, smiling and partly dressed and all but nude ... lively and gay... ready for a night.

That studio certainly exuded something of its owner's joyous passion – both in his work and in his life. I was enchanted – with the man and his home.

* * * * * * * *

Forty-three years later I went there again. It had become The Sir Alfred Munnings Art museum run by the Castle House Trust. This was in accordance with his wish that his home and all the pictures in his possession should be left to the nation in a Trust which Violet set up.

By then I knew most of the innermost and most intimate secrets of his life having long since written his biography. Yet once again there were the initial misgivings. This was because the cream frontage of his house as I had first seen it and as he had immortalised it in his famous painting *My Wife, My Horse and Myself* had been painted a pale Suffolk pink. It seemed to be breaking trust with the past. What other anomalies should I find?

Once through the small Tudor entrance hall, however, and into the large loftier Georgian one I well remembered, I was reassured. It was almost as if time had stood still. Facing me was one of his proudest possessions, the tall ormolu grandfather clock, one of the first antiques and greatest bargains he ever acquired; He had found it in a Suffolk inn at the turn of the century and bought it along with a pair of period portraits and some embroidered silk pictures of girls holding birdcages. Afterwards he had sold the portraits and pictures for the same amount as he had paid for the lot so the grandfather clock had cost him nothing.

Dominating the hall was a huge canvas of his favourite model, Shrimp the gypsy boy leading a string of ponies across a Norfolk farm. Looking down from half way up the fine staircase was another large and very familiar Newmarket racing picture, *Under Starter's Orders.*

'Always the start, never the finish,' he had said of his racing pictures.

On my first visit I remembered seeing a large selection of his pictures on the walls but not nearly as many as there were now. I reckoned there were at least two hundred on show including many of his finest works. This must surely form one of the greatest collections of his work in the world and, I learned, was constantly changing because the Museum borrowed paintings, in a reciprocal arrangement, from other museums and from private collections for its annual exhibitions.

He had owned most of the pictures but, I learned, the Trust had bought twenty-eight others, chosen to fill in the gaps in his life's work.

There were two of their purchases in the drawing room; *The Path to the Orchard*, a sun-filled picture of one of his most famous equestrian models, his white pony Augereau, being led along the river bank at Mendham by a blue-frocked girl in a white linen cap and apron. This was exhibited in the 1909 Royal Academy. Also *Tagg's Island*, shown in the 1920 Academy, a conversation piece portraying three of Munnings's artist friends with four girl models enjoying a champagne party beside the river Thames.

'Friends of my bachelor life' was how Munnings had described the sitters, ignoring the fact that he had been married and widowed six years before it was painted.

Also in the drawing room was a version of the theatrical self portrait *My Wife, My Horse and Myself* and *The White Canoe* showing Violet and a friend, both twenty-eight-years old, enjoying the summer sunshine in a Canadian canoe moored in the river at Dedham. Munnings painted several versions of both these pictures and, one suspects, for sentimental reasons they were among his favourites.

The Trust aims to show Castle House much as it was when Alfred and Violet lived there and he would surely have approved of the way his lifetime collection of antiques had been restored and displayed. The elegant dining room leading from the drawing room seemed waiting to receive guests with its eight Chippendale chairs surrounding the eighteenth century dining table set with a pair of silver candelabra. Small silver treasures were displayed in a pair of little glass cabinets.

It was evident that Alfred Munnings, one of the first British painters to gain financial recognition in his own lifetime, had used his money well. He need have had no misgivings.

The house seemed so lived in that I felt almost a sense of intrusion on entering the little circular morning room where Violet's notebooks were displayed on her very feminine small mahogany writing bureau. This intimate room was the place where they often chose to have breakfast and supper. Equally comfortable was the small library whose bookshelves displayed Munnings's taste in reading; Tolstoy and Trollope, George Eliot and Smollett ...

And there was the same sense of intrusion on entering the small bedroom where Munnings died, although this is now an office, whose blue walls were hung with more of his favourite paintings; an Exmoor scene and Dedham Church, *Cherrybounce* the bay mare he bred who inspired his fifty-one verse ballad, *Cheena* his wife's old mare and a study for a portrait of Mrs J. V. Rank's horse *Southern Hero*, perhaps a reminder of the time he stayed at her home Druid's Lodge when it was heavily bombed during World War II.

French windows led out onto a balcony with a wide view of the garden where well-kept lawns and flower beds had replaced the horse-filled paddocks I remembered from his time. The thirty horses he kept there were reduced to two, kept just to retain the flavour of the place.

The view, recorded by Munnings in *From My Bedroom Window*, the name of two pictures painted in winter and summer, were actually painted from the next door bedroom window, the room he shared with Violet. The view in winter took two days to paint but the summer version took two years. It was painted from scaffolding erected outside the window to shield him from the afternoon sun but, because of the unseasonable summer, it took two years to finish. Moreover, the monkey puzzle tree in the foreground took him a long time to master and, in summer, he also had to contend with its shadow.

Castle House today certainly reflects Munnings's painting history. From his early days and dominating the newly-formed Tudor Gallery is the study of the father of Munnings's first patron, John Shaw Tomkins, the managing director of A. J. Caley and Sons who commissioned it when Munnings was a teenage lithographer. Facing it is one of his few nudes, a model painted when he was studying art in Paris.

As for my initial misgivings ? The house today seemed more elegant and dignified than I remembered it from my first visit. The fine rugs Munnings collected now stand on carpeted floors and, although the casual disarray and clutter has been tidied away, this in no way detracts from the feeling that Munnings might walk in at any moment, survey the scene and be not displeased.

The studio too looks much as I remembered it; paint-spattered overalls, jars of brushes and painting paraphenalia and, hanging from the roof, alongside the jockeys' silks, hunting kits above a row of well-worn riding boots.

Dominating it all is the plaster cast of the first work Munnings did in his newly-enlarged studio, the model of Edward Horner commissioned for the chapel at Mells Church. When he did it, there had been room in the studio for Patrick, the bay horse who modelled for the young hussar's charger, to stand there day after day.

Munnings's sketch books, some early posters and a fine bust of his father are dwarfed by the canoe seen in many of the summer scenes he painted on the river at Dedham. It is a reminder of peaceful harmonious days in contrast to the controversial *Does the Subject Matter?* standing on an easel and giving visitors a chance to study the anger and bitterness in his detailed lampoon on modern art which was the talking point of the 1956 Royal Academy.

For anyone wanting to understand the real Alfred Munnings a visit to Castle House is essential, for it is impossible to overestimate its importance in his life.

He himself acknowledged this when he wrote:

'Where a man makes his headquarters is the main thing in his existence, the perfect spot where he would like to dwell and pass away is often not to be found, is out of reach, unobtainable. Should he discover it, it is only chance or accident that leads him there.'

He did discover it and described its finding as 'the main event of my life. A married man,' he added, 'should say that meeting his wife was the main event, but what is the use of meeting a wife if you have no house? Everyone must have a house, be he married or single.'

He often waxed lyrical about the day he found it:

'I was rivetted in the drawing room with its Regency bow windows looking out across peaceful meadows with chestnut trees and cows grazing. The dining room was all I could have wished for – Regency windows, one looking out over a laurel fence across the valley to East Bergholt, the other looking on to lawn and meadows ... I had indeed found my dream house, river and all ... what advantages were mine then and for years onwards!'

No set tours of The Sir Alfred Munnings Art Museum intrude on the atmosphere of a home that still seems lived in while invigilators in each room will answer questions about the man some of them knew personally.

Visitors are free to wander at will around the house and grounds, study some of his great paintings and absorb the atmosphere of the place that helped him to create them; the place he loved more than anywhere in the world and where, one senses, his spirit still lingers.

JG 2000

Book for
Sale

BIBLIOGRAPHY

Allthorpe-Guyton, Marjorie and Stevens, John, *A Happy Eye,* Jarrolds, 1982

Asquith, Herbert Henry, *Memories and Reflections 1852–1927*, Cassell, 1928

Bedford, Hugh, *Frank Gascoigne Heath and his 'Newlyn School' Friends at Lamorna*, Hugh Bedford, 1995

Bell, Adrian, My *Own Master,* Faber & Faber, 1961

Booth, Stanley, *Sir Alfred Munnings 1879–1959,* Sotheby, 1978

Collis, Maurice, *Stanley Spencer,* Collins Harvill, 1950

Duff, David, *Queen Mary,* Collins, 1985

Du Maurier, George, *Trilby,* Collins, 1953

Dunbar, Janet, *Laura Knight,* Collins, 1975

Ewart Evans, George, *Ask The Fellow Who Cut The Hay,* Faber & Faber, 1956

Ewart Evans, George, *The Days That We Have Seen,* Faber & Faber, 1975

Ewart Evans, George, *Horse Power and Magic,* Faber & Faber, 1979

Fox, Caroline and Greenacre, Francis, *Painting in Newlyn 1880–1930*, Newlyn Orion Gallery, 1985

Goodman, Jean, *Edward Seago – The Other Side of the Canvas,* Collins, 1978

Grunche, C. Philippe, *Géricault's Horses,* Sotheby, 1985

Heron, Roy, *Cecil Aldin, The Story of a Sporting Artist,* Webb & Bower, 1981

Holroyd, Michael, *Augustus John* (Vol. II), Heinemann, 1975

Hough, Richard, *History of the Garrick – Ace of Clubs,* André Deutsch, 1986

Hutchison, Sidney, *History of the Royal Academy,* Chapman & Hall, 1968

Knight, Laura, *Oil Paint and Grease Paint,* Ivor Nicholson and Watson, 1936

Knight, Laura, *The Magic of a Line,* William Kimber, 1965

Lindsay, Lionel, *A. J. Munnings, R.A. (An Appreciation),* Eyre & Spottiswoode, 1927

Mottistone, Lord, *Adventure,* William Heinemann, 1930

Mottistone, Lord, *Fear and Be Slain,* Hodder & Stoughton, 1931

Mottistone, Lord, My *Horse Warrior,* Hodder & Stoughton, 1934

Munnings, A. J., *An Artist's Life,* Museum Press, 1950

Munnings, A. J., *The Second Burst,* Museum Press, 1952

Munnings, A. J., *The Finish,* Museum Press, 1952

Munnings, A. J., *Ballads and Poems,* Museum Press, 1957

Munnings, Violet, *The Diary of a Freeman,* Cassell, 1953

Pelling, Henry, *Winston Churchill,* Macmillan, 1974

Pound, Reginald, *A Maypole in the Strand,* Ernest Benn, 1948

Pound, Reginald, *The Englishman,* Heinemann, 1962
Vulliamy, C. E., *Calico Pie,* Michael Joseph, 1940
Walke, Bernard, *Twenty Years at St Hilary,* Methuen, 1935
Wentworth Day, James, *Norwich Through the Ages,* East Anglian Magazine Co., 1976
Whistler, Laurence, *The Laughter and the Urn,* Weidenfeld & Nicolson, 1985
Williamson, Henry, *The Gale of the World,* Macdonald, 1969

Various magazines and newspapers including:

Country Life; East Anglian Daily Times; Eastern Daily Press and Evening News; The Field; The Framlinghamian (school magazine of Framlingham College); *The Guardian; Illustrated London News; London Evening News,* 1949; *The Listener; The Observer; The Studio; The Times.*

Introductions to various Exhibition Catalogues, as mentioned, and extracts from Company House Magazines.

Unpublished Sources:
Family letters, notebooks and personal papers in the possession of the Munnings Trust; BBC tape recording and transcript; the writings of Marjorie Coppin, Eversley Belfield and Stanley Wade. Diaries of Gilbert Evans in the possession of David Evans.

ALFRED MUNNINGS'S PAINTINGS EXHIBITED IN THE ROYAL ACADEMY

Year	No.	Title
1899	460	PIKE FISHING IN JANUARY.
	817	STRANDED.
1900	391	AN OLD FAVOURITE.
	952	IN THE SUFFOLK MARSHES.
1901	679	WOOD CUTTING IN OCTOBER.
	877	FEEDING THE CHICKENS.
	902	A SUFFOLK HORSE FAIR.
1902	15	THE VAGABONDS.
	73	THE GOSSIPS.
1903	348	THE LAST OF THE FAIR.
	476	SALE BY AUCTION, MICHAELMAS.
	583	A COUNTRY HORSE-FAIR.
	628	A GALA DAY.
	751	THE WOOD CUTTER.
1904	649	WHITSUNTIDE.
1905	195	LEAVING THE FAIR.
	234	THE LOW MEADOWS.
1906	416	PONIES AT A HORSE FAIR.
	340	THE MEET AT 'THE BELL'.
1907	436	CHARLOTTE'S PONY.
	569	GOING TO THE MEET: CAPT. AND MISS CHAMBERLIN.
	597	INTO THE SPINNEY.
1908	254	ON THE ROAD.
	556	THE OLD GRAVEL-PIT.
1909	474	THE EDGE OF THE WOOD.
	748	THE PATH TO THE ORCHARD.
1910	530	THE WATERING.
	651	THE ROVING LIFE.
1911	80	A ROMANY BOY.
	114	THE SHADY GROVE.
	690	THE FORD.
1912	78	SHADE.
	136	THE WIND ON THE HEATH.
	718	A NORFOLK SANDPIT.
1913	235	AUTUMN AFTERNOON.
	637	A NORFOLK HILLSIDE.
	873	PIGS IN A WOOD.
1914	385	A CHECK BY THE CROMLECH.
	659	DEPARTURE OF THE HOP-PICKERS.
1915	508	GIPSY GROUP.
	727	COUNTRY RACES: THE START.
	777	THE FAIR.
1916	790	GONE TO THE CLIFF.
	816	THE FIR WOOD.
	1529	THE PIPER.
1917	191	THROUGH THE WOOD.
	245	A MODERN BILLY PRINGLE.
1918	341	THE BARN.
	478	THE GIPSIES.
	589	THE HUNTSMAN.
(Elected ARA 1919)		
1919	1	EVELYN.
	576	ZENNOR HILL, CORNWALL.
	598	DRAWING FOR AN APRIL FOX.
1920	27	EPSOM DOWNS: CITY AND SUBURBAN DAY. (CHANTREY WORK).
	51	BRIG.-GEN. THE EARL OF ATHLONE, GCB, GCVO, DSO.
	76	PORTRAIT OF THE PAINTER'S WIFE.

304 MAJOR ERIC BONHAM, MVO, LATE SCOTS GREYS.
341 MRS PEEL'S 'POETHLYN' AT BRYNYPYS, WINNER OF GRAND NATIONAL, 1918 & 1919.
585 TAGG'S ISLAND.

1921 82 ROBIN BOLITHO ESQ., SENIOR MASTER OF FOXHOUNDS TODAY.
374 THE GREY COB.
443 BLACK AND WHITE.
547 THE ARTIST'S WIFE.
554 THE GREEN WAGGON.
557A HRH THE PRINCE OF WALES ON 'FOREST WITCH'. (PRESENTED BY 'THE FIELD' TO HIS ROYAL HIGHNESS, AND PLACED IN THE EXHIBITION 9 JUNE 1921).

1922 111 MRS ROBERT RANKIN AND HER DAUGHTERS.
208 ISAAC BELL ESQ., AND HIS FOXHOUNDS, KILKENNY.
216 JOHN MOWBRAY ESQ., EX-MFH, BEDALE, AND HIS WIFE. PRESENTATION PORTRAIT.
400 MRS LEOPOLD DE ROTHSCHILD.
424 P.G. BENSON ESQ., MASTER, TAUNTON VALE FOXHOUNDS.
665 THE DRUMMER OF HIS MAJESTY'S FIRST LIFEGUARDS.

1923 84 'HUMORIST' AND DONOGHUE GOING OUT FOR THE DERBY, 1921.
178 A MAY MORNING AT SOUTHCOURT.
223 THOROUGHBRED STALLION 'RADIUM'.
229 BROOD MARES AND FOALS AT SOUTHCOURT STUD.
387 KILKENNY HORSE FAIR.
360 'MY HORSE IS MY FRIEND.'

1924 10 LORD & LADY MILDMAY OF FLETE, HELEN & ANTHONY.
98 THE GREY HORSE.
200 THE DUCHESS OF WESTMINSTER WITH HER HARRIERS.
276 ROSEMARY AND EDDIE DE ROTHSCHILD.
298 THE DUKE OF MARLBOROUGH AND LORD IVOR SPENCER CHURCHILL.
318 THE WHITE CANOE.

1925 21 THE RIDE TO THE CHATEAU.
103 THE WHIP.
200 THE COMING STORM.
269 F.H. PRINCE ESQ. AND THE PAN FOXHOUNDS.
344 HORSES AT GRASS.
385 JULY.

(Elected R A 1925)

1926 52 GYPSIES ON EPSOM DOWNS, DERBY WEEK.
97 THEIR MAJESTIES' RETURN FROM ASCOT.
148 THE ASCOT PROCESSION CROSSING WINDSOR PARK.
237 'SAUCY SUE' WINNING THE OAKS, 1925.
406 THE ROYAL CARRIAGE WAITING FOR THEIR MAJESTIES AT DUKE'S LANE, WINDSOR PARK, ON ASCOT GOLD CUP DAY.
431 KILKENNY HORSE FAIR. DIPLOMA WORK.

1927 41 PHYLLIS AND RACHAEL, DAUGHTERS OF LT.-COL.

H.H. SPENDER-CLAY, CMG, MC, MP.
64 BEFORE THE RACES.
108 EXERCISING IN THE SNOW.
146 THE OLD OAK.
226 W. RILEY-SMITH ESQ., CHANGING PONIES.
325 MRS W. RILEY-SMITH ON 'SNOWFLAKE'.

1928 84 SIR JOHN RUTHERFORD'S 'SOLARIO'.
92 SADDLING UP FOR THE GRAND NATIONAL, 1919: BEFORE THE SNOWSTORM.
198 THE BRAMHAM MOOR HOUNDS.
235 MRS RONALD TREE AND HER SON.
305 MR R.G. SHAW ON 'LEE BRIDGE', WINNER OF THE GRAND MILITARY, 1925.
311 SIR ABE BAILEY'S 'SON-IN-LAW'.

1929 51 SKATING AT FLATFORD.
66 MR ANTHONY DE ROTHSCHILD'S MARE 'PILLION' WITH FOAL, AND KENT THE STUD GROOM.
80 VISCOUNT ASTOR'S MARE 'BOOKLAW'.
165 EARLY MORNING AT NEWMARKET: THE HON. GEORGE LAMBTON AND HIS SON.
182 DAFFERN SEAL ON 'CANARY'.
212 FRANK FREEMAN, HUNTSMAN TO THE PYTCHLEY, ON 'PILOT'.

1930 23 FROM MY BEDROOM WINDOW. (CHANTREY WORK).
132 HRH PRINCESS MARY COUNTESS OF HAREWOOD AND THE EARL OF HAREWOOD, MFH, WITH THE BRAMHAM MOOR.
140 THE PRESENTATION OF STANDARDS TO THE HOUSEHOLD CAVALRY BY HM KING GEORGE V, JUNE 1927.
227 MILLICENT BARON ON 'MAGPIE'.
239 LADY BUCHANAN JARDINE'S HORSE 'NOTHING VENTURED'.
351 THE NEW STANDARDS AT THE PRESENTATION OF STANDARDS TO THE HOUSEHOLD CAVALRY BY HM KING GEORGE V, JUNE 1927.

1931 15 UNSADDLING AT EPSOM.
49 GOING OUT AT EPSOM.
86 HRH PRINCESS MARY COUNTESS OF HAREWOOD.
99 ON THE MOORS.
129 THE PADDOCK, EPSOM.
286 NOVEMBER MORNING.

1932 53 FROM MY BEDROOM WINDOW.
97 THE FULL RIVER.
145 A CORPORAL OF HORSE.
186 FLOOD WATER AT FLATFORD.
283 MR JOHN DEWAR'S HORSE 'CAMERONIAN', WINNER OF DERBY AND TWO THOUSAND GUINEAS, 1931.
456 CHANTILLY.

1933 14 MY WIFE IN THE GARDEN.
79 ELEVEN O'CLOCK.
131 ON THE DOWNS.
135 MISS BETTY BARON ON 'FRECKLES'.
158 THE HON. IRWIN

LAUGHLIN AND SON AND DAUGHTER NEAR SAN SEBASTIAN.
263 'A FOX FOR A HUNDRED!'
1934 37 A TROOPER, SCOTS GREYS, 1807. FROM THE PAINTED STATUETTE BY PILKINGTON JACKSON IN THE NATIONAL SCOTTISH MUSEUM, EDINBURGH.
69 MR W.W. ASTOR WITH THE OXFORD UNIVERSITY DRAGHOUNDS.
74 WINTER AT FLATFORD.
106 (PENDANT OF NO. 37).
116 A LUNCHEON PARTY WITH MINE HOST AT 'THE HIND'S HEAD', BRAY.
156 HORSES AND ELDER BLOSSOM.
1935 82 GROUP OF MY HORSES (1).
148 PORTRAIT GROUP: MRS. HELEN CUTTING AND THE MISSES BRADY.
162 GROUP OF MY HORSES (2).
219 SIR HAROLD WERNHER'S HORSE 'BROWN JACK'.
402 AT BUCKHURST.
420 MY WIFE, MY HORSE AND MYSELF.
1936 14 ERNEST HEATLEY ESQ., MASTER OF THE ESSEX UNION, ON HIS HORSE 'CONRAD'.
19 SKETCHING AT WISTON BRIDGE.
60 A FARM IN SUFFOLK.
144 FLOOD WATERS.
167 CHESTNUT TREES IN BLOOM.
623 EARL STONHAM CHURCH, SUFFOLK.
1937 49 LORD ASTOR'S HORSES, 'TRAFFIC LIGHT', 'RHODES SCHOLAR' AND 'EARLY SCHOOL', WITH JOE LAWSON, TRAINER, AT MANTON, WILTS.
61 SADDLING 'MAHMOUD', THE DERBY WINNER, 1936.
87 THE POLISH RIDER.
105 AFTER THE RACE.
154 HM KING GEORGE V ON HIS PONY 'JOCK' AT SANDRINGHAM.
239 THE COUNTESS FORTESCUE.
1938 59 THE HON. ANTHONY MILDMAY ON 'DAVY JONES'.
71 THE EARL OF DERBY'S HORSE 'HYPERION', WINNER OF THE DERBY AND THE ST LEGER, 1933.
185 STUDY: AFTER THE RACE.
252 THE NEIGHING STALLION: MR MACALMONT'S GREY HORSE 'MR. JINKS'.
521 AT MESSRS WHITBREAD'S BREWERY, CHISWELL ST., EC.
543 THEIR MAJESTIES' RETURN FROM ASCOT, 1925. (CHANTREY WORK). (SAME AS 1926. NO. 97).
1939 22 SNOW LANDSCAPE.
38 JUNE EVENING.
131 BARKER, THE PYTCHLEY HUNTSMAN.
167 'WHY WEREN'T YOU OUT YESTERDAY?'
175 STEPHEN DONOGHUE, 1921.
460 THE LANDLORD OF 'THE HIND'S HEAD'.
1940 19 DRIFTING.
48 JOCKEYS AT THE START (2).

72 JOCKEYS AT THE START (1).
178 FEEDING THE BIRDS.
565 THE EARL OF DERBY'S HORSE, 'FAIRWAY'.
569 THE EARL OF DERBY'S HORSE, 'HYPERION'.

1942 3 ON THE DOWNS.
4 START AT NEWMARKET.
34 OCTOBER LANDSCAPE.
36 'WEIR WATER', AT OARE.
115 A SWIMMING POOL.
178 MRS J.V. RANK'S HORSE, 'LE MAESTRO'.

1943 63 A SUMMER EVENING: LORD ASTOR AT THE CLIVEDEN STUD (1939).
75 EXMOOR LANDSCAPE AT OARE.
90 THE DELANEYS.
146 A PARTISAN, 1940.
396 STUDIES OF MARES AND FOALS AT THE CLIVEDEN STUD.
401 GORSE ON WINSFORD HILL, EXMOOR.

(Elected PRA, 1944 and knighted same year)

1944 2 WINTER MEETING.
44 START AT NEWMARKET.
56 THE PYTCHLEY KENNEL HOUNDS FEEDING.
63 HAWTHORN STUDY.
64 EXERCISING.
67 THE WHITE CANOE.
208 EXMOOR LANDSCAPE.

1945 2 BAGSWORTHY WATER AT CLOUD.
19 ELMS ON THE ACLAND ESTATE.
22 LANDSCAPE AT OARE, EXMOOR.
23 FEBRUARY THAW.
103 THE ENGLISH SCENE: LOOKING FROM SELWORTHY OVER COUNTRY GIVEN BY SIR R. ACLAND, BT., TO THE NATIONAL TRUST.
136 START OF A STEEPLECHASE.
140 PADDOCK SCENE: SUMMER MEETING.

1946 2 GOING TO THE START.
19 CHANTILLY.
86 WINTER ON EXMOOR.
141 THE OLD SAND PIT.
148 THE WHITE CANOE.
218 AFTER THE RACE.

1947 2 AUTUMN.
18 THE SADDLING PADDOCK, CHELTENHAM, MARCH MEETING.
81 EXMOOR SHEPHERD.
118 STUDY FOR 'THE SADDLING PADDOCK', CHELTENHAM MARCH MEETING.
212 SKETCH OF A NEWMARKET START.
221 THE FRISIAN BULL.

1948 18 GOING TO THE START.
37 MY GARDEN IN WINTER.
76 GOING OUT.
128 DAYS OF YORE.
204 SEPTEMBER AFTERNOON.
212 HORSE CONVERSATION PIECE, 1940: MR J.V. RANK'S THREE HORSES, 'SOUTHERN HERO', 'BLACK SPECK' AND 'KNIGHT'S ARMOUR'.

1949 3 HIS OLD DEMESNES.
18 COMING OFF THE HEATH, EARLY MORNING, NEWMARKET.
84 UNDER STARTER'S ORDERS, NEWMARKET (NO. 2).
88 KEMPTON PARK.
140 THE ARTIST'S WIFE.
220 UNDER STARTER'S

ORDERS, NEWMARKET (NO. 1).

1950 40 STABLE LADS.

140 NOT YET A DUMPING GROUND FOR TINS AND RUBBISH.

156 BRIGHTWORTHY CROSSING, EXMOOR.

200 THE FROZEN RIVER.

203 EARLY MORNING, NEWMARKET (2).

207 EARLY MORNING, NEWMARKET (1).

1951 15 THE PASSING THE HORSE AND THE PIG.

18 L'ECOLE DE NEWBURY.

110 THE ARTIST IN HIS SPOT.

114 'WHEN THE EVENING SUN IS LOW'.

127 SIXTEEN-YEAR-OLD SUFFOLK STALLION.

147 OCTOBER DAY.

1952 57 GIPSY LIFE.

169 IN THE ROOM: A PROBLEM PICTURE.

184 THE LATE PERCY WHITAKER ON 'SILVO'.

220 BEFORE THE START, NEWMARKET.

232 HAMPSHIRE HOP-PICKERS.

237 SEPTEMBER AFTERNOON.

1953 2 MORNING EXERCISE, NEWMARKET.

153 DEDHAM.

171 OUR MUTUAL FRIEND THE HORSE.

183 THE WHITE CANOE.

593 'MINE ANCIENT ENEMY THE SEA HAS BUT RETIRED FOR A WHILE.'

675 STUDY: JOCKEYS AT THE START, NEWMARKET.

1954 7 BEFORE THE START: OCTOBER MEETING.

58 A CORPORAL OF HORSE.

139 MAY BLOSSOM ON EXMOOR.

214 ARRIVING AT EPSOM: A SCENE OF THE PAST.

230 MOVING UP UNDER STARTER'S ORDERS: OCTOBER MEETING, NEWMARKET.

266 NEWMARKET INCIDENT: THE RUNAWAY.

1955 20 A SHADY CORNER.

151 WHO'S THE LADY?

163 THE BAY HORSE AND OURSELVES.

167 A WINNER AT EPSOM.

563 ASCOT POSTILLION ON BAY LEADERS.

652 LINING UP UNDER STARTER'S ORDERS, NEWMARKET.

1956 14 LAND OF MY DREAMS.

157 SEPTEMBER AFTERNOON, 1939 (VERSION No. 4).

172 THE WHIP.

209 HAPPY DAYS.

283 DOES THE SUBJECT MATTER? 'AND WHY NOT PURCHASED FOR THE STATE? THE STATE, ALAS, HAS COME TOO LATE. BECAUSE THE SUBJECT'S SO PROFOUND 'TWAS SOLD FOR TWENTY THOUSAND POUND!'

992 'AROUND ME HOWLS A WINTRY SKY THAT BLASTS EACH BUD OF HOPE AND JOY; AND SHELTER, SHADE NOR HOME HAVE I SAVE IN THOSE ARMS OF THINE LOVE.' (ROBERT BURNS)

1957 13 WINTER'S MORNING.

148 HER MAJESTY THE QUEEN AND HER HORSE 'AUREOLE', WITH THE

TRAINER, CAPTAIN BOYD-ROCHFORD.
181 DEDHAM CHURCH: STUDY NO. 2.
219 THE OLD GRAVEL PIT ('AUGEREAU', THE PONY, PAINTED 1911; THE BOY PAINTED 1956).
229 A NEWMARKET START: CRIES OF 'NO, NO, SIR! NO, NO, SIR!'
305 EARLY MORNING ON WARREN HILL, NEWMARKET.

1958 52 GOING OUT AT KEMPTON.
174 GOING OUT AT EPSOM.
179 START AT NEWMARKET: STUDY NO. 4.
364 KEMPTON PARK.
561 AUTUMN TAPESTRIES.
662 NEWMARKET AGAIN.

1959 80 HER CARAVAN.
99 A WINNER AT EPSOM.
264 GYPSY TALES.
331 BRIGHTWORTHY FORD.
515 WARREN HILL, NEWMARKET.
632 BEFORE THE START, NEWMARKET.

(The late Sir Alfred J. Munnings, KCVO, PPRA)

1960 64 STUDY FOR A 'START'.
212 HOUNDS CROSSING DUNKERY BEACON.
269 MY WIFE IN THE GARDEN.
281 THE FORD.
285 NEW YEAR MORNING IN A CHELSEA STUDIO.
654 THE OLD GRAVEL PIT (THE PONY PAINTED IN 1911, THE BOY IN 1956).

Blinkers
French nose band
6 plaits
floor hoss!
Gilbert
Alfred

INDEX